Elusive Citizenship

To Professor Hing,
with great
thanks & admiration.

John

CRITICAL AMERICA

General Editors: Richard Delgado and Jean Stefancic

Elusive Citizenship

Immigration, Asian Americans,
and the Paradox of Civil Rights

John S. W. Park

NEW YORK UNIVERSITY PRESS

New York and London

NEW YORK UNIVERSITY PRESS
New York and London
www.nyupress.org

Library of Congress Cataloging-in-Publication Data
Park, John S. W.
Elusive citizenship : immigration, Asian Americans, and the paradox
of civil rights / John S. W. Park.
p. cm. — (Critical America)
Includes bibliographical references and index.
ISBN 0-8147-6714-1 (cloth : alk. paper)
1. United States—Emigration and immigration—History.
2. Asia—Emigration and immigration—History.   3. Asians—
United States—History.   4. Immigrants—United States—History.
5. Emigration and immigration law—United States—History.
I. Title.   II. Series.
JV6450.P35   2004
325.73'095—dc22   2003026400

New York University Press books are printed on acid-free paper,
and their binding materials are chosen for strength and durability.

Manufactured in the United States of America

10 9 8 7 6 5 4 3 2 1

This book is dedicated to the loving memory of my mother, Soo Boon Kim

Contents

Acknowledgments

This book began at its end, when my brother Edward saw on my desk a seminar paper I had written for Angela Harris at Boalt Hall, and now a version of it appears here as the conclusion for this book. Edward told me to submit the original paper for publication. I did as he suggested (as I'm always inclined to do), and it was subsequently published in the *Michigan Journal of Race and Law*. Professors Richard Delgado and Jean Stefancic saw the piece there, and they gave me the encouragement to turn the ideas from that article into this book. They became my editors, and they helped me secure a book contract with New York University Press. At the same time, my graduate advisors at Berkeley—Samuel Scheffler, Robert Kagan, Angela Harris, and Michael Omi—helped shape the article into a dissertation in political theory, public law, and race theory. And so in this way, that seminar paper for Professor Harris turned into an extended, extended project that I took with me from Berkeley, to Austin, and then to Santa Barbara, where my wife, Gowan Lee, told me in no uncertain terms to send off the manuscript or else. I owe my sincerest appreciation to everyone mentioned in this paragraph, although Edward and Gowan deserve my deepest thanks. Without Edward, this project would not have gone anywhere, and without Gowan, it probably would never have ended.

I have received tremendous support during the many years I have lived with this project. At Berkeley, in addition to my dissertation advisors, I owe many thanks to several terrific professors, including Marianne Constable, Jeremy Waldron, and Ling-chi Wang. I took four courses at Cal with Professor Constable; she is by far the best professor I have ever had. She was the first to teach me how to look at law in an unconventional, multi-disciplinary way. Professor Waldron's writings and seminars on liberal theory were inspirational, and his encouragement had a lasting effect on many of his students long after he had left Berkeley. Professor Wang pushed me to become a better teacher by helping me design my first courses, and then by offering me my first job as a lecturer in the Department of Ethnic Studies. He also introduced me to several intriguing areas of research in Asian American Studies, many of which I am still pursuing.

In Austin, I owe my deepest thanks to several colleagues. Arthur Sakamoto was instrumental in helping me get my first tenure-track academic appointment, and he supported me through every step of my first two years as an Assistant Professor. Mia Carter, who was Art's successor as the Director of the Center for Asian American Studies, was also incredibly supportive professionally and personally. She showed by her example how a skilled administrator could steer an infant, contentious program through impossible challenges. Her leadership will always amaze me. In the Department of American Studies, I was fortunate to have the support of several colleagues and friends, especially Jeff Meikle, Shelley Fisher Fishkin, Mark Smith, Janet Davis, and Steven Hoelscher. Over the two years I was at the University of Texas, they were simply wonderful to me and my family, and understanding of the difficult challenges we were facing. Like Art and Mia, they taught me by their example that a good colleague is first of all a caring friend. And it was terrific to be in a department that was so encouraging of eclectic, interdisciplinary, and multidisciplinary work.

I owe thanks to other colleagues at Berkeley and at Austin. My two Deans at UT, Richard Lariviere and Brian Roberts, each offered crucial support during different stages of this project. They gave me what every young academic needs: a good job and a summer off. Others were just as kind in different ways. Brigid Tung and Margo Rodriguez helped me in innumerable ways throughout my time at Berkeley; Janice Bradley, Barbara Jann, and Cynthia Frese helped me do everything at UT, and they also created a happy work environment in both of my home departments.

My newest colleagues at the University of California at Santa Barbara have been very supportive as well. Jon Cruz, Susan Koshy, Xiaojian Zhao, Diane Fujino, Celine Parreñas Shimizu, Hung Cam Thai, and Douglas Daniels have been most kind, and each have shown me and my family a great deal of warmth, as did Sucheng Chan when I first arrived in Santa Barbara. I am especially appreciative that I even have this job in this spectacular corner of the world, and I am deeply grateful to these folks for hiring me and for taking a risk on my academic work. Patricia Fenwick Miller, Sally Foxen, Doris Phinney, and Arlene Phillips helped me navigate my new institution. Patty was especially helpful in the transition from Texas to California, organizing travel, housing, and office space.

Over several years now, a number of people at the New York University Press worked very hard to produce this book. My first editor at NYU, Niko Pfund, steered the article into a book proposal, which was brutally but fairly criticized by an anonymous reviewer. After more work and extensive revision, the new proposal became a generous book contract under Mr. Pfund's direction. A few years later, Deborah Gershenowitz, my current editor, sent the finished manuscript out again to yet another anonymous reviewer who said rather nice and supportive things, but with some additional excellent suggestions for review. All the while, Emily Park and Jennifer Yoon facilitated correspondence and otherwise helped me through the process, and then Despina Gimbel and Nicholas Taylor oversaw the final edits and production. Everyone was very kind to me, and except for that first anonymous reviewer, they were all very kind in a most pleasant way. I owe thanks to all the good people at the Press, especially the two anonymous reviewers for their contributions to the substantive content of this book.

Finally, I am so happy to acknowledge the people closest to me. My family has been terrific, I have had many great friends, and it's just a pleasure to acknowledge all of their love and support. I owe special thanks to Janet Shim, Dat Ly, Phong Le, Ramie Dare, David Chiu, Debby Lu, TD Huynh, and Miles Becker. They've been so supportive in so many different ways that it would be impossible to list them all. My sister-in-law, Reiko Furuta, made many difficult sacrifices so that I could finish graduate school. My own in-laws have folded me into their loving family: my father-in-law and mother-in-law, Hung Ku Lee and Joung Sun Lee, are so kind to me that I hardly know how to thank them. Earl, Ajean, and Sulggi have been kind, sweet, and forgiving, and I am most fortunate to have them as my siblings. (So many times, these friends and family have asked me, "So, John, where's the book?" Well, here it is.)

My brother Edward deserves his own paragraph. Ed raised me when we were kids, sacrificed much of his own childhood for the sake of mine, and he introduced me to a world of books and ideas that shaped who I am. He got me my first library card, turned me on to Shakespeare and Marx, hid from me all of his bad habits like any good parent, and gave me all kinds of love and support. He has been my best friend, my biggest influence, and my greatest mentor.

My wife, Gowan Lee, deserves her own paragraph. She has been my most constant companion—and that has really not been easy for her. She has been through a lot with me, a fact that many of those who know us will recognize as a profound understatement. Yet Gowan has always shown great strength even through the most difficult times. I hope that our lovely daughters, Zoe, Sophia, and Isabel, grow up to be like their mom. If a good life requires more than anything a great measure of good luck, then I know I have been immensely lucky to have my family.

My mother passed away four years ago, but her enduring love animates everything I have done and everything I will do. Some day, I hope to write the story of my mother's remarkable life. She was an amazing woman. I miss her every day.

1

"A Subclass within Our Boundaries"

In June of 1982, the United States Supreme Court issued its decision in *Plyler v. Doe*, a case from Texas involving the education of undocumented alien children in that state. Since 1975, the Texas Legislature had authorized the withholding of state funds for the education of undocumented children, and had also allowed local school districts to deny enrollment to such children.[1] In part, the state had passed these restrictions to discourage illegal immigrants from settling there. The plaintiffs in the original suit in 1977 were undocumented, school-age children in Texas "who could not establish that they had been legally admitted into the United States." Although their very presence was in violation of several federal immigration rules, they still pressed their suit, as anonymous "Does" against the Superintendent Plyler, on the grounds that the Texas rule violated the Constitution: "The question presented by these cases is whether, consistent with the Equal Protection Clause of the Fourteenth Amendment, Texas may deny to undocumented school-age children the free public education that it provides to children who are citizens of the United States or lawfully admitted aliens."[2] The Court divided as evenly as it could, with five Justices supporting the plaintiffs, the other four the State of Texas; altogether, there were five separate opinions from the Court, including the dissent by Chief Justice Warren Burger.

"Fundamental Conceptions of Justice"

In his majority opinion, Justice William Brennan immediately rejected the claim by the State of Texas that undocumented children, simply because of their immigration status, were not "persons" within the meaning of the

Fourteenth Amendment. Citing several precedents, a few from the late 19th century, Brennan said "aliens, even aliens whose presence in this country is unlawful, have long been recognized as 'persons' guaranteed due process of law by the Fifth and Fourteenth Amendments."[3] Brennan quoted from Justice Stephen Field, who had once rejected a similar argument about the scope of Fourteenth Amendment protections in an early Chinese Exclusion Case almost a hundred years earlier: "The contention that persons within the territorial jurisdiction of this republic might be beyond the protection of the law was heard with pain on the argument at the bar—in face of the great constitutional amendment which declares that 'no State shall deny to *any person* within its jurisdiction the equal protection of the laws.'"[4] Clearly, according to Brennan, these undocumented children were "persons" in the eyes of the Constitution, and as persons they could invoke the Equal Protection Clause of the Fourteenth Amendment.

Yet Justice Brennan expressed appreciation for the strangeness of this situation, of applying the Constitution to persons who were within the territorial jurisdiction of the United States, but without the nation's consent. It would seem odd that these illegal immigrants could be entitled to anything, let alone the protection of the nation's highest law. These persons were of a "special status," their very presence a sign of the nation's failure to police its lawful boundaries. "Sheer incapacity or lax enforcement of the laws barring entry into this country, coupled with the failure to establish an effective bar to the employment of undocumented aliens, has resulted in the creation of a 'shadow population' of illegal immigrants—numbering in the million—within our borders." Their continued presence outside the law could still evolve into a potentially larger political problem. "This situation raises the specter of a permanent caste of undocumented resident aliens."[5] The threat of a special caste might be especially true of undocumented children, Brennan said, who were of an even more peculiar subclass among this "shadow population": "The children who are plaintiffs in these cases 'can affect neither their parents' conduct nor their own status.'"[6] The Texas rule was unjust, he argued, because by targeting children, it "imposes its discriminatory burden on the basis of a legal characteristic over which children can have little control." In other words, the rule functioned to "[penalize] these children for their presence in the United States."[7] "Even if the State found it expedient to control the conduct of adults by acting against their children, legislation directing the onus of a parent's misconduct against his children does not comport with fundamental conceptions of justice."[8] Brennan wrote that the Texas rule violated the essence of the Equal Protection Clause, which had been conceived to abolish "governmental barriers presenting unreasonable obstacles to advancement on the basis of individual merit."[9]

The barriers were "unreasonable" precisely because they involved public education, which, according to the Court's earlier precedents, wasn't quite a "fundamental right," but an "important governmental interest."[10] The interest was an important one because of the special role of public education in American public life. Citing *Brown v. Board of Education* from 1954, perhaps the most important Supreme Court decision of the Civil Rights Era, Justice Brennan said that "education is perhaps the most important function of state and local governments. . . . It is required in the performance of our most basic public responsibilities, even service in the armed forces. It is the very foundation of good citizenship."[11] Public education served to assimilate children into the prevailing norms of society, to help them cope with their lives in the United States, and to participate in the economic and political life of the country. "What we said twenty-eight years ago in *Brown* still holds true."[12] Moreover, citing Justice Hugo Black, Brennan insisted that this precedent ought to apply for all persons, including undocumented children.

After all, the Texas rule "imposes a lifetime hardship on a discrete class of children not accountable for their disabling status," and "forecloses any realistic possibility that they will contribute in even the smallest way to the progress of our Nation."[13] Perhaps like many Americans, Brennan conceded in part that the "lifetime hardship" faced by the undocumented children would most likely occur within the nation's borders, because the children might never leave the country. "There is no assurance that a child subject to deportation will ever be deported." First of all, they were hard to detect. Most were of Mexican ancestry, but so were a very large number of their peers in the public school districts. In terms of their educational costs and needs, the lower federal courts had already found that undocumented children were "basically indistinguishable" from the children of American citizens. In addition, recent federal rules had "legalized," or "provided amnesty," to persons who were once undocumented, and so it was clearly possible that, in the future, "An illegal entrant might be granted federal permission to continue to reside in the country, or to even become a citizen."[14] Unless determined otherwise, undocumented children thus had an "inchoate federal permission to remain"; given that many of them would remain in Texas,

Brennan suggested that a policy of denying them public education made no rational sense.

Brennan also predicted that the rule would succeed only in creating a perpetual class of unassimilated, poor, and hostile outsiders: "It is difficult to understand precisely what the State hopes to achieve by promoting the creation and perpetuation of a subclass of illiterates within our boundaries, surely adding to the problems and costs of unemployment, welfare, and crime."[15]

Chief Justice Burger half agreed that the Texas rule did appear irrational in this way, but he objected to the majority's willingness to substitute its version of the best social policy over the judgments of the Texas Legislature. "Denying a free education to illegal alien children is not a choice I would make were I a legislator," but "the fact that there are sound *policy* arguments against the Texas Legislature's choice does not render that choice an unconstitutional one." In other words, Texas had a sovereign right to make this public choice even though its choice may be all wrong. Burger implied that the Court's majority was merely privileging its choice impermissibly, over the legitimate decisions of popularly elected officials.[16]

In addition, Burger argued that as far as the immigration and fate of illegal aliens was concerned, the Court had traditionally played a very limited role. According to settled precedents in American immigration law, again dating back to the Chinese Exclusion cases, "Congress . . . bears primary responsibility for addressing the problems occasioned by the millions of illegal aliens flooding across our southern border." "Similarly, it is for Congress, not this Court, to assess the 'social costs borne by our Nation when select groups are denied the means to absorb the values and skills upon which our social order rests.'"[17] As sad and miserable as the fate of uneducated, undocumented families and children might be, "it is but one segment of a larger problem, which is for the political branches to solve."[18] The majority in *Plyler*, Burger argued, had acted in a manner beyond its traditional role in immigration law, by intervening in an area normally reserved for legislatures. That Congress should have "plenary power" over immigrants and immigration had its roots in the late 19th century, with the early Chinese cases.

Membership and Belonging in Liberal Political Theory and American Public Law

The *Plyler* case introduces the main themes of this study because of its very strangeness—how is it possible that a state like Texas could be *required* to educate persons who had no permission to be in the country in the first place? Granted, on the one hand, the case involved "innocent children," as Brennan had pointed out, but on the other hand, they or their parents had clearly violated federal rules by coming into the United States without the nation's consent. That Brennan had cited cases from the late 19th century for the proposition that all persons had rights—no matter the manner of their entry—was offset by Burger's allusions to national sovereignty and congressional authority over matters of immigration, which were also legal precedents that dated to the late 19th century. Ironically, both sets of precedents were, as we shall see, authored by a single Justice, the same Justice Field, confused himself over these very issues. Confronted by "barbarians" who seemed "unassimilable," the Supreme Court created a strange and contradictory body of law that both sides evoked in the debate over *Plyler*.

But these contradictions were far more basic, as the first section of this study attempts to show. Most scholars can agree that Anglo-American law has been based on various strains of liberal political theory, the philosophies of the Enlightenment articulated by John Locke, Jean-Jacques Rousseau, and John Stuart Mill, and carried forward into our own day by influential scholars like John Rawls and Ronald Dworkin. First of all, this study explains how this political theory supports within it conflicting commitments between principles of equality and fairness on the one hand, and principles of national sovereignty within bounded political communities on the other. These theoretical tensions can largely explain the muddled origins of federal immigration law in the late 19th century, as well as why Texas was required to educate illegal immigrants in the late 20th century. These tensions remain unresolved, and are perhaps irresolvable.

The second section of this study explores the first federal efforts at a resolution, undertaken by Justice Field, the primary author of several of the most important immigration precedents in American history. Field served on the Supreme Court before, during, and well after the Civil War, when questions of federal sovereignty and race-based citizenship were most intense. In response to a rising tide of anti-immigrant sentiment directed against migrants from Asia, Field at first defended the rights of all persons irrespective of their immigration status, but then eventually supported Chinese Exclusion. Even as the Chinese Exclusion Act became a precedent for other immigration rules and legal disabilities directed at Asians, Field hesitated in his support of racially hostile immigration rules. In the end, he expressed intense sympathy for the very immigrants he had worked so hard to exclude. Near his death, Field affirmed their common humanity and condemned his colleagues and government for their harshness and severity.

Finally, the last section of this study shows how Asian immigrants—the last group of immigrants legally forbidden from becoming American citizens—managed to cope with a wide variety of racially hostile rules in the United States. Many of these rules depended on the idea that some persons, namely Asians, were so different from the current American citizens that they themselves could never become American citizens. As "aliens ineligible from citizenship," Asian immigrants were constantly harassed in American law. Until recently, Asian American legal scholarship often focused on what happened to these immigrants, as relatively passive victims to the battery of horrible state and federal rules that brutalized, stigmatized, and harassed them. More contemporary scholarship has remedied this tendency by focusing on the courageous ways that Asian immigrants fought at every turn against practically all the discriminatory statutes passed against them. This study shows something in between, by detailing the ways that specific actors and litigants evaded, fought, and embraced American law, first when they were told that they could not belong, and then, ultimately, when they were told that they could. Their story is one of resisting *and* embracing the principles of white supremacy, which were (and perhaps still are) at the core of American citizenship.

Altogether, this study attempts to explain how theoretical tensions within liberal theory are reflected in American public law, which in turn shaped the legal strategies of those treated as racial pariahs. The study concludes by suggesting that the experiences of Asian Americans from the late 19th century to the mid-20th century reveal the triumph of a civil rights discourse, where equality and fairness before the law remain the privilege of those who belong—or at least those capable of belonging. Despite whatever theoretical confusion, we still live in a legal regime where liberal notions of sovereignty often precede liberal notions of equality. Rather than conceiving of immigration status as an arbitrary characteristic that should not be used as the basis for legal disabilities, immigration status remains a compelling disability. That would explain why, for example, the schoolchildren in *Plyler* remained safely anonymous, even as they made their public claims for equality. Immigration status may be a morally arbitrary characteristic, but it is not a legally insignificant one. That has not changed since the late 19th century. What has changed in American immigration and naturalization law since Chinese Exclusion is merely the universe of "barbarians" who are conceived as capable of joining the political community. That shift, as we shall see, came at a very heavy price for generations of Asian immigrants and Asian Americans.

PART I

Theory

2

"Characteristics Arbitrary from a Moral Point of View"

Conflicting Commitments

In this section I outline why immigration rules pose significant problems for liberal theory and liberal democratic societies. I argue here that the problems arise, fundamentally, from within liberal theory itself, and from two different types of liberal commitments. On the one hand, liberal theorists have articulated ideas of equality and fairness in a way that rejects arbitrary factors as a ground for greater rights or privileges. On the other, liberal theorists have either insisted on, or assumed the need for, a bounded nation-state, with enforceable borders and a relatively clear set of rules to determine membership. At the outset, these values would seem not to conflict—ideally, a liberal nation-state, with a fixed and determinate membership, would guarantee equality and fairness to all members irrespective of qualities such as race or gender or some other arbitrary criteria. But what happens in less than ideal circumstances, when persons cross national boundaries and find themselves in liberal societies that either do not want them or treat them unfairly? On what grounds can liberal nation-states *deny* the claims and needs of persons who, by accident of birth, were not "born" as members?

This chapter approaches these questions by examining briefly the nature of the first of the two liberal commitments in question. I shall refer to the first principle as the principle against ascriptive status: briefly, the principle holds that persons should not be entitled to a greater share of privileges or opportunities, nor be denied basic rights and opportunities, based on characteristics that are morally arbitrary. This principle reflects notions of equality, but does not necessarily begin with the premise that all persons are morally equal in one sense or another. Rather, the idea relies more on an understanding of what the principle of "equality" requires—that no person ought to enjoy political or social advantage, or suffer similar disadvantage, based on morally arbitrary characteristics. In other words, the principle is normative, not descriptive: it does not say, for example, that all persons are morally equal, but it says that no one ought to be treated advantageously, or disadvantageously, based on a characteristic for which he or she is not responsible.

An explanation of the second, competing principle in liberal theory is contained in the following chapter, but to sketch it briefly here, it is the principle of sovereignty, understood to mean that liberal nation-states have the right to self-determination and territorial integrity, which would necessarily entail control over their boundaries and membership. The principle is grounded on notions of self-determination—the basic idea that once political communities are properly organized, their members have a presumptive right to pursue collectively what is in their own self-interest. In classic accounts of this principle, as we shall see, the right of self-determination is often simply asserted, as though formal justification were either unnecessary or self-evident. Notions of territorial integrity, cohesion within political communities, appeals to cherish and protect a distinctive political culture, and the right of self-defense against aggression—these all stem from this fundamental commitment, and liberal nation-states have long operated as though the principle has long been descriptive as well as normative.

To clarify further how these commitments are expressed in liberal theory, this section focuses on three influential theorists in particular—John Locke, John Stuart Mill, and John Rawls—while drawing from the works of other contemporary theorists as their arguments reflect or criticize the dominant themes presented in the primary works of these important thinkers. Locke, Mill, and Rawls are certainly not the only important liberal theorists for this type of study, but because they represent to some extent the libertarian, utilitarian, and egalitarian strains of liberalism, a discussion of central themes that run throughout their work can illustrate recurring, dominant themes in much of liberal theory overall. This section is certainly not intended as an exhaustive discussion of the basic values of liberalism, if such a thing is even possible; rather, the point is to describe how liberal commitments to equality and fairness rest on mitigating the effect of characteristics that seem "arbitrary from a moral point of view," to use Rawls' phrase, while at the same time showing how ideas of sovereignty and self-determination remain a central facet of liberalism, even when they rely tacitly on arbitrary circumstances. To use a phrase from

Locke, the liberal nation is conceived as "one body," a united commonwealth with a shared political culture that the commonwealth itself may defend, protect, or offer as an example to the world. In the next section I attempt to show how the recurring tensions between the two types of commitments explains in large measure the varying oscillations in American public law, between claims of basic rights, and equally compelling claims of national sovereignty. In this first section I will show how these oscillations are rooted within liberal theory itself.

"Man Has a Natural Freedom . . . and Ought to Partake in the Same Common Rights and Privileges"

To a surprising extent, theorists of liberalism have worried extensively about luck, fortune, and fate. So much of liberal theory has attempted to confront the arbitrariness of life. For example, for John Locke, nothing could have seemed more arbitrary than hereditary monarchy. Indeed, Locke devoted considerable attention to the idea of equality in the context of a political and theological debate with and against defenders of hereditary monarchy like Sir Robert Filmer, Locke's intellectual nemesis in the *First Treatise*. As Locke's contemporary in the late 17th century, Filmer had defended the divine right of kings, which stated that a proper reading of theology would point to monarchy as the only appropriate political system for persons in the world, as it was the only one sanctioned by God. Locke found the argument morally abhorrent at a time when Filmer's arguments had many supporters. If as Filmer had suggested, God had "chosen" not only monarchy, but a particular monarch, at a particular historical moment, for a specific people, then debating political consent was largely irrelevant. At the very least, it became a religious question. Obedience to God required obedience to His chosen monarch; opposition to a "rightfully chosen" monarch was itself an opposition to God, something going beyond simple political dissent and toward moral and political heresy. Human equality, if there was such a thing, occurred only among those who shared a common obedience to a monarch, who himself (or herself) was *above* other persons, his or her political and moral *inequality* justified by God Himself.

It was against this view of political authority that Locke argued for the basic equality of all persons, approaching the question in such a way as to question all claims of such "natural" or divinely sanctioned inequality.

Nowhere was this more evident than in the *First Treatise*, written in large part as a reply to Sir Robert Filmer's work, *Patriarchia*, published in 1680.[1] In many respects, both works claimed some of the same things from a similar Christian perspective: that initially, political authority had evolved from paternal authority; that the original father of mankind was Adam, and God his divine Creator; and that subsequent political rulers in the Christian world either attempted to trace, or could trace, their authority to the first father—either Adam, or, after the flood—Noah.[2] Filmer argued from there that this justified and supported the notion of absolute sovereignty by a monarch over his people, much as a father could claim sovereignty over his children.[3] To this, Locke replied: "Scripture or reason, I am sure, does not anywhere say so, notwithstanding the noise of divine right, as if divine authority hath subjected us to the unlimited will of another."[4] Rather, Locke insisted that when God gave dominion over the earth to man, "it was not Adam in particular, exclusive of all other men; whatever dominion he had thereby, it was not a private dominion but a dominion in common with the rest of mankind."[5] In other words, Locke insisted that God had not given an exclusive grant of sovereign authority to one person, where it would pass on his death to his immediate descendant. Locke's vision of human equality rested on the opposite premise: God gave the world to all mankind, and as God's children, all are in a position of rough equality before God. No one was entitled to rule over anyone else based on some accident of birth.

The idea extended beyond political authority. In other cases, Locke argued that the circumstances of birth did not endow anyone with a greater right over others. For Filmer, monarchy was an extension of patriarchy, and to buttress the argument for monarchy, Filmer had claimed that because fathers produced their own children, they had a right to rule over them. Again, Locke denied the claim. Although in the course of human history children may have consented to the rule of their fathers, and in that way "the natural fathers of families by an insensible change became the political monarchs of them too," this did not mean that consent was unimportant, nor entirely absent. In fact, consent was everything; tacit consent marked a *legitimate* patriarchy, and without that consent, a patriarchy could not persist. And throughout, all men were "at liberty what government he will put himself under," such that it was "very evident [that] man has a *natural freedom*."[6] Thus, being the father of someone did not necessarily give the father any political authority. Even if such a right did exist, Locke argued, then mothers had a legitimate claim to authority on the same grounds.[7] However, neither parent, as parents, could claim his or her child as his or her own creation, and thus claim over the child permanent authority and right. Because neither men nor women could animate life, all credit was due to God.[8] In any case, when the children eventually became adults, they were at liberty to pursue political and other arrangements and to secure their best interests, sometimes despite parental authority.[9]

Other aspects of patriarchy, even the differences between men and women, did not involve a divinely sanctioned inequality between men and women, as Filmer had also suggested.[10] Locke suggested that God did not necessarily grant men dominion *over* women.[11] When He drives Adam and Eve from paradise, God merely "foretells" what will happen between men and women, but does not directly justify it. And despite whatever "conjugal power" men might have over their wives, Locke thought it was hardly analogous to political authority: "[It is] not a political power of life and death over her, much less over anyone else."[12]

These examples illustrated an inescapable conclusion: all persons shared an equality of right irrespective of the circumstances of birth. The summary of Locke's argument against Filmer was laid out thus, in one very long sentence in the *First Treatise*:

> But if Creation, which gave nothing but a being, made not Adam prince of posterity; if Adam was not constituted lord of mankind, nor had a private dominion given him exclusive of his children, but only a right and power over the earth and inferior creatures in common with the children of men; if also God gave not any particular power to Adam over wife and children, but only subjected Eve to Adam as a punishment, or foretold the subjection of the weaker sex in the ordering of the common concernment of their families, but gave not thereby to Adam, as to the husband, power of life and death, which necessarily belongs to the magistrate; if fathers by begetting their children acquire no such power over them; and if the command, "Honor thy father and mother," give it not, but only enjoins a duty owing to parents equally, whether subjects or not, and to the mother as well as the father—if all this be so, as I think by what has been said is very evident, then man has a *natural freedom*, notwithstanding all our author [Filmer] confidently says to the contrary, since all that share in the same common nature, faculties, and powers are in nature equal and ought to partake in the same common rights and privileges, till the manifest

appointment of God, who is "Lord over all, blessed forever," can be produced to show any particular person's supremacy, or a man's own consent subjects him to a superior.[13]

As God did not make such a "manifest appointment," naked monarchy under the guise of divine right could hardly be justified. The notion of consent, developed further in the *Second Treatise*, would remain for Locke the only legitimate grounds for political power.

"Government . . . For the Benefit of the Governed"

Since the time Locke first articulated his theory of property and his theory of political consent, his critics, then and now, have given numerous reasons for why both accounts are less than plausible.[14] But the importance of these accounts lies not so much in whether they are plausible, either as real or theoretically satisfying ways of viewing property or political membership; rather, so much of the significance of Locke's work lies in the fact that he wanted so much for both political membership and property to hinge on choice, conduct, and other forms of conscious action, rather than things more arbitrary, such as the circumstances of birth, social status acquired by birth, mere geography, or tradition and common practice. Nowhere is this more evident than in his discussions of private property.

Locke suggested that social inequality could rightfully exist when some persons labored more than others. For example, the use of money, Locke speculated, arose out of a desire to save the surplus of legitimate labor and exchange, so that an industrious man could keep more than he needed for the moment and enlarge his possessions, yet without harming anyone.[15] Similarly, Locke reasoned that a poor man was poor due to his own bad behavior: in the midst of a bountiful economy, he wrote in one essay, "the growth of the poor must . . . have some other cause, and it can be nothing else but the relaxation of discipline and corruption of manners; virtue and industry as being as constant companions on the one side as vice and idleness are on the other." To help the poor, the state may need to set "a restraint on their debauchery," and shut down those "superfluous brandy houses and unnecessary alehouses."[16] Remedies for poverty were desirable insofar as they could discipline the poor to work, and thereby encourage or at least frighten within them a penchant for good behavior. Locke recommended a few measures: send them off as maritime laborers; export them to plantations; create working schools for poor children; maim a thief publicly for forgery; and open more houses of correction.[17] Locke was not always so harsh; he did insist, for example, that charity required a man with means to share what he could with another in need, so that no matter how poor, a man in need need not starve.[18] Yet, for the most part, in much of his work, Locke argued for how wealth and poverty *should* depend on conduct and not be the result of something less.

Locke's view of social distribution worked also in the other direction, as was underscored by his analysis of inheritance. The distribution of a person's wealth after his death, he insisted, should have some fairness to it, and also depend on conduct. According to Locke, being the first-born male did not entitle a child to inherit everything: "Every man is born with a double right: first, a right of freedom to his person, which no other man has a power over, but the free disposal of it lies in himself; secondly, a right, before any other man, to inherit *with his brethren* his father's goods."[19] Among the brethren, moral desert should matter the most: "The possession of the father being the expectation and inheritance of the children, ordinarily in certain proportions according to the law and custom of the country, yet it is commonly in the father's power to bestow it with a more sparing or liberal hand, according as the behaviour of this or that child hath comported with his will and humour."[20] Again, "behaviour" should determine reward.

By that same standard, an irresponsible man who risked everything— perhaps a man who engaged foolishly in adventure and war—could rightfully lose his life and property to his enemy, and still, a just adversary would spare the innocent victims of the irresponsible man's actions. Admitting that his argument was hardly ever the rule for most conquerors, Locke still appealed for the "innocent wives and children."[21] Again, those who did nothing should not lose everything because of the conduct of some husband or father. The just conqueror, having some right to the property of a rebel for restoring his own property, should nevertheless yield "to the pressing and preferable title of those who are in danger to perish without it."[22] The same theme persisted: one's enjoyment of property should depend on one's own conduct, not someone else's. At a time when this principle was rarely observed, in Europe or anywhere else, Locke's separation of individual culpability and group responsibility appeared distinctive.[23]

Locke's justifications for rightful acquisition, property, and inheritance helped to explain why, in terms of political membership and obligation, he was deeply offended by nonconsensual monarchy. The trouble with monarchy by inheritance lay in the fact that right conduct often had nothing to do with it. A monarch could simply be born into the position without having "done" anything to deserve it. The king of France could inherit an entire kingdom and his subjects could be bound to obedience as though *they* were objects of *his* property. "The great mistakes of late about government [have] arisen from confounding these distinct powers. . . . Government, being for the benefit of the governed and not the sole advantage of the governors, cannot be inherited by the same title that children have to the goods of their father."[24] Monarchy by inheritance did in this way tend to reduce men to cattle by reducing men to a form of property. The thought of a mere child, born to a king, having done nothing to inherit a kingdom, enormous wealth, the obedience of everyone in the realm—all of this appeared grossly offensive. As a Protestant skeptic, Locke could not believe such a fiction.[25]

In that light, Locke's arguments for the grounds of *legitimate* government would appear more compelling. A proper understanding of political relationships could free men of thinking as though they should be content with fate. Collectively and self-consciously, persons could establish a common government for themselves for their own sake. Such a government, rather than limiting their freedom, was actually the primary expression of their freedom, as well as an expression of their desire for a fair and impartial enjoyment of their liberties. In this type of government, men best expressed to one another their position as moral equals. Any inequality between them would occur because of conduct, or by mutual consent; only those who labored would be rewarded, in rough proportion to their labor; and only those who had had the approval of their peers could exercise political power. Politically, equality would occur through elective schemes where the decisions of the majority would determine particular rules, "or else this original compact, whereby he with others incorporates into one society, would signify nothing and be no compact, if he be free and under no other ties than he was before in the state of nature."[26] Logistically, the consent of everyone for specific decisions would be impossible, and to require it would mean the unraveling of commonwealths. Instead, everyone's vote would count as one; majorities of votes would settle particular decisions. The benefits of the end products—clear rules about what was and was not permissible within the commonwealth, and impartial judges to settle disputes—outweighed the uncertainties associated with a vague law of nature, or even the "liberty" of persons to decide in the state of nature how to settle disputes and ambiguities, sometimes with resort to personal violence. Altogether, living in a well-regulated commonwealth, men could come to experience one another as moral equals and also escape the endless cycles of violence and predation that had plagued their history. To keep the peace and to give order, men could rely on *each other* rather than capitulating as they had so often done to all-powerful monarchs. And in such a commonwealth, right conduct—everyone *doing* the right thing—could give men a framework in which to pursue their fortunes rather than be themselves the victims of arbitrary fortune.

"The Fruit of a Thousand Years' Experience"

These same preoccupations with fortune and arbitrary circumstances troubled John Stuart Mill, perhaps the most important English political theorist of the 19th century. In one of his most famous essays, "The Subjection of Women," he wrote that among "one or two of the most advanced nations of the world," "we now live . . . in a state in which the law of the strongest seems to be entirely abandoned as the regulating principle of the world's affairs." Of the rule of force, "nobody professes it, and, as regards most of the relations between human beings, nobody is permitted to practice it."[27] In place of force, Mill pointed to law and order and other values synonymous with Enlightenment principles—including equality, merit, and moral desert. Indeed, in looking through Mill's statements on gender equality in his own country, or his staunch opposition to slavery in other nations abroad, one could hardly guess that the same person could easily approve of colonial rule in India or conquest in North America (which he did). Curiously, his statements about the principles to which a liberal society *ought* to be committed mark him as a defender of those who were, during his time (and even in ours), considered pariahs, savages, and inferior beings. Underlying Mill's defense of the downtrodden was a moral disdain for a power acquired through status, birth, or some other "accident." In fact, Mill and Locke had much in common on these issues.

In "The Subjection of Women," Mill articulated a different attitude toward luck, an attitude that correspondingly marked for him the difference between primitive and modern societies. "For, what is the particular character of the modern world—the difference which chiefly distinguishes modern institutions, modern social ideas, modern life itself, from those of times long past?"

> It is, that human beings are no longer born to their place in life, and chained down by an inexorable bond to the place they are born to, but are free to employ their faculties, and such favorable chances as offer, to achieve the lot which may appear to them most desirable. Human society of old was constituted on a very different principle. All were born to a fixed social position, and were mostly kept in it by law, or interdicted from any means by which they could emerge from it. As some men are born white and others black, so some were born slaves and others freemen and citizens; some were born patricians, other plebeians; some were born feudal nobles, other commoners and *roturiers*. A slave or serf could never make himself free, nor, except by the will of his master, become so.[28]

"The fruit of a thousand years of experience" seemed to Mill to suggest that persons' lives ought not be so profoundly determined by such accidents of birth. People themselves should determine for themselves the terms of their lives while respecting "the rights of others."

Under this theory, continuing the practice of privileging men over women betrayed a lack of commitment to this newly emergent principle: "If the principle is true, we ought to act as if we believed it, and not to ordain that to be born a girl instead of a boy, any more than to be born black instead of white, or a commoner instead of a nobleman, shall decide the person's position through all life."[29] In other words, "The principle of the modern movement in morals and politics, is that conduct, and conduct alone, entitles to respect: that not what men *are*, but what they *do*, constitutes their claim to deference; that, above all, merit, and not birth, is the only rightful claim to power and authority."[30] Applied to gender, "the ideas and institutions by which the accident of sex is made the groundwork of an inequality of legal rights, and a forced dissimilarity of social functions, must ere long be recognized as the greatest hindrance to moral, social, and even intellectual improvement."[31]

Mill's equally powerful rejection of ascriptive status can be found in his opposition to slavery, both British and American.[32] Against apologists of slavery in Great Britain, who claimed that places like the West Indies ought to be dominated by white, English landowners, Mill asserted what seemed to him the more legitimate claim of African slaves who had provided the "thews and sinews" for developing the colony. Following a Lockean view of ownership and claim, Mill implied that the mixing of African labor with the land had given Africans a legitimate right to determine the fate of that same land. The English colonists, with their "fopperies of so-called civilization," had a less legitimate claim to places like the West Indies. Most of them did nothing while their slaves worked.[33]

Mill also argued that one could see even more clearly the injustice of the slavers' arrangements by noting its "modern" rigidity. For Mill, American slavery seemed clearly worse than slavery in the past: "[Slavery] is divested of one of its worst features when it is compatible with hope: enfranchisement was easy and common [in Rome]: enfranchised slaves obtained at once the full rights of citizens, and instances were frequent of their acquiring not only riches, but latterly even honors."[34] What was so particularly awful about American slavery was that the slaves inherited their status and could do practically nothing about it—they quite literally came into and exited the world as slaves. In that sense, there was no more awful or terrifying manifestation of ascriptive status, employed in a nation that purported to be "modern" and "advanced." When he witnessed how the Americans had engaged themselves in a civil war over the fate of this peculiar institution, Mill made very clear the direction of his sympathies: "War, in a good cause, is not the greatest evil which a nation can suffer. War is an ugly thing, but not the ugliest of things: the decayed and degraded state of moral and patriotic feeling which thinks nothing *worth* a war is worse."[35] Like gender equality, racial equality remained a noble aspiration, something to fight for: "Let us hope that . . . before the lapse of another generation, the accident of sex, no more than the accident of skin, will not be deemed a sufficient justification for depriving the possessor of the equal protection and just privileges of a citizen."[36]

"The Most Powerful of All Determining Circumstances Is Birth"

In several other respects, most particularly in his analysis of social inequality, Mill expressed similar concerns about the possibility for equal citizenship beyond ascriptive status. While supportive of the principles of private property, for example, Mill nevertheless did not believe that those same principles supported the harsh realities of poverty in his own society. "Suffice it to say that the condition of a number of people [in] civilized Europe, and even in England and France, is more wretched than that of most tribes of savages who are known to us."[37] The most troubling thing about this profound economic inequality, for Mill, appeared to be that the institution of private property—so cherished in advanced societies—could make poverty worse by entrenching it across generations.

Mill said that "private property, in every defense made of it, is supposed to mean the guarantee to individuals of the fruits of their own labor and abstinence," and the subsequent "right to the disposal of what he or she have produced by their own exertions, or received either by gift or by fair agreement, without force or fraud, from those who have produced it."[38] Working from those principles presented two kinds of problems. First, "the principle of private property has never yet had a fair trial in any country; and less so, perhaps, in this country than in some others."[39] Mill argued that throughout all of Europe, there had been too much "conquest and violence," and "the system still retains many and large traces of its origin." This would suggest that very many property holders (most?) had illegitimate rights to their property, such that a strict enforcement of the original premise would tend to condemn present arrangements. Second, work and property often appeared inversely related: "The reward [of labour], instead of being proportioned to the abstinence of the individual, is almost in an inverse ratio to it: those who receive the least, labour and abstain the most."[40] If the original premise of private property hinged on enjoying the fruits of one's own labor, then "the very idea of distributive justice, or of any proportionality between success and merit, or between success and exertion, is in the present state of society so manifestly chimerical as to be relegated to the regions of romance."[41] Rather than condemning the poor as Locke did, Mill underscored the way in which the institution of private property in practice could undermine its very foundations in theory. Instead of work, industry, frugality, and abstinence, there could be blind, stupid luck, leading some to luxury and others to lifelong poverty.

And so the defense of property posed this broader problem for Mill: How could it be possible that certain persons could be "born into" luxury, perhaps ill-acquired by their ancestors in the first place, without having "done" anything for it? Many of his contemporaries avoided the uncomfortable question; it seemed to Mill that among those who addressed it, it was usually the wealthy that most righteously defended the right to property. Did they deserve it? "It is true that the lot of individuals is not

wholly independent of their virtue and intelligence; these do really tell in
their favour, but far less than many other things in which there is no merit
at all. . . . The most powerful of all determining circumstances is birth."[42]

> The great majority are what they are born to be. Some are born rich
> without work, others are born in a position in which they can become
> rich *by* work, the great majority is born to hard work and poverty
> throughout life. . . . Next to birth the chief cause of success in life is acci-
> dent and opportunity. When a person not born to riches succeeds in ac-
> quiring them, his own industry and dexterity have generally contributed
> to the result; but industry and dexterity would not have sufficed unless
> there had been also a concurrence of occasions and chances which falls
> to the lot of only a small number.[43]

Were the regime of private property more open to the second possibility—the chance of becoming "rich *by* work"—rather than just chance itself, Mill would not have objected so strongly. But because in his view of
his own society, economic stability could not be had "without the aid of
fortunate accidents," the system of private property could appear unjust
and unfair even in cases where persons had demonstrated "industry and
dexterity."[44] For principles of private property to be meaningful, good
conduct was required—but without a fortunate set of circumstances,
good conduct would not be enough, and in some cases, fortune alone
would be enough without any good conduct whatsoever. Above all, luck
was necessary for a good life.

From a rhetorical point of view, Mill saved his harshest venom for
those who refused to think more critically about the role of *good* luck in
their lives. Mill expressed contempt for those who lived in an unexam-
ined, sheltered luxury while at the same time looking down on those who
were less well off. Such people were filled with the worst possible vices,
"the worst sort of pride."[45] Given to "self-worship" and "fopperies," this
class routinely attempted to reinforce its advantageous position through
"class legislation" and through organizing "government intended for . . .
the immediate benefit of the dominant class, to the lasting detriment of
the whole."[46] Speaking against this "evil," Mill sounded like a true revolutionary: "All privileged and powerful classes, as such, have used their
power in the interest of their own selfishness, and have indulged their
own self-importance in despising, and not in lovingly caring for, those
who were, in their estimation, degraded, by being under the necessity of

working for their benefit."[47] In several places, Mill clearly indicated both his aversion to existing property rules that tended to reinforce social inequality, and his sympathy for alternative arrangements that attempted to alleviate the plight of the less fortunate.[48] Indeed, Mill seemed to have loathed the members of the class "who never worked at all," but continued to lean on unearned privileges and self-serving interpretations of private property principles.

As did Locke, Mill noted that inheritance was one primary way that persons "who never worked at all" received most of their wealth. In a substantial chapter in his *Principles of Political Economy*, Mill devoted his attention to this problem along similar lines of analysis. Having established that riches could often lead to hubris and bad manners, Mill challenged the bases for inheritance: "Whatever fortune a parent may have inherited, or, still more, may have acquired, I cannot admit that he owes to his children, merely because they are his children, to leave them rich, without the necessity of any exertion."[49] Inheritance should occur within reasonable limits. "Without supposing extreme cases, it may be affirmed that in a majority of instances the good not only of society but of the individuals would be better consulted by bequeathing to them a moderate, than a larger provision."[50] One should be generous, but not too generous, lest he harm the recipient with excessive good fortune. In any case, if desert and property must be positively correlated, then it followed that inheritance and bequest ought to be correspondingly limited. Again, this was the same theme. In an ideal society, no one would come into enormous fortunes without having done *something*, or know poverty despite labor.[51]

Finally, and perhaps most surprisingly, in his theory of politics and representation Mill also attempted to link political participation more closely with desert. Many of his contemporaries favored property as a qualification for voting; not surprisingly, Mill opposed such a policy. Instead, he insisted that education ought to give a citizen a better claim to exercise the right of participation. The argument unfolded along familiar lines, in the context of a debate concerning the best method for apportioning "plural" votes in local, and possibly national, elections in Great Britain: "The [property] criterion is so imperfect; accident has so much more to do than merit in enabling men to rise in the world. . . . It is impossible for any one by acquiring any amount of instruction, to make sure of the corresponding rise in station, that this foundation of electoral privilege is always, and will continue to be, supremely odious."[52]

Because education did not correlate positively with subsequent enjoyment of property, property qualifications should not be the decisive criteria for the franchise. If some were to be rewarded with plural voting rights, then education itself should be the qualification.[53] Perhaps deflecting charges that his scheme would itself be exclusionary and elitist, Mill suggested that there ought to be openness to all comers, which "would not necessarily be repugnant to any one's sentiment of justice." For workingmen who could not attend the universities or afford time for a course of study, Mill recommended "voluntary examinations at which any person whatever might present himself, might prove that he came up to the standard of knowledge and ability laid down as sufficient, and be admitted, in consequence, to the plurality of votes."[54] In any case, tying suffrage to "superiority of mental qualities" was preferable to suffrage by property, or even universal suffrage. Like other goods, the right to vote should be something to be achieved. Political equality would be tied in this way to equality of opportunity, not accidents of birth, and certainly not through property acquired without labor.[55]

These arguments about equality and political authority suggested that for Mill as well as for Locke, the principle against ascriptive status moved in two directions. First, ascriptive characteristics such as race or gender did not justify deprivations of basic rights or opportunities. To the extent that legal and political systems disadvantaged persons based on such criteria—rendering certain people "unlucky"—these systems were unjust and morally repugnant. Similarly, the problem with institutions like private property or practices like inheritance was that in their operation, fortune often played a greater role than moral desert. These institutions and practices violated the same principle against ascriptive status, by conferring *advantages* on some simply because they were born lucky. Separated by over a century, Locke and Mill shared a common preoccupation with luck, fortune, and chance. In a surprising number of ways, they each tried to imagine liberal societies that mitigated the fact of arbitrariness in the world.

"The Basic Structure of Society"

The same concerns over luck and chance appear in contemporary liberal theory, and the work of John Rawls provides an excellent example. Few works of political theory have been as influential as *A Theory of Justice*, published in 1971. Rawls' objective was at once limited and ambitious—to propose principles of justice appropriate for "the basic structure of society, or more exactly, the way in which the major social institutions distribute fundamental rights and duties and determine the division of advantages from social cooperation."[56] Though deliberately narrowed in scope in this way, the theory of justice as fairness was nevertheless broad and ambitious.[57] Rawls intended to capture and to reinterpret the essence of social contract theory, to recover from it a sense of how it might be possible for free and equal persons to agree on principles of justice appropriate for the basic structure of society.[58]

To do this, Rawls introduced several imaginative theoretical devices, most notably "the original position" and its attendant "veil of ignorance." Rawls made clear that neither of these devices was intended to capture reality—neither "exists" in any place but in the mind, and both were intended to engage the imagination rather than describe a certain state of affairs, either historical or possible.[59] The original position denoted the parameters of an interesting and compelling thought experiment. First, "it is important that the original position be interpreted so that one can at any time adopt its perspective."[60] As a hypothetical experiment, it was not historically contingent. Second, the crucial element of the original position was that it simulated the circumstances for collective decision making: under this "perspective" one imagines being one of many parties considering a variety of possible options for the basic structure of society—utilitarianism, perfectionism, or other moral or political doctrines. It was an "original" position to the extent that persons taking this perspective were free to consider any and all possible doctrines that may be appropriate for governing society, as though their decision were *prior to* and essential for the foundations of that society. Third, in coming to a decision, parties were to be situated fairly, as equals. "The original position is defined in such a way that it is a status quo in which any agreements reached are fair. It is a state of affairs in which the parties are equally represented as moral persons and the outcome is not conditioned by arbitrary contingencies or the relative balance of social forces."[61]

In other words, no one in the original position took this perspective with vested interests to protect, nor was one party more advantaged than another. Given these conditions of fairness, the "agreement" that would emerge from the deliberations would be conceived as fair. Finally, once that agreement was reached, it was binding. Persons in the original position were ultimately free to choose whatever doctrine seems most appropriate to govern their society, but they were bound by their decision, whatever eventualities may occur.

Of these parameters, the third element of the original position received the most elaboration. Without too much effort, one could imagine or recall a nascent society, where persons or their representatives gather prior to the creation of a state to determine a constitution or some other fundamental rules to govern the society in which they will live. But in such cases, rarely were the parties or their representatives in a situation of complete equality, and given that fact, rarely were the proceedings or results untainted by imbalances of power or resources. Yet, the ideas of equality and fairness were essential to the Rawlsian thought experiment. And so, to control for the "arbitrary contingencies" and "the relative balance of social forces" that may skew preferences for one or another principle of justice, Rawls introduced the "veil of ignorance": in deciding on binding principles to govern their lives, "no one knows his place in society, his class position or social status, nor does any one know his fortune in the distribution of natural assets and abilities, his intelligence, strength, and the like."[62]

> Nor, again, does anyone know his conception of the good, the particulars of his rational plan of life, or even the special features of his psychology such as his aversion to risk or liability to optimism or pessimism. More than this, I assume that the parties do not know the particular circumstances of their own society. That is, they do not know its economic or political situation or the level of civilization and culture it has been able to achieve. The persons in the original position have no information as to which generation they belong.[63]

Still, Rawls indicated that behind the veil of ignorance, persons do know "the general facts about human society. . . . They understand political affairs and the principles of economic theory; they know the basis of social organization and the laws of human psychology. Indeed, the parties are assumed to know whatever general facts affect the choice of the principles of justice."[64] Defined in this way, the original position and the attendant veil of ignorance combined to present the parties with thrilling uncertainties—in the original position, one knew generally that any particular society could include Christians and Muslims, persons of different races, rich and poor, and so on, but once "outside" the original position, one did not know exactly which, or what combination of characteristics may eventually describe him. Or her.[65]

Having set out these parameters, Rawls proceeded to argue that under these conditions, persons in the original position would clearly reject certain moral and political principles as inappropriate for the basic structure of society. Most importantly, persons would reject various forms of consequentialism, including the utilitarianism of Bentham, Mill, and Sidgwick.[66] This would be the case because, under a utilitarian morality, some persons' "happiness" may be sacrificed for an increase in "happiness" experienced by others. Moreover, under a utilitarian morality, virtually nothing was immune "to political bargaining or to the calculus of social interests," not even basic liberties and rights.[67] Rawls argued that rational parties—knowing that *they* may potentially be the candidates to make severe sacrifices, including the surrender of basic rights and liberties, all for the sake of the happiness of *others*—would reject utilitarianism and other forms of consequentialism. Similarly, analogous doctrines of perfectionism—under which only a few persons' skills and potential were cultivated, while the others existed merely to support the aspirations of the chosen—would appear undesirable in the original position.[68] Knowing in advance that one might spend one's entire life as Thomas Jefferson's slave, rather than as Jefferson himself, perfectionism would appear distinctively unappealing.

Moreover, "if the parties are conceived as themselves making proposals, they have no incentive to suggest pointless or arbitrary principles."

> Inevitably, then, racial and sexual discrimination presupposes that some hold a favorable place in the social system that they are willing to exploit to their advantage. From the standpoint of persons similarly situated in an initial situation that is fair, the principles of explicit racist doctrine are not only unjust. They are irrational.[69]

Again, the idea would be that even the most racist and sexist person, provided there were a certain level of rationality and the right conditions for deliberation, would quickly drop racist or patriarchal arrangements if *that person* had to face truly the possibility of being the pariah in society. Persons in the original position would presumably reject, then, *any* use of ascriptive characteristics as the foundation for distributing social advantage.

At the heart of *A Theory of Justice* lies an explanation and defense of justice as fairness, the conception that included "the two principles of justice" that Rawls proposed rational and reasonable persons *would* adopt in the original position. Within the book itself, and in his subsequent work, Rawls has articulated the two principles in various forms, but essentially, they were as follows: "Each person is to have an equal right to the most extensive basic liberty compatible with a similar liberty for others.[70] . . . Social and economic inequalities are to be arranged so that they are both (a) to the greatest benefit of the least advantaged and (b) attached to offices and positions open to all under conditions of fair equality of opportunity."[71]

The exact content of the two principles might vary, depending on how "our considered judgments [are] duly pruned and adjusted."[72] Also, according to Rawls, the first principle ought to have priority over the second, chiefly because persons in the original position would not sacrifice their basic rights and liberties in favor of greater social or economic advantages. Again, unlike in a consequentialist ethics, the lexical ordering of the two principles expressed the idea that some things—namely the basic rights and liberties of all persons—would be off limits in routine political calculations from the perspective of persons fairly situated in the original position.[73]

Rawls devoted a substantial part of his work explaining why the two principles of justice would appear more satisfying to persons considering the very terms on which they will live with one another. For Rawls, one of the primary reason why they would choose these principles, and order them serially, lay in the binding and more or less permanent nature of the original (hypothetical) agreement: once persons decide on the terms for the basic structure of society, they must be prepared to live with whatever they chose. Deciding on the two principles helped them live with such a profound decision.[74] By ensuring, first, an extensive, basic set of rights and liberties which may not be sacrificed in a consequentialist way, the parties ensured a fundamental equality of right and liberty among one another. Also, by agreeing to the difference principle, the parties acted "to mitigate the influence of social contingencies and natural fortune on distributive shares, . . . by arranging inequalities for reciprocal advantage and by abstaining from the exploitation of the contingencies of nature and social circumstances within a framework of equal liberty."[75] Together, the idea of justice as fairness for Rawls best captured the possibility for conceiving persons as retaining their moral worth, while at the same time engaging in a society conceived as a fair scheme of social cooperation: "Another way of putting this is to say that the principles of justice manifest in the basic structure of society men's desire to treat one another not as means only but as ends in themselves."[76] And, moreover, "one might say, in view of our discussion, that a common understanding of justice as fairness makes a constitutional democracy."[77]

"Those Aspects of the Social World That Seem Arbitrary from a Moral Point of View"

Embedded deep within the theory of justice as fairness was a commitment to an egalitarian vision of society that was quite remarkable. It was a vision far more pronounced than in Locke or in Mill. By framing the original position as he did, Rawls immediately engaged the imagination, while at the same time encouraging persons to take a more sober look at diverse, multifaceted societies. Differences in race, class, gender, "natural" disabilities and talents, including intelligence, physical strength, and the like, as well as reasonable, comprehensive conceptions of the good—these were all within the realm of possibilities that persons taking the original position were aware of. And once they found themselves facing the possibility of being a racial minority, impoverished, a woman, a person with limited talents or abilities, or a member of a religious minority, they were at once tempted to embrace a level of tolerance and a commitment to equality that in real, liberal societies has yet to exist. In a Hobbesian state of nature, with chaos lurking everywhere, persons immediately rushed not to God but to the protection of a conceivably Godless Leviathan; but in a Rawlsian original position, with its own unsettling possibilities, persons—being rational—rushed to secure basic rights and liberties and to arrange for a system of social cooperation that would account for the worst-off in society in case it should happen to be them.[78] Faced with a myriad of possibilities, those in the original position were forced to confront every possibility and, in the process, to determine principles that would adequately account for their plurality and diversity. More importantly, though, the two principles of justice "express the result of leaving aside those aspects of the social world that seem arbitrary from a moral point of view."[79]

But what was "arbitrary"? To Rawls, the morally arbitrary appeared precisely in those characteristics—like race, class, gender, physical strength, and intelligence—that were normally ascribed to persons, but were not the result of their own doing. One does not choose one's own race or gender, or the level of one's native intelligence or strength.[80] They appear "arbitrary from a moral point of view" because they occurred without any volition; they were a matter of blind luck, void of conduct. Much as Locke had insisted that God did not grant to one person in a political system the right to rule over all others, by virtue of birth or divine right, no one was entitled, in a Rawlsian scheme, to a greater set of rights and liberties due to similar accidents of nature. Characteristics such as race and gender—which, in liberal societies, *have* served as the bases for social advantage, often within the basic structure of those societies—did not lead to similar entitlements in justice as fairness. Here, Rawls' framework echoed Mill's call for an enlightened society where status and power were divorced from morally arbitrary contingencies.

Moreover, other types of "natural" differences, such as strength and intelligence and the like, that may lead to social inequality were accounted for in egalitarian ways through the difference principle. For Rawls, the initial premise was the same: "No one deserves his greater natural capacity nor merits a more favorable starting place in society."[81] The difference principle accounted for this and allowed for social inequality, but only as part of a broader conception of society, taken as a fair scheme of cooperation.

> We see . . . that the difference principle represents, in effect, an agreement to regard the distribution of natural talents as a common asset and to share in the benefits of this distribution whatever it turns out to be. Those who have been favored by nature, whoever they are, may gain by their good fortune only on terms that improve the situation of those who have lost out. The naturally advantaged are not to gain merely because they are more gifted, but only to cover the cost of training and education and for using their endowments in ways that help the less fortunate as well.[82]

Once again, in the Rawlsian paradigm, persons in the original position fundamentally agreed to share their fate. "Natural accidents" did not occur in different people in the same way—life and fate just aren't that fair or "egalitarian"—but Rawls argued that persons in the original position would agree only to inequality that somehow can mitigate these vagaries of life. Since no one "deserved" his or her natural talents, the social structure ought to be arranged in a way that leveraged all natural talents for the benefit of society, with a view to the improvement of the conditions of the least well-off. The circumstances of life were never fair, but persons could choose to confront such fortunes by first acknowledging the role of luck, then by agreeing to treat one another fairly in light of it.

In Rawls' articulation of liberal theory, the recurring principle against ascriptive status has perhaps its most novel expression. By showing how morally arbitrary characteristics may be addressed in deliberations about the basic structure of society, Rawls insisted that rational persons would create a framework that accounted for the "throwness" of life. It was immediately evident that under the constraints of the original position, no one could possibly consent to a political system such as a hereditary monarchy, nor to institutions or practices such as chattel slavery or patriarchy. Rather, persons in the original position come to see that the only fair choice—in the midst of all of life's uncertainties—would be to agree on a scheme that mitigated luck and fortune, such that those who were fortunate in some circumstances would share their fate with those who weren't. They would cooperate not because of benevolence or pity, but as a matter of justice. For Rawls, that reasoned sense of justice began first by accounting for blind, dumb luck.

"Had You or I Been Born in the Bay of Soldania"

Altogether, the separate works of Locke, Mill, and Rawls strongly suggest a common aversion to ascriptive status deep within the core of liberal political theory. Whether expressed as a moral revulsion toward hereditary monarchy or as a rational strategy within a hypothetical agreement about the basic structure of society, the principle against ascriptive status captures important elements of liberal conceptions of equality, justice, and fairness. In illustrating examples of how nonliberal arrangements relied too heavily on ascription, each of these theorists grappled with the vagaries of life, and each theorized liberal societies to address questions of fate and chance; their separate concerns revolved around the central idea that neither luck nor birth ought to determine the scope of political authority, the enjoyment of basic rights and liberties, and presumptive social advantage or disadvantage. Inheritance of wealth and property posed the same type of problem as the "inheritance" of political authority—in a liberal society, an "enlightened society," right conduct and mutual consent ought to replace fate and fortune as the grounds for inequalities of fortune or formal authority. On these matters, all three theorists shared remarkably similar concerns.

But in light of these concerns, it is striking that none of these theorists discussed at length the significance of determining political membership by birth, which is arguably one of the most basic identities of persons in the world. For the most part, conventional legal practices have assigned political membership at birth, either through physical birth within the territory of a particular state, through the "blood" or ancestry of one's parents, or some combination of both. These practices of assigning political membership are all ascriptive. Moreover, few would disagree that this system of assigning membership has tremendous consequences; political membership itself often shapes opportunities and life chances, as some are born into wealthy democratic republics, while others to despotism, and still others to varying forms of political organization, some palatable and some not.[83]

Certainly, questions of political membership and political obligation were not totally ignored in the arguments of these important theorists. In several places, Locke expressed unease about the ascriptive nature of political membership. For example, Locke insisted that birth alone was insufficient to determine political allegiance for persons already born into a particular society, and he did outline in some detail the relationship between various acts and signs to varying degrees of political obligation. Persons born into a commonwealth always retained the right to leave: "if he disclaim the lawful government of the country he was born in, he must also quit the right that belonged to him by the laws of it and the possessions there descending to him from his ancestors if it were a government made by their consent."[84] Also, political obligation required something more than mere existence on the territory of the commonwealth: "Submitting to the laws of any country, living quietly and enjoying privileges and protection under them, makes not a man a member of that society."[85] For political obligation to occur, rather, one required something definitive: "Nothing can make any man so but his actually entering into it by positive engagement and express promise and compact."[86] In a number of such examples, the consequences of presumptive membership are limited or mitigated by subsequent conscious actions, and these are suggestive again of Locke's aversion to ascriptive status.

Mill, too, suggested that membership in a political community should be reflective of certain types of conduct, not mere circumstance. "Half-savage relics" could, if they tried, evolve toward membership in progressive civilization. On the borders of France, for example, the "savage," ethnic Basque could be better off by actively becoming a French citizen.

> Nobody can suppose that it is not more beneficial to a Breton, or a Basque of French Navarre, to be brought into the current of the ideas and feelings of a highly civilized and cultivated people—to a member of the French nationality, admitted on equal terms to all the privileges of French citizenship, sharing the advantages of French protection, and the dignity and *prestige* of French power—than to sulk in his own rocks, the half-savage relic of past times, revolving in his own little mental orbit, without participation or interest in the general movement of the world. The same remark applies to the Welshmen or the Scottish Highlander, as members of the British nation.[87]

Civilized nations like France ought to remain open to such admixture and absorption, for it was "a benefit to mankind." "The united people, like a crossed breed of animals (but in a still greater degree, because the influences in operation are moral as well as physical), inherits the special aptitudes and excellencies of all its progenitors, protected by the admixture from being exaggerated into neighboring vices."[88] Of course, Mill said, civilized peoples ought to protect against being overrun by savages: "The absorption of Greece by Macedonia was one of the greatest misfortunes which ever happened in the world: that of any of the principle countries of Europe by Russia would be a similar one."[89] Beyond these rather harsh observations, though, Mill devoted little to problems of political membership as an ascriptive phenomenon. Although he devoted considerable attention to the proper relationship between "civilized" and "savage" peoples, he did not defend or explain why political membership in general ought to be assigned at birth. And of course his casual insults against the Basques, the Welsh, the Scottish, the Russians, and the Macedonians left no doubt that he himself was grateful to have been born in London.

In Rawls' work, because he largely circumscribed the parameters of the "thought experiment" in the original position, problems of membership and belonging do not appear at all. The hypothetical society he contemplated was by design completely closed and self-sufficient: "Entry into it is only by birth and exit from it is only by death." For purposes of the Rawlsian thought experiment, "we have no prior identity before being in

society; it is not as if we came from somewhere but rather we find ourselves growing up in this society in this social position, with its attendant
advantages and disadvantages, as our good or ill fortune would have
it."[90] In this way, problems of membership and belonging simply are not
integral to Rawls' project.

Even when Rawls extended his theory of justice to cover international
realities, membership and belonging remained relatively static and unproblematic. In a revealing, prefatory passage in his book, *The Law of
Peoples*, Rawls admitted that "there are numerous causes of immigration," but that ideally, "they would disappear in the Society of liberal and
decent Peoples." This would be because in a "realistic utopia," governments would address some of the fundamental causes of migration, either
within their own borders, or in conjunction with other nations. Thus,
persons would have no reason to migrate.[91] The attendant problems of
adjusting political allegiance and the right of societies to deny political
membership from potential seekers do not appear as compelling issues in
Rawls' work. Rather, the focus is on societies and governments and their
duty to create a structure viable enough such that the persons within it
would not want to migrate: "People must recognize that they cannot
make up for failing to regulate their numbers or to care for their land by
conquest in war, or by migrating into another people's territory without
their consent."[92] In essence, Rawls framed international migration as resulting from a failure of governments to achieve justice or fairness within
their own territories. But nowhere does Rawls question why political
membership should be assigned at birth, nor does he give a justification
for why existing political communities can or should exercise their right
to exclude others, particularly the less fortunate.

The omission is more notable because Rawls, perhaps even more than
Locke or Mill, acknowledged deeply the vagaries of life and the elements
of luck necessary to make a good life possible. In Locke's words, "Had
you or I been born at the Bay of Soldania, possibly our thoughts and notions had not exceeded those brutish ones of the savages that inhabit
there; and had Tottepottemay been educated in England, he had perhaps
been as zealous a Christian and as good an architect as any in it."[93] And
from Mill, there was the recognition that "the most powerful of all determining circumstances is birth," and "next to birth the chief cause of
success in life is accident and opportunity." For Rawls, no one "deserved" a more favored starting position in life, because no one "deserves" the natural endowments that may give advantage, nor did one

"deserve" the fortunate circumstances that make enjoyment of those advantages possible. That was why, after all, as a matter of justice, persons in the original position would consent to treat all such advantages as though they were "common assets," to be accounted for in the two principles. Indeed, given that all three theorists recognized the compelling role of luck, chance, fortune, or fate, it is somewhat remarkable that they gave such scant attention to how political obligation did have in their own time, and does have in ours an undeniably strong connection to accidents and circumstances of birth.

Instead of confronting the relationship between political obligation and the circumstances of birth on the basis of considerations about justice, all three theorists devoted considerably more attention to defending the integrity of commonwealths and nation-states once they were created. Indeed, their very creation represented a noble grappling with the harshness and arbitrariness of life and the fruition of free and autonomous desires to confer security and stability in an unstable, dangerous world. Precisely because commonwealths represented such things, their protection and integrity were yet another important aspect of liberal theory, as we shall see. Irrespective of some of the confusion over exactly how membership ought to be assigned or denied, notions of sovereignty dominate liberal political discourse. In the following chapter I will attempt to explain exactly why Locke, Mill, and Rawls so valued political community, and why the sovereignty of liberal nation-states remains so compelling.

3

"One Body in the State of Nature"

"The Advantage of the Commonwealth"

For Locke, one premise seemed obvious: it was clearly just for a commonwealth to protect itself from persons it did not want. This was first because the original creation of a commonwealth, as he saw it, "harmed no one." Everyone else in the state of nature was still free to make his own commonwealth through mutual consent.[1] Of the existing commonwealths, the fact that they were created was a remarkable thing in and of itself. That men could join together for self-protection and reject mutual predation was so *against* the natural tendencies of so many men, perhaps all of humanity, that when such a society arose, it was a rare thing indeed and worthy of protection.[2] As for those outside such an auspicious and beneficial set of relationships, the commonwealth had no duty to accept them, nor did they have any presumptive right to be admitted. Of course, such persons could be admitted, but according to guidelines that account primarily "for the advantage of the commonwealth." "What is done in reference to foreigners, depending much on their actions and the variations of designs and interests, must be left in great part to the prudence of those who have this power committed to them, to be managed by the best of their skill for the advantage of the commonwealth."[3] The commonwealth may assert a "federative power" to deal with strangers and other governments. "The whole community is one body in the state of nature in respect of all other states or persons out of its community."[4] Locke stated further that because existing states had no duty to accept strangers, strangers seeking membership ought to make themselves more attractive as potential members.

And so, for example, potential immigrants should "depend only on what they bring with them, either their estates or industry, both of which are equally profitable to the kingdom"; they should not be likely to become a public charge.[5] Overall, the Lockean commonwealth truly was "one body," organized in such a way as to provide stability and protection in the midst of a chaotic, predatory world. In this type of world, where even Christians routinely victimized "innocent" savages and violence and wrong marked the most civilized cultures, it was no small thing that a commonwealth would "prevent or redress foreign injuries, and secure the community from inroads and invasion."[6] Here, where Locke's work indicated a sobering admission of men's savagery as well as a faith in their ability to rise above it, the survival of the commonwealth depends on the right to protect itself against very real threats.

Moreover, for Locke, the existence of the bounded commonwealth gave men a special place to articulate and confront differences without treachery. One of the advantages of a commonwealth was that it could provide a common forum for articulating the law of nature and be at the same time a place of tolerance in matters of conscience or religious belief. Locke spoke from personal experience: in a world in which secular affairs were routinely rendered bloody and vicious on account of religious difference, the Lockean commonwealth could be a place where men did not impose matters of conscience on one another. Among themselves, they could practice tolerance.[7] Also, in the same way, the trouble with the state of nature was not the absence of law, but rather the ambiguity of the law of nature, since reasonable men could differ of the exact requirements of that law. The bounded commonwealth was essential in this regard because it gave its members the space to articulate and bind one another to a settled meaning of the law of nature, so as to give themselves determinate rules that did not exist before in the state of nature.[8] In this regard, an *unbounded* commonwealth would be both illogical and unwieldy. In size and scope, it would be no different than the state of nature, and perhaps for that reason it does not appear as a legitimate or workable option anywhere in Locke's work. Conversely, settling questions of justice and fairness, such as those that the members of a commonwealth pursue, presupposed some closed, bounded framework.

"The Due Growth and Development of a People Further Advanced in Improvement"

For Mill, the bounded nation-state was necessary for other similar reasons, namely, for the members within it to develop among one another the feeling of mutual concern necessary for a free, liberal society to flourish. The defense of national autonomy appeared here as being analogous to the protection of a particular type of culture. There was, for Mill, a clear distinction between "civilization" and "savagery," as we have seen. Those lucky enough to have been born into the former had a duty to protect themselves from the latter. This was Mill's advice to European colonists, whose lives among the savages should be devoted toward "higher stages of improvement" for the savages, and an aversion toward the "inclinations of savage life."[9] "Savages" did not have a similar right to sovereignty or cultural integrity. For the barbarians, "independence and nationality, so essential to the due growth and development of a people further advanced in improvement, are generally impediments to theirs."[10]

On the other hand, liberal political culture as it appeared to him in his own native England wasn't so much an "accident" as a type of cultural achievement to be cherished and protected.[11] Mill insisted that culture helped to make liberal citizens possible; in turn, those citizens had a duty to protect that heritage. For example, as "the agency of national education," a liberal government "is to be judged by its actions upon men . . . by what it makes of the citizens, and what it does to them; its tendency to improve or deteriorate the people themselves."[12] Thus, the protection of liberal culture against external threats was rather indispensable to the very survival and flourishing of liberal societies, and not necessarily reflective of a more base liberal chauvinism. Indeed, to insist that this was not chauvinism, Mill said that liberal societies had "a sacred duty" to work toward the "future permanent improvement" of "backward" or "inferior" peoples unlucky enough to have been born into their "inferior" societies. Mill suggested that liberal societies had the duty to deny self-government for such "savages," like the people of India, for their own good, and in place of self-rule, the "civilized nations" had the burden of instituting among the savages liberal habits, customs, and institutions.

Should the savages come to live among more civilized people, the importance of a cohesive, unified political culture was substantial enough to require an aggressive assimilation of the former into the latter. Again, there are the familiar and jarring phrases from Mill: "half-savage relics," once content to live within their own "little mental orbit," but now crawling out from under their barbaric "rocks" to join civilized peoples in the "general movement of the world." Civilized peoples had to be open enough or liberal enough to accept such relics into their societies, but with the understanding that the relics would conform to *their* culture and way of life. Nothing could be worse, on the other hand, than if the savages were to overwhelm the civilized natives. Yet, if assimilation of the savages could be possible, the new amalgamation of peoples within a civilized nation with liberal institutions could be even better than the past, unadulterated composition of liberal citizens. The new peoples would have "special aptitudes and excellencies of all its progenitors."

Underlying all of these observations and concerns was Mill's argument about the necessity for a common political culture, for a people to be "united among themselves by common sympathies, which do not exist between them and any others."[13] Without a sobering, realistic appreciation for liberal culture, and without that aggressive assimilation toward that culture, and without the openness to create the possibility for new combinations and varieties of liberal peoples, there would be the constant, persistent threat of civil war, mutual animosity, and internal chaos. In this sense, Mill was certainly not a liberal theorist confident about the health and survival of multiracial or multicultural liberal societies. For Mill, it would appear as though values like liberal tolerance—for matters of conscience and points of view—could only be possible within a framework of shared affiliations and mutual belonging, fixed primarily in a sense of common nationality which ought to be defended as a matter of survival. Whenever possible, nationality and statehood ought to be linked presumptively.

"A World Government . . . Would Either Be a Global Despot or Else Rule over a Fragile Empire Torn by Frequent Civil Strife"

In Rawls' work, while he explicitly rejected the idea that a multiracial state could not survive, he retained the idea of having and protecting a common *political* culture, and that, too, was reflective of the same type of concerns expressed by Locke and Mill. So much of Rawls' theory of justice relied also, quite explicitly, on a shared sense of community and affiliation among disparate members. Once persons in a closed, self-regenerating political community came to understand how luck and fortune gave some advantages over others that were not "deserved," they would consent, Rawls argued, on the basis of considerations about justice, to treat all talents as though they were common assets, the benefits of which ought to be shared and distributed among members. They would also mitigate, or try to mitigate, the role of luck by establishing and then prioritizing the principle of justice that provided for a complete set of basic rights merely as a condition of belonging.

But this unproblematic sense of belonging must be bounded. Stretching those boundaries to include, say, the entire world would be self-defeating and destructive to Rawls' two principles of justice. He explicitly rejected it in *The Law of Peoples*:

> Here I follow Kant's lead in *Perpetual Peace* (1795) in thinking that a world government—by which I mean a unified political regime with the legal powers normally exercised by central governments—would either be a global despot or else rule over a fragile empire torn by frequent civil strife as various regions and peoples tried to gain their political freedom and autonomy.[14]

Like Locke and Mill, Rawls tended to agree that too much diversity and too much inclusiveness would result in kind of disaster. Although he did not specify the lines along which this "civil strife" would occur, Rawls' later comments about different types of societies suggested that too much plurality would be unwieldy, or even dangerous. Through the original position and the veil of ignorance, Rawls' theory of justice *assumed* a liberal society emerging, composed of persons committed to liberal principles; the theory did not assume a union with the world, a world consisting of liberal as well as nonliberal peoples. In Rawls' work, there was more than a hint that the world—as Locke had suggested—was still full of predators.

In *The Law of Peoples*, Rawls offered a typology of various kinds of peoples and states—"liberal peoples" and "decent hierarchical peoples," which are "well-ordered," and "outlaw states," "societies burdened by unfavorable conditions," and "benevolent absolutisms," which are typically nonliberal.[15] Of these, outlaw states posed the greatest problem, and their existence was perhaps the best argument for protecting the autonomy and integrity of liberal states. Rawls argued that self-defense was a proper justification for war, and in circumstances where outlaw states posed significant dangers to the neighbors and to the world, liberal nations were justified in defending themselves militarily. Moreover, even against decent societies and other nonliberal peoples, Rawls suggested that liberal societies can and must cherish their liberal political culture, often to the point of setting a desirable example for nonliberal peoples to follow. Persons in a liberal state may show a "proper patriotism" for their society's achievements and history—they were the result of many generations of collective, coordinated acts, all toward a noble purpose. In these ways, Rawls evoked tactfully much of what Mill or Locke put more bluntly—instead of "savages," Rawls talked of "decent societies," "burdened societies," or "outlaw states," and instead of suggesting a coercive conquest of nonliberal peoples, Rawls implied persuasion toward a liberal example.[16] At each turn, Rawls embraced the notion of sovereign, independent states, as well as the necessity for the political boundaries that they entailed, even though they may seem artificial or arbitrary.[17] To the extent that all persons and peoples in the world are not yet liberal, and that some were actually hostile, Rawls suggested throughout that liberal nations can and should protect those values that make them distinctive. This implied the freedom to act independently as collective bodies.

Also, like Locke and Mill, Rawls indicated the need for certain types of institutions within states to help create the liberal self. He did give a sense of how a person's "moral development . . . might occur in a well-ordered society." Rawls wrote of how a sense of justice and concern for others begins from attachments that were more immediate—from one's family, and from one's own local community—and then grew into general and perhaps more abstract and universal concerns over time.[18] Moral and liberal sentiments, once connected to immediates and fellow citizens, develop further such that they are "no longer connected solely with the well-being and approval of particular individuals and groups." Eventually, "our moral sentiments display an independence from the accidental circumstances of our world."[19] And yet, the account Rawls gave suggested that these initial, more narrow concerns were actually quite indispensable and that that was why, no matter how general and universal our moral sentiments and sense of justice become eventually, "our natural attachments to particular persons and groups still have an appropriate place." In a liberal society, members do develop concern for others, but always from within a more intimate core of belonging without which those universal concerns might not be possible.[20] For those reasons, smaller communities and more immediate political associations may be what allow liberal selves to appreciate the two principles and the entire theory of justice as fairness.

Citizenship and Ascription

Because all three theorists discussed nation-states as essentially bounded, closed political communities, their discussion of the relations among these nation-states largely assumed no changes in constitutive membership other than by natural increase. In Locke and in Mill, persons did migrate, but neither theorist addressed the issue as though it might raise fundamental problems of assigning or denying political membership. Entry into a Lockean society was at the discretion of the federative power of the commonwealth, never a matter of right nor based on claims of justice. For Mill, the primary issue of diverse political communities appeared to be how the "civilized" peoples of the world should control or resist the culture of the "savages," either through an aggressive assimilation of the savages when they came within the jurisdiction of the civilized, or through a period of "tutelage," where the civilized quite literally took over the political destiny of the savages for their own good. In his more elaborate theory of the law of peoples, Rawls rejected Mill's dichotomy of "civilized" and "savage" peoples as well as the argument for colonialism. But for the most part, he assumed national boundaries as fixed and political membership across societies as relatively unproblematic. Among recent commentators, including Rogers Smith, Rawls' failure to address these types of questions, regarding political obligations, exclusion, and national sovereignty, was "inexcusable."[21] But the primary goal for Rawls was to provide an account of how persons in a *hypothetically* bounded, closed community could live peacefully among one another based on familiar principles of justice. As mentioned before, in Rawls' ideal world, there would not be any significant migration across borders, and thus no need to sort through whether exclusionary immigration or naturalization policies may ever be justified in liberal societies. As in his original, influential work, persons were simply born into societies and exited only by death.

Yet, this tendency to avoid addressing seriously the facts of international migration and the problems of political obligation that they raise leave fundamental ambiguities about liberal commitments to principles of equality, fairness, and political community. There is simply no direct account for why it is just—for persons who have the misfortune to be born into a collapsing society—to be assigned *permanent* political membership there, rather than seeking new membership in another society somewhere else. There is no direct account for why it is just to deny such persons membership in a flourishing liberal society with a burgeoning economy, society, and political life. Liberal justifications—in an inherent sovereignty and right, in the protection of liberal culture, or in a rejection of "borderless" nation-states—either fail to address these types of questions adequately, or, when they suggest an approach toward an answer, various liberal precepts and principles lead toward different conclusions. On the one hand, as Locke, Mill, and Rawls all agree, there could be nothing more arbitrary than the circumstances of birth, and as such, there would appear to be no basis in liberal theory to treat such circumstances as though they should be the grounds for advantage or disadvantage in the distribution of basic opportunities and rights. As we have seen, one of the most central, recurring themes that ran throughout the works of Locke, Mill, and Rawls was the idea that such circumstances of birth should *not* dominate one's fortunes nor determine the scope of one's basic rights. There might not be any justification, then, for attaching political membership in such a manner as to limit the context of choices for all people in the world.

Nor does there appear to be just grounds to grant presumptive membership to those born fortunate enough to be members without having done anything to "earn" their membership. One wonders why political membership designated in that way should not raise, as in Locke, or Mill, objections similar to the ones they had about inheritance, for example, or race and gender. Political membership thus assigned would appear like an undeserved "feudal privilege," as the contemporary political philosopher Joseph Carens has suggested.[22] Without question, the vast majority of citizens in powerful modern nation-states did nothing to earn their citizenship—they were merely lucky to be born within the territorial borders, or had parents who were fortunate to have such status. Current rules tend to confer the parents' citizenship on their children as well. On average, such children acquire tremendous relative advantages on the basis of their citizenship status compared to children born into poorer states and societies. There would appear to be no reasonable way to argue that this type of advantage was related, in any way, to moral desert; indeed, it seems disappointing that this particular privilege is not treated more seriously as another type of illegitimate privilege, based on the basic premises of liberal theory.

Instead, to protect the achievement that is the commonwealth, or the culture that liberal societies need in order to flourish, or the communities that make the enlightened, liberal self possible, liberal theorists like Locke, Mill, and Rawls assumed the ability or right to exclude outsiders to some extent, to protect the types of political communities that these liberal theorists value. Indeed, Locke, Mill, and Rawls all presumed a bounded, closed political community. They did so for disparate reasons, but they assumed at least a tacit right to exclude in order to make some components of their separate liberal theories intelligible. The pervading idea was that a liberal society that relinquished the right to exclude outsiders was a liberal society that had no future, as it became overrun by "savages," or became too politically and culturally unmanageable or destructive of the very institutions that made liberal persons and societies possible.

But in a world where persons have migrated routinely across international borders based on reasons ranging from a perception of better economic opportunities, to abject poverty, political persecution, social dislocation, war, famine, or some other catastrophic upheaval, the lack of a satisfactory resolution is deeply troubling in light of the tremendous problems such migrations can cause. The absence of a clear resolution may be understandable in the context of appreciating the fundamental values in liberal theory that are at stake in any resolution. That liberal values and interpretations of such values often conflict is hardly surprising, and yet the conflicts that arise here are quite basic. Can liberal societies justly exclude persons from entry or membership without violating principles of equality? Can they exclude on the basis of race, or culture, as Mill might argue, or exclude simply as a matter of right? Even if exclusion were grounded on a liberal account of national self-determination, would this justify the disparate or discriminatory treatment of persons who—for whatever reason—entered a liberal state anyway, either with or without formal permission? Can the state treat such persons as "perpetual strangers," relying on their immigration status alone to justify legal, political, or economic disabilities? Or, paradoxically, can liberal societies give up the right to exclude without jeopardizing the culture, institutions, and communities they value? Because of the chaos that an unregulated migration may cause, can liberal states impose boundaries to protect the very institutions that many members regard as social and political *achievements*? On what grounds can exclusion be possible, just, or necessary?

"Fellow Members as Partners in a Shared Way of Life"

These questions have reemerged in liberal political theory, especially in light of ever more contentious public discussions over immigration and multiculturalism. Among political theorists writing in the liberal tradition, as well as theorists critical of liberalism, questions of migration, and issues of racial and ethnic diversity, in addition to issues of liberal plurality and national sovereignty, have received great attention in recent years. As Will Kymlicka and W. J. Norman have observed, there is a "return of the citizen," a renewed interest in what citizenship and political membership mean in an increasingly mobile, dynamic world, where single nationalities rarely correspond with homogeneous political units largely because of widespread migration.[23] Some writers, including Bruce Ackerman and Joseph Carens, have answered restrictionist objections to migration by questioning the very bases for immigration restrictions in liberal societies, including the United States.[24] Ackerman has suggested that to the extent that the United States is a liberal democracy, dedicated to discursive practices of political participation, the nation should essentially be as open as possible to all persons willing "to participate in the conversation," irrespective of their racial or cultural background. "In an ideal theory, all people who fulfill the dialogic and behavioral conditions have an unconditional right to demand recognition as full citizens in a liberal state."[25] Carens has noted that liberal states are far from such an ideal and that, in fact, the very legal system that assigns presumptive membership to citizens in a liberal democracy, thereby giving them a collective "right" to select or even discuss the desirability of new members, amounts to the protection of a kind of "feudal privilege" that should be rejected under liberal tenets. "Liberals objected to how feudalism restricted freedom, including the freedom of individuals to move from one place to another in search of a better life. But modern practices of citizenship and state control over borders ties people to the land of their birth almost as effectively. If the feudal practice was wrong, what justified the modern ones?"[26]

To that question, other writers (some of whom are critical of liberalism itself for not caring enough about such boundaries), including Yael

Tamir and Michael Walzer, have replied that liberal political theory has *always* been nationalistic and particularist, despite claims of universality. Liberal citizenship has always required a sense of communal membership; citizens have always seen "fellow members as partners in a shared way of life, as cooperators they rely on." Citizenship mediates moral duties, and that is not just descriptively accurate, but morally permissible, perhaps even necessary.[27] In one defense of this "liberal nationalism," Tamir wrote: "Assuming that individuals have a right to preserve the uniqueness of their communal life, it would make sense to place some restrictions on membership and claim that we, who already belong, should do the choosing 'in accordance with our own understanding of what membership means in our community and of what sort of a community we want to have.'"[28] For Michael Walzer, "The primary social good that we distribute to one another is membership in some human community. And what we do with regard to membership structures all our other distributive choices: it determines with whom we make those choices, from whom we require obedience and collect taxes, to whom we allocate goods and services."[29] By its very nature, that membership cannot be universal. While it may be true, as Walzer conceded, that international migration, conquest, or other political realities may have created states with "multiple selves"—by nationality, race, or religion—this would not necessarily mean that such states should then forgo the exercise of the right of self-determination by controlling their boundaries.

Clearly, these debates among political theorists—including attacks on liberalism itself, from communitarians and civic republicans—have been inspired in part by the presence of new immigrants, many profoundly different culturally and politically from the citizens of existing liberal states.[30] Their very presence has inspired Western political theorists to rethink basic liberal commitments and, in some cases, to reaffirm what liberalism is, or should be, committed to. Many influential scholars have questioned liberal commitments to homogeneity with respect to "culture" within a nation-state. For example, Joseph Raz, one of the most eminent contemporary liberal theorists, insisted that in fact, liberal principles *require* an embracing of multicultural realities, not a rejection of them: "Multiculturalism requires a political society to recognize the equal standing of all the stable and viable cultural communities existing in that society." Furthermore, "a political society, a state, consists—if it is multicultural—of diverse communities and belongs to none of them."[31]

Yet other theorists have echoed Mill's concerns that multicultural or multinational liberal states may not survive.[32] Even among liberals, the idea of being *required* to live with multicultural realities violates other important liberal values. After all, particularist ties and national attachments—especially those based on a shared culture—may in fact be essential to the health of liberal societies, such that exclusionist sentiments may not be taken as so terribly inconsistent with liberalism. "It is," Neil Mac-Cormick has suggested, "those who have a decent and moderate love of their own families, country, colleagues, co-religionists or whatever who can alone recognize as equally legitimate the love others bear for their own."[33] Protecting a national culture, even if it means excluding those not of the same culture, might mean protecting the very grounds on which persons can become free and autonomous. And so, why shouldn't liberalism support a system of national sovereignties respecting the right of people *not* to become multicultural or multinational in the first place? If, as most liberals would agree, one of the fundamental tenets of liberalism is popular sovereignty, shouldn't the people of a particular state have the *right* to determine who should or shouldn't be allowed to join, even if they make that decision for race-based or "cultural" reasons?[34] Given the constant state of war among ethnic groups that had once been cobbled together, and given now their bloody attempts to restore national sovereignty, some prominent theorists have argued that "legalized self-determination could quite conceivably contribute to order and stability, not anarchy."[35]

Whatever the answer, there is among contemporary theorists some agreement that American immigration policies, naturalization rules, and other similar areas are now hopelessly confusing, theoretically inconsistent, and in some measure "irrational" when measured against liberal ideals. Theorists have talked about the necessity for "soft" borders (as opposed to more coercive "hard" borders), the relationship between welfare economics and immigration restrictions, and the balancing of the needs of compatriots against the demands of "strangers."[36] Rogers Smith and Peter Schuck, both legal historians, have argued that confusion in the matter of immigration restrictions and formal membership reign in the field, and yet their own attempts to provide theoretical consistency—in light of problems such as illegal immigration or refugee movements—have received as much criticism as praise.[37] And in one important article published over thirty years ago, Roger Nett described the right of free movement across international boundaries as "the civil right we are not ready for." Optimistically, "at some future point in world civilization, it may well be discovered that the right to free and open movement of people on the surface of the earth is fundamental to the structure of human opportunity and is therefore basic in the same sense as free religion, speech, and the franchise."[38] Balancing the two competing commitments at the core of liberal theory, between an aversion to ascriptive status and the necessity for national sovereignty, has proved exceedingly difficult. We have not yet arrived at that future point.

Public Law for the Other

The next section of this book explores how American public law displayed many of the theoretical inconsistencies and problems that have plagued liberal theory for over three centuries. In order to appreciate the dilemmas of having to explain and defend laws restricting membership and belonging, while acknowledging at the same time the arbitrariness of immigration status as an ascriptive identifier of persons, the next section of this study examines the original public justifications for immigration restrictions in the United States. That section explores how various facets of liberal theory were originally applied to these problems through institutions whose purpose was to provide such reasonable justifications. Specifically, the key decisions of Justice Stephen Field—one of the primary architects of Chinese Exclusion—offer an interesting glimpse of a time when the United States was engaged in its first serious attempt to answer questions of belonging on a national level. As we shall see, important jurists like Field were torn between competing principles, and this in part explains why the law of immigration and naturalization that they defended became so confusing and contradictory. A thorough reexamination of that jurisprudence might explain why such rules *remain* so inconsistent into our own time.

In this section I have attempted to show how liberal principles of equality, founded on an aversion to ascriptive status as the basis for rights or disabilities, can conflict squarely with liberal commitments to national sovereignty. In the next section I will attempt to show how American immigration law grew, in part, in the midst of that tension, both reflecting and amplifying it. Here, a reexploration of the American experience with problems of migration and belonging can be highly instructive: exactly what were the public justifications given by American leaders when their ostensibly liberal society was confronted with large numbers of persons who are culturally distinct, politically different, and noticeably nonliberal, at least initially? In having to confront real-life immigrants in the public sphere, the "answer" of a thoughtful American jurist—charged with somehow making legislation regarding migration and belonging consistent with the fundamental law of the land—can tell us a great deal about the prevailing tendencies and anxieties that arise within liberal societies when confronted with these types of problems. Liberal institutions had to struggle with these problems, and an analysis of their struggles can prove extremely helpful in clarifying some of the important issues at stake.

To that end, we will now revisit the period of Chinese exclusion, when the national government took the first serious steps toward restricting migration and membership to the United States. As we sift through the development of a national policy on migration and political membership, we hope that an examination of earlier juridical rules about immigration and naturalization will prove illuminating and helpful in understanding *why* such problems remain so compelling and intractable for those committed to a rational, consistent understanding of liberal political theory, as well as those interested in matters of justice and fairness in immigration law and policy. In this analysis, the tensions between liberal principles of equality and fairness, and liberal commitments to closed political communities, reemerge, in ways that suggest both the limits of liberal political theory in addition to its profound power and imagination.

PART II

Law

4

"They Do Not and Will Not Assimilate"

Stephen Johnson Field had a spectacular career. Leaving the relative security of his brother's law office in New York, he set out for California in 1849 after news of the Gold Rush. A year later, he was elected to the State Legislature, and in 1857, he was appointed to its highest court, then served as Chief Justice only four years later.[1] When President Lincoln nominated him to the United States Supreme Court in 1863, Field would become one of the youngest men ever appointed. He served there for over thirty-four years, one of the longest tenures in the Court's history. Justice Field's profound influence on American jurisprudence has been well documented in several accounts, although in most he has been most noted and often criticized for laying the intellectual foundations for the *Lochner* era.[2] He is less well known as one of the most important jurist to defend and articulate justifications for federal immigration law, beginning at the critical period of Chinese Exclusion. His decisions regarding the Chinese in America span the length of his career, from his days on the California Supreme Court, until one year before his retirement in 1896. Few Justices exerted such profound influence over immigration jurisprudence. And few wrestled so poignantly with the fate of early Asian migrants to the United States, "the strangers from a different shore."

In his efforts to find some solution to the "Chinese Question," Justice Field confronted the difficulties of maintaining a just balance between an impartial rule of law irrespective of ascriptive status, and the intense desire among many of his countrymen to exclude newcomers because of their purported differences in culture and manner. On the one hand, Field seemed truly to believe that basic rights were God given, and that the government he represented was charged with protecting and securing basic rights, not creating or granting them. Field was hardly a civil rights advocate for people of color—he was a Democrat when a huge segment of that party openly supported slavery. But in his decisions with respect to the Chinese, he employed a language of rights that broadened their scope, which in turn protected Chinese immigrants from hostile legislation despite the fact that these immigrants were not American citizens and could never naturalize into citizenship. Confronted with rights claims made by strangers to the United States, Field often replied as though their immigration status ought to be immaterial to the impartial rule of law. On many occasions, he admonished his countrymen for their zealous harassment of Asian immigrants.

Yet even as he defended the Chinese, Field was sympathetic toward the political movement that eventually led to their exclusion. The Chinese would be the first racial group in American history subject to federal exclusion rules. Proponents of exclusion—whether from organized, white labor unions or opportunistic national politicians—based their claims on the cultural, political, and social differences between American civilization and the Chinese immigrants. If American society represented a refinement of Western culture, white racial dominance in economy and society, and a commitment to representative government, then the Chinese were a threat to all of these aspirations. The historian Andrew Gyory noted that, in an open letter to the *New York Tribune*, John Stuart Mill worried about how Chinese immigration in the United States could result in "a permanent harm" to the "more civilized and improved portion of mankind."[3] Field obviously shared Mill's prejudices. He openly and also tacitly lobbied for the national government to limit Chinese migration decisively, and when Congress finally passed the Chinese Exclusion Act in 1882, Field spoke for the Court to uphold the law. He was *the* author of *the* Chinese Exclusion Case. Many of his formal justifications for excluding the Chinese were cultural in nature, and Field complained in the case itself that the Chinese "will not assimilate with our people." Like Mill, Field was sympathetic to a logic that separated the "savages" from the "civilized," and to a policy that defended "the inestimable benefits of our Christian civilization." Like many liberal theorists, he conceived the exercise of national sovereignty as unproblematic: "That the government of the United States, through the action of the legislative department, can exclude aliens from its territory is a proposition which we do not think open to controversy."

Field's jurisprudence in immigration law would be less interesting if this were the extent of it. But in time, as federal rules grew ever harsher and as both federal and state governments began to penalize Chinese immigrants for their very status, Field changed in his manner and tone yet again. Toward the end of his career, Field defended the rights of Chinese immigrants in passionate dissents, often against Justices who quoted his own opinions as precedents for positions he detested. As Field came to believe that the brutal mechanisms of exclusion reflected terribly on the character of the nation, he later found offensive much of what his own country was doing. He kept dissenting, insisting that the Chinese had rights that the American government could not violate. Ultimately, then, his decisions concerning the Chinese reveal him as torn between a commitment to basic rights even as he was committed to the idea of national sovereignty. The course of his career showed that while Americans may have felt their political culture endangered by the arrival of the Chinese, dealing harshly with these immigrants meant sacrificing some of their core values. We turn to Field because he measured these losses better than most.

"Certain Inherent Rights Lie at the Foundation of All Action, and upon a Recognition of Them Alone Can Free Institutions Be Maintained"

Like Stephen Field, large numbers of Chinese immigrants came to California to make their fortune. According to Ronald Takaki, 325 Chinese immigrants landed in California during the first year of the Gold Rush. "A year later, 450 more Chinese arrived in California; then suddenly, they came in greatly increasing numbers—2,716 in 1851 and 20,026 in 1852."[4] White settlers became alarmed and immediately supported rules to discourage the Chinese. Wielding their influence in the State Legislature, anti-Chinese lawmakers offered several measures to make their lives as difficult and as costly as possible. From as early as 1852, the State Legislature passed discriminatory legislation, including a series of taxes against Chinese and other foreign miners, but "aimed primarily at the Chinese."[5] Three years later, the state approved a head tax on immigration, through "An Act to Discourage the Immigration to This State of Persons Who Cannot Become Citizens Thereof."[6] In 1862, the Legislature passed another law, titled, more bluntly, "An Act to Protect Free White Labor Against Competition with Chinese Coolie Labor, and Discourage the Immigration of the Chinese into the State of California."[7]

Such laws evoked the experience of slavery and suggested both class-based and race-based resistance to the Chinese.[8] But in some of the earliest cases involving the Chinese, Justice Field appeared neither hostile nor friendly in a state that was clearly becoming more and more hostile to the newcomers from Asia.

In response to these types of laws, Justice Field rarely took issue with the Legislature's intent. He voted to uphold state taxes on the landing of Chinese immigrants—against clear legal precedents—and yet he also voted to read narrowly the scope of other discriminatory taxes such as the Foreign Miners' Tax. In these early cases, whether his decisions happened to favor the Chinese or not, he seemed not to have given much thought to the rising animus that was building against the Chinese.[9]

Yet, by the time he returned to California in 1872, having been appointed to the U.S. Supreme Court some nine years earlier, Field could not ignore the rising level of animosity directed at the Chinese. The noted historian Sucheng Chan has written that it was only after the completion of the transcontinental railroad—large portions of which had been built by Chinese laborers—that whites moved to California in greater numbers. "As more and more Euro-Americans appeared in California, they began to compete with the Chinese for jobs. Their resentment helped to fan the flames of an anti-Chinese movement." Lucy Salyer observed that "as the 1870s wore on, [an economic] depression became more severe for Californians, reaching crisis proportions in 1877. A long, devastating drought exacerbated an already difficult time for workers."[10] In turn, race-based animus against the Chinese grew worse, and as anti-Chinese politicians and activists stepped up their efforts to legislate against the Chinese, the "Chinese Question" emerged as one of the most compelling issues on the West Coast. The Chinese themselves were not passive in response to these attacks, as Charles McClain has argued; rather, the Chinese organized a formidable resistance and challenged in federal courts virtually every law, procedure, and official action directed against them.[11]

Field's response toward these developments was originally rather cosmopolitan, and even compassionate. Every spring since his appointment to the Supreme Court, Justice Field made the difficult trip from Washington, D.C. to San Francisco to preside as the Chief Justice of the newly created Ninth Circuit Court of Appeals. During one visit in 1872, he spoke about the Chinese Question as though "there may be reasonable differences of opinion with respect to the wisdom and policy of encouraging the immigration to this country of persons, between whom and our people there is such marked dissimilarity in constitution, habits, and manners." But insofar as commercial and political relations with China remained important, "it is the duty of the government to exert its power, its entire power if necessary, to enforce its obligations in this respect."[12] Field alluded to the Burlingame Treaty and the obligations of the American government to protect Chinese subjects in America, as well as the promise of enlarging commerce for American businesses. Like Mill, though, Field acknowledged that "reasonable people" could have some anxiety about allowing the migration of persons so different "in constitution, habits, and manner." Aside from these issues, there were others.

> Independently of all such considerations of duty or interest, it is base and cowardly to maltreat these people whilst they are within the jurisdiction of our government. If public policy requires that they be excluded from our shores, let the general government so provide and declare, but until it does so provide and declare, they have a perfect right to immigrate to this country; and whilst here they are entitled, equally with all others, to the full protection of our laws. It is unchristian and inhuman to maltreat them, as has been sometimes done by disorderly persons, we are sorry to say, in this district.[13]

At a time when anti-Chinese sentiments were proving politically popular in California and across the West, Field did not attack the Chinese. Although he suggested the possibility of restricting their migration "if public policy requires," Field clearly indicated his aversion to the growing numbers of "disorderly persons" behaving in a shameful way toward the Chinese. Several historians have noted that the "guarantees of equal protection by treaty and by federal law had little or no effect on what happened in society . . . [where] the Chinese remained vulnerable, victims of racial discrimination and violence." But Field's words did suggest a "humanitarianism" toward them that was certainly not common in California at the time.[14] And Field must have known that the adjectives "base and cowardly," "unchristian and inhuman" had been used recently to describe chattel slavery.

That they had rights was especially compelling for Justice Field. In the same year that he gave his jury instructions, Field had suggested that basic rights were God given—they were acknowledged and embodied in documents like the Declaration of Independence and the Constitution, but they were not "made" or "granted" by the sovereign power of the nation-state. In his famous dissent in the first of the controversial *Slaugh-ter-House Cases*, he had said: "The immortal document which pro-claimed the independence of the country declared as self-evident truths that the Creator had endowed all men 'with certain inalienable rights, and that among these are life, liberty, and the pursuit of happiness; and that to secure these rights governments are instituted among men.'"[15] In addition, "[the Fourteenth] amendment was intended to give practical ef-fect to the declaration of 1776 of inalienable rights, rights which are the gift of the Creator, which the law does not confer, but only recognizes."[16] In another opinion, in the second round of the *Slaughter-House Cases*, he made his views more explicit:

> As in our intercourse with our fellow men certain principles of morality are assumed to exist, without which society would be impossible, so cer-tain inherent rights lie at the foundation of all action, and upon a recog-nition of them alone can free institutions be maintained. These inherent rights have never been more happily expressed than in the Declaration of Independence, that new evangel of liberty to the people: "We hold these truths to be self-evident"—that is so plain that their truth is recog-nized upon their mere statement—"that all men are endowed"—not by edicts of Emperors, or decrees of Parliament, or acts of Congress, but "by their Creator with certain inalienable rights"—that is, rights which cannot be bartered away, or given away, or taken away except in pun-ishment of crime—"and that among these are life, liberty, and the pur-suit of happiness, and to secure these"—not grant them but secure them—"governments are instituted among men, deriving their just pow-ers from the consent of the governed."[17]

Here, Field echoed Thomas Jefferson, who in turn had echoed John Locke. Like Locke, Field believed firmly that it was the *acknowledging* of "inalienable rights"—as prior to government, God given, and self-evi-dent—that held free institutions together. Throughout his life, Justice Field would reiterate this understanding of rights and of government in speech after speech.[18] Under this theory, ascriptive qualities should not impede the enjoyment of basic rights, and so the Chinese should be able to invoke them just like all other persons. In his conceptions of human equality and rights, Field had much in common with Locke.

In 1874, in the case, *In re Ah Fong*, Field became the first Justice to apply the Fourteenth Amendment's due process and equal protection clauses to noncitizens in order to protect Chinese women from state rules prohibiting the landing of "lewd and debauched women."[19] For Field, the state rule was clearly enforced only against Chinese women: "I have little respect for that discriminating virtue which is shocked when a frail child of China is landed on our shores, and yet allows the bedizened and painted harlot of other countries to parade our streets and open her hells in broad day, without molestation and without censure."[20] More specifically, the Fourteenth Amendment, according to Field, was designed to eliminate just this form of discrimination—"it . . . enacts that no State shall deprive *any* person (dropping the distinctive designation of citizens) of life, liberty of property, without due process of law; nor deny any person the equal protection of the laws." And so, "discriminating and partial legislation, favoring particular persons of the same class, is now prohibited . . . . [and] equality of protection is the constitutional right of all persons."[21] Here, Field was applying directly the logic of his opinions in the *Slaughter-House Cases* to protect from hostile state and local legislation a group of immigrants who would soon be rendered perpetual strangers.

In 1878, in a case entitled *In re Ah Yup*, the federal court in San Francisco, speaking through Circuit Court Judge Lorenzo Sawyer, held that Chinese immigrants could not become naturalized citizens because they were neither white nor of African descent.[22] The ruling closed the possibility that Chinese immigrants could use the polls to protect themselves through the political process, and this left them even more vulnerable to discriminatory legislation and violence. If, as Justice Field had suggested elsewhere, "frequent and fair elections by the people furnish the only protection, under the Constitution, against the abuse of acknowledged legislative power," the Chinese were now denied that protection even more.[23]

Sensing the vulnerability of the Chinese, public policy makers moved against them, and in San Francisco municipal regulations were becoming particularly offensive and harsh. The City already punished the Chinese with a host of discriminatory taxes and rules, including taxes on laundries, a tax on bones exhumed for burial in China, rules against overcrowded living quarters, and even one prohibiting persons from carrying anything attached to a pole. In April 1876, the Board of Supervisors passed a law that allowed for the sheriff to cut off the queues of Chinese prisoners in the county jails.[24] In challenging these laws, the Chinese took advantage of one modest legal reform. In 1872, the State Legislature had revised its Civil Procedure Code to allow for the testimony of Chinese witnesses in noncriminal proceedings.[25]

Aware of this change in procedure, Ho Ah Kow, a Chinese man who had had his queue severed in the county prison by Sheriff Matthew Nunan, sued for civil damages in federal court. He had been in the city jail for two simple reasons: he had lived in a room with less than five hundred cubic feet of air per person; and he had refused to pay the $10 fine for living in such a room. With the backing of leading organizations among the Chinese, including the Chinese Six Companies, Ho Ah Kow and several other plaintiffs filed similar suits for relief in federal court, and the matter appeared before Justice Field in 1879. His reply was unambiguous: he deplored the "base and cowardly" ordinance, and characterized the City's lawmakers as "unchristian and inhuman."[26] "Nothing can be accomplished . . . by hostile and spiteful legislation on the part of the state, or of its municipal bodies, like the ordinance in question—legislation which is unworthy of a brave and manly people."[27]

The lawyers for the plaintiffs were apparently familiar with Field's decision in past cases: they charged that the ordinance was "special legislation imposing a degrading and cruel punishment upon a class of persons who are entitled, alike with all other persons within the jurisdiction of the United States to the equal protection of the laws."[28] In his opinion, Field repeated the plaintiffs' arguments almost verbatim and rejected entirely the arguments on behalf of the sheriff: "The cutting of the hair of every male person within an inch of his scalp, on arrival to the jail, was not intended and cannot be maintained as a measure of discipline or as a sanitary regulation."[29] Rather, Field believed that "the ordinance was intended only for the Chinese in San Francisco" despite the absence of any language specifically indicating such intent.[30]

> When we take our seat on the bench we are not struck with blindness, and forbidden to know as judges what we see as men; and where an ordinance, though general in its terms, only operates upon a special race, sect or class, it being universally understood that it is to be enforced only against that race, sect or class, we may justly conclude that it was the intention of the body adopting it that it should only have such operation, and treat it accordingly.[31]

The regulation was, therefore, unconstitutional.

In our country hostile and discriminatory legislation by a state against persons of any class, sect, creed or nation, in whatever form it may be expressed, is forbidden by the fourteenth amendment of the constitution . . . [which] enacts that no state shall deprive *any person* (dropping the distinctive term citizen) of life, liberty or property, without due process of law, nor deny *to any person* the equal protection of the laws.[32]

Field emphasized again the broad scope of the new Constitution: "It is certainly something in which a citizen of the United States may feel a generous pride that the government of his country extends protection to all persons within its jurisdiction, . . . whatever country he may come from, or whatever race or color he may be."[33]

But the queue ordinance case, *Ho Ah Kow v. Nunan*, was also remarkable for reasons related to the scope and application of important constitutional principles. Apparently, Field believed two important arguments for the plaintiff: that "the deprivation of the queue is regarded by [the Chinese] as a mark of disgrace, and is attended, according to their religious faith, with misfortune and suffering after death"; and that the City and the sheriff "knew of this custom and religious faith of the Chinese, and knew also that the plaintiff venerated the custom and held the faith."[34] In this light, Justice Field emphasized the cruelty and harshness of the queue ordinance:

The reason advanced for its adoption, and now urged for its continuance, is, that only the dread of the loss of his queue will induce a Chinaman to pay his fine. That is to say, in order to enforce the payment of a fine imposed on him, it is necessary that torture should be superadded to imprisonment. . . . Probably the bastindo, or the knout, or the thumbscrew, or the rack, would accomplish the same end; and no doubt that the Chinaman would prefer either of these modes of torture to that which entails upon him disgrace among his countrymen and carries with it the constant dread of misfortune and suffering after death.[35]

Ten dollars compared poorly with eternal misfortune—"the ordinance acts with special severity against the Chinese prisoners, inflicting on them suffering altogether disproportionate to what would be endured by other prisoners if enforced against them. . . . Upon the Chinese prisoners its enforcement operates as 'a cruel and unusual punishment'"; it was akin to forcing Jewish prisoners to eat pork.[36]

What is important here is not that Field correctly assessed the religious significance of the queue, but rather his sympathy for the deeper principles at stake. His words suggested the language and spirit of the First and Eighth Amendments—as though religious tolerance, freedom of religion, and freedom from "cruel and unusual punishment," were, like due process and equal protection, rights not just for American citizens, but meant for everyone. That the San Francisco Board of Supervisors had not only known of the religious feelings of the Chinese but had intentionally exploited them for the purpose of inflicting "a cruel and unusual punishment" was absolutely reprehensible. Here, Field's sensitivity to the religious beliefs of the Chinese appeared, at least in the words of his opinion, truly genuine, and so, too, his indignation with the Board of Supervisors: "It is not creditable to the humanity and civilization of our people, much less to their Christianity, that an ordinance of this character is possible."[37]

In this part of his opinion, Field reflected one of the most central themes of liberal theory—a complete moral aversion toward public rules denying basic rights to persons based only on some ascriptive characteristic. Applying a theory of universal basic rights, he treated the Chinese as moral beings in a position to make demands for fairness and equality of treatment—in spite of the fact that they were not full members and legally forbidden to become so. Aware that the Chinese were in a precarious legal position, Field offered the protection of the federal courts for all "persons."

The Chinese and their antagonists had, of course, widely different reactions to Field's decision. As if to make his position utterly clear, Field took the unusual step of reading his opinion "in open court on July 7, 1879."[38] A well-coordinated Chinese resistance had paid off in this widely publicized legal victory, and the Chinese themselves took Field as their ally. "A memorial, beautifully lettered in gold, was sent to Field."[39] For anti-Chinese agitators in San Francisco, the relationship between Field and the Chinese was a source of derision: "Justice Field was such a zealous advocate of the Chinese, the *Examiner* said, that there was no need for a Chinese litigant to employ counsel in any case where he sat as judge."[40] The present case "raised a storm of abuse against its author. It seemed as though, for the time, reason had fled from the minds of the people of the State."[41] In one commentary, "very mild and sane, as compared to the many others," Field was accused of defending "the soul of a soulless heathen," "vermin in a pagan's hair," "the Asiatic coolie," "the incoming host of barbarians who threaten our civilization and our government." Field's "sickly sentimentality" was worse than "the prejudice and passion of the ignoble mob."[42] His holding was "ridiculous," "too absurd for us to seriously consider."[43] Field had expressed some ambition to run for president of the United States, but his friend, John Pomeroy, a professor of law at Hastings College in San Francisco, later conceded that this decision probably doomed his nomination.[44]

"It Would Be Better . . . That the Immigration Be Stopped"

In subsequent years, Field proved that both the Chinese and their antagonists were quite wrong about him. Even as he had issued decisions ostensibly favorable to the Chinese, Field had suggested and intimated a number of measures designed to stop their migration and thus "settle" the politically volatile Chinese Question. He had remarked in his jury instructions that restricting the migration of the Chinese could be done by the federal government. In *Ah Fong*, the case of the lewd and debauched women, he had suggested the same thing, even as he had ridiculed local and state rules harassing the Chinese. His suggestions in both instances proved prophetic. In fact, in response to the Supreme Court's decision in *Chy Lung v. Freeman* (which upheld *Ah Fong*), Congress had passed the Page Law in 1875, which among other things provided for the exclusion of women arriving in the United States "for lewd and immoral purposes," or "imported for the purpose of prostitution."[45] Led by congressional leaders from California, the law would be the first of many federal exclusion laws targeting the Chinese.

Like many anti-Chinese activists, Field himself thought that their exclusion might be appropriate in light of their "unassimilability," as they appeared to him to have "such marked dissimilarity in constitution, habits, and manners." Looking at his decisions more closely, such fears appeared in every major opinion he had authored concerning the Chinese. In *Ah Fong*, he had said: "I am aware of the general feeling prevailing in this state against the Chinese, and in opposition to the extension of any encouragement to their immigration hither. It is felt that the dissimilarity in physical characteristics, in language, in manners, religion and habits, will always prevent any possible assimilation of them with our people." Exclusion, though, had to be done in a particular way: "If their further immigration is to be stopped, recourse must be had to the Federal government, where the whole power over this subject lies."[46]

Following logic similar to Mill's, Field considered "any possible assimilation . . . with our people" an important criterion in picking which newcomers ought to be admitted the United States. Even in the Queue Ordinance Case, Field expressed the same concerns about "their dissimilarity in physical characteristics, in language, manners and religion." Field evinced sympathy with those who would exclude the Chinese: "Thoughtful persons, looking to the millions which crowd the opposite shores of the Pacific, and the possibility at no distant date of their pouring over in vast hordes among us, giving rise to fierce antagonisms of race, hope that some way may be devised to prevent their further immigration."[47] Again, Field shared Mill's pessimism toward a multiracial society—such a society would be prone to tear itself apart through "fierce antagonisms of race." In the past, Field had reserved blame for antagonisms of race on "disorderly persons," whites who had targeted and harassed the Chinese. Here, Field characterized the Chinese immigrants as though *they* were the menace—"millions . . . pouring over in vast hordes among us," overrunning the Caucasian, Christian civilization in America.

About a month after his decision in *Ho Ah Kow*, Justice Field granted an interview with the *Argonaut*, one of the more popular newspapers based in San Francisco. In that interview, the Justice discussed a wide range of subjects related to the Chinese, including the provisions of the Burlingame Treaty, the military power of China, the cessation of further Chinese immigration to the United States, and the fate of the Chinese immigrants already there. Whether Field had intended to defend himself against his critics is uncertain, but his statements indicated that he shared their concerns and was busy himself thinking of a "solution": "This question can not be solved by San Francisco nor California, nor is it a local one, nor are its consequences to be confined to this side of the Continent."[48]

Given that this was a national question, the exercise of national sovereignty, not state or local rules, was most appropriate.[49] As Locke himself might have suggested, the "federative power of the commonwealth" was the logical agent for dealing with outsiders.

Also, Field noted that although the Burlingame Treaty did foster trade, "commercial intercourse with China is a one-sided affair, and that the English, German, and American merchants are being driven out of the Chinese trade."[50] "It is not equal. . . . Now what is the remedy? To me it seems plain." It was a modification of the existing treaty with China, so that the Chinese could come to the United States to trade, visit, or acquire an education, but not reside, compete, or "engage in the general industries of our country."[51] Field recommended a compromise of sorts—merchants, tourists, and students could still enter the United States, but permanent residents and laborers would be excluded. Those already here would be relegated to the bottom of economy and society; lost was the Burlingame Treaty's original language of "the inherent and inalienable right of man to change his home and allegiance, and also the mutual advantage of free migration and emigration of their citizens and subjects."

But Field suggested that such an amicable relationship between the United States and China no longer existed, and that this was the fault of the Chinese. "There is danger in a military point of view. . . . China is purchasing armor-clad war vessels from England. . . . She is importing and manufacturing arms of precision, is increasing, arming, and drilling her army and navy."[52] Strangely, Field did not mention that the government of China had been under constant assault by Western powers, and that the Chinese had lost much of their sovereignty to foreign encroachment ever since their loss to the British in the Opium Wars of the 1830s and 1840s.[53] But like many other Westerners, Field inverted the political and military realities of East Asia: the Chinese, not the Western powers, were the menace. And like many other Westerners, Field did not or would not separate the actions of the government of China with the fate of the Chinese immigrants in the United States.

In March of the following year, Justice Field had received a copy of an editorial written by General John Miller in which Miller had complained of the gravity of the Chinese Question and the arrogance of the federal judiciary in protecting the Chinese. Miller had been the chairman of a special committee on Chinese immigration to California when he had been a representative to the state's constitutional convention in 1879, and he was widely known as a particularly vicious opponent of the Chinese. In his interview with the *Argonaut*, Justice Field had said of the Chinese who had become permanent residents, "It is perhaps well enough to allow [them] to remain."

> If there are one hundred thousand of them, they will disappear in a short time from natural causes; many will return voluntarily; they will be absorbed. What forty millions of white people will do with any part of one

hundred thousand male Chinese, is not a consideration of consequence, and will soon be disposed of.[54]

Field noted that the present population of Chinese immigrants would likely not produce a second generation—they were overwhelming male. Miller, on the other hand, had suggested something more aggressive: that the Chinese be "cut out." Moved by the veiled attack made by General Miller, Field responded with an open letter published in the *San Francisco Morning Call*, where he agreed "that it is our duty 'to preserve this land for our people and their posterity forever; to protect and defend American institutions and republican government from the Oriental gangrene. And this is the duty of every American citizen.'"[55] It appeared that Field and Miller were not, after all, too far apart—their primary difference was deciding what to do with the "Oriental gangrene," either cut it out or let it die off. For now, though, they agreed that further immigration should not continue. Following Field's advice about pursuing a solution through the federal government, "Miller began a campaign for the modification of the treaty with China, a task which was probably made easier by the support of Field," according to Carl Brent Swisher.[56]

In Congress, legislators from California had been lobbying for restrictive legislation against the Chinese for over a decade, and in 1879, they succeeded in passing a bill that "[limited] to ten the number of passengers who could be landed by vessel at any U.S. port."[57] President Rutherford Hayes vetoed the bill, but sent an emissary to China to renegotiate the Burlingame Treaty. On November 17 of the same year, the two governments agreed to modifications: the new treaty "permitted the U.S., whenever it determined that it should be in its interest to do so, to *suspend* for a reasonable period of time, but not absolutely prohibit, the coming of Chinese laborers into the United States." Chinese laborers already in the United States could "'go and come of their own free will,' and were guaranteed the 'rights, privileges, immunities, and exemptions' accorded to subjects and citizens of the most favored nation."[58] This was a compromise of sorts, but in 1881, legislators from California moved a bill to establish a national identification system for all Chinese laborers in the United States, and to suspend Chinese immigration for twenty years. The new President, Chester Arthur, vetoed both measures.

When newspapers in California attacked President Arthur, Field sent a letter to Professor Pomeroy, his friend in San Francisco. Field was amused because his fellow Californians had attacked him openly when he quietly floated the idea of his own presidential candidacy against no less a personage than Chester Arthur. Turning to the serious matter of Chinese immigration, Field revealed that, had the anti-Chinese forces been better informed of his present position, they would hardly have opposed him:

> I see that California is very much excited over the veto of the Chinese Bill by the President. I do not wonder at it. It must be apparent to every one, that it would be better for both races to live apart—and that their only intercourse should be that of foreign commerce. The manners, habits, modes of living, and everything connected with the Chinese prevent the possibility of their ever assimilating with our people. They are a different race, and, even if they could assimilate, assimilation would not be desirable. If they are permitted to come here, there will be at all times conflicts arising out of the antagonism of the races which would only tend to disturb public order and mar the progress of the country. It would be better, therefore, before any larger number should come, that the immigration be stopped.

And then, this:

> You know I belong to the class, who repudiate the doctrine that this country was made for the people of all races. On the contrary, I think it is for our race—the Caucasian race. We are obliged to take care of the Africans; because we find them here, and they were brought here against their will by our fathers. Otherwise, it would be a very serious question, whether their introduction should be permitted or encouraged.[59]

Like Benjamin Franklin, who had suggested a hundred years ago that the United States be preserved for the "lovely White," Field wished to leave the nation as much as he could for "the Caucasian race."[60] The presence of Africans could not now be helped, but the Chinese were a different matter. Field assumed that as a sovereign nation-state, the United States had the right (if not the duty) *not* to become more racially diverse.

As for the exact method of excluding the Chinese, in May of 1882, Justice Field's insights proved accurate. President Arthur signed a revised federal immigration law that excluded Chinese laborers from coming to the United States for ten years. Although there was no national identification system, customs officials at U.S. ports were authorized to issue identification certificates for Chinese laborers leaving the United

States on or before August 4, 1882, as proof of their right to reenter. Treaty and law had changed, the federal government had acted, just as Field had suggested, and the appeals for exclusion were not "ultimately disregarded." The Chinese exclusion law was the first of its kind—the first federal law to exclude specifically the immigration of any particular race, ethnic group, or nationality from American soil. It was also the first of many exclusion laws directed at the Chinese. But over the course of the next fifteen years, Justice Field had new doubts about the extent of this exclusionist tendency in the law, even as he began vigorously enforcing the exclusion of Chinese immigrants.

"The Whole Purpose of the Law . . . Was to Exclude from the Country Laborers of the Chinese Race"

For the next decade, most of the cases coming before the federal judiciary involved habeas corpus petitions brought by Chinese litigants, most of whom were challenging the terms under which they were excluded by what was now commonly referred to as the Chinese Exclusion Act. Again, in his capacity as a Circuit Court judge, Justice Field was in a particularly influential position to apply and to interpret the Act. The early decisions were important because through them, Field largely shaped the Act to make it a more refined instrument to exclude certain categories of Chinese altogether, while preserving the rights of others to enter, reenter, or work. These early cases are also striking because through them, Field evoked Lockean ideas about the federative power of the commonwealth—the idea that what should be done with "outsiders" ought to coincide primarily with the best interests of the commonwealth. The rights and interests of the sovereign people of the United States emerged as more compelling than the inalienable rights of man, or the enjoyment of those rights irrespective of ascriptive status. And above all, there was the racial logic of Chinese exclusion through which Asian immigrants were framed as barbarians threatening American civilization and culture.

The early immigration cases challenging the Exclusion Acts were dispensed in federal court as early as 1882, but they did not always result in exclusion. Field upheld the right to land for Chinese laborers working on American vessels; so long as they worked aboard American ships, he said, they had never really left the United States.[61] In another case, where Chinese workers aboard an American vessel had disembarked temporarily in

Sydney, Australia, although "without severing or intending to sever their connection with the vessel," Field did not read literally the Exclusion Act's prohibition against Chinese laborers embarking from a "foreign port or place." He ordered such persons released.[62]

Along the same lines, during the debates about the Exclusion Act, one of the key issues was how the Act would affect another central economic concern—trade with China. As he had said in the *Argonaut*, Field had favored the entry of merchants, "allowed the privilege of crossing our continent in pursuit of business," but not laborers "to engage in the general industries of our country," or those who might "come into competition with our laborers." Just as he had hoped, the Exclusion Act of 1882 had preserved the distinction between merchants and laborers and allowed the former to enter for commercial reasons while excluding the latter. In one case, customs officials under the Act had detained a Chinese merchant, Low Yam Chow, originally employed for a firm based in San Francisco; he had been away on business to South and Central America for fifteen years before his return to San Francisco in 1882. Issuing his decision in the case, Justice Field reviewed the history of the Exclusion Act against the Chinese:

> It was discovered that the physical characteristics and habits of the Chinese prevented their assimilation with our people. Conflicts between them and our people, disturbing to the peace of the country, followed as a matter of course, and were of frequent occurrence. Chinese laborers, including in that designation not merely those engaged in manual labor, but those skilled in some art or trade, in a special manner interfered in many ways with the industries and business of this state. Their frugal habits, the absence of families, their ability to live in narrow quarters without apparent injury to health, their contentment with small gains and the simplest fare, gave them great advantages in the struggle with our laborers and mechanics, who always and properly seek something more from their labors than sufficient for a bare livelihood, and must have and should have something for the comforts of a home and the education of their children.[63]

Again, as he had before, Field suggested that the Chinese—particularly Chinese laborers—through "their frugal habits," "contentment with small gains and simplest fare," were the ones who caused the conflicts with whites, "disturbing the peace of the country." In other words, the poorest Chinese caused trouble by working too hard and asking for too little, and their labor hindered, rather than furthered, the development of a free market. Chinese laborers ruined the chances that white citizens could pursue "the comforts of a home and the education of their children."

Field did say, however, that Chinese *merchants* were of a different class because of their unique role in the commercial relationship between the United States and China. In one case, Field noted that "Commerce with China is of the greatest value, and it is constantly increasing." Some immigration inspectors were "possessed of more zeal than knowledge."[64] Field himself cited some compelling figures: the total value of trade between the United States and China amounted to roughly $15.4 million in 1868, $27.8 million in 1881. "Of this latter amount $16,185,165 of the merchandise passed through the port of San Francisco, and 70 per cent of it was shipped by Chinese merchants."[65] Given the importance of this class of migrants, Field reminded officials that "The [Exclusion] act, conforming to the supplementary treaty, is aimed at against the immigration of *Chinese laborers*—not others."[66] "The petitioner," a Chinese merchant, "must be discharged."[67]

Yet, the poorest Chinese were not so lucky, and they represented the vast majority of petitioners. A year after *Low Yam Chow*, a Chinese laborer from Hong Kong pled in his writ of habeas corpus that he was wrongfully detained under the Exclusion Act. "The petitioner is a Chinese by race, language, and color, and has all the peculiarities of the subjects of China . . . but he was born on the Island of Hong Kong after it was ceded to Great Britain."[68] As a British subject, he claimed that he was exempt from the Exclusion Act. Field disagreed, saying that the framers of the Exclusion Act "knew, as we all knew, that Hong Kong would pour such laborers into our country every year in unnumbered thousands, unless they were also covered by the restriction act."[69] Field repeated the claims that Chinese laborers presented "a competition degrading in its character," and that they "[endangered] good order" by their mere presence in California and the United States.[70] Therefore, *"any Chinese laborer from any foreign port or place"* was excludable, and "the whole purpose of the law, which was to exclude from the country laborers of the Chinese race, would be defeated by any other construction."[71]

His opinion suggested that the Exclusion Act was clearly race based, and it represented in that way a mixture of concerns for Field that were also expressed by Locke and Mill—laborers would be excluded because they would be a net drain on society, but merchants would be included because they would benefit American society. In general, though, the Exclusion Act quite explicitly rejected the possibility of a well-ordered, multiracial society, and Field understood this as an overt, public act—populated in part by "degrading" races, such a society would be antithetical to "good order."

From 1884 through 1885, Justice Field excluded every Chinese laborer who appeared before him. So zealous was he that the United States Supreme Court overruled Field's Circuit Court opinion on one or two separate occasions (depending on one's point of view). If there was, in his heart, "a clear strain of sympathy for the unfortunate and oppressed [Chinese]," it did not reveal itself in his decisions during these two years.

To make matters worse for Chinese immigrants, Congress amended the Exclusion Act in 1884 to "require *all* merchants and others exempt Chinese to present a . . . certificate" of residence as a condition of entry, and made the certificate "the only evidence permissible to establish a right of re-entry," both of which effectively overruled Field's decision in *Low Yam Chow*.[72] Perhaps because of this move toward more aggressive enforcement of the Exclusion Act, Field excluded the wives of Chinese laborers, Chinese laborers who were abroad when residency certificates were issued, Chinese laborers who had presented a "tag" entitling them to a certificate of residence, rather than the certificate itself.[73] Literally, any Chinese laborer who could not prove residence in the United States prior to the Exclusion Act—exactly according to the letter of the law— was found excludable. Field also refused to rely on Chinese testimony in exclusion cases, although several federal decisions allowed for such testimony.[74] In the case of one laborer, Cheen Heong, who could not possibly have procured a residency certificate because he had been out of the country when the Exclusion Act was enacted, Justice Field rather insisted on the "suspicious character of the testimony [he] produced, from the loose notions entertained by the witnesses as to the obligation of an oath."[75] And in one particularly cruel moment, he tersely refused to grant bail to a Chinese woman whom he had ordered excluded, a woman who had traveled for months to reunite with her husband.[76] Field suggested she was a prostitute. Before her departure back to China, Mrs. Ah Moy had spent two more months at an immigration detention center, and even as this type of detention was becoming a more regular feature of immigration procedure, Field did not regard this as punishment nor "a gross violation of her personal rights."[77] As in this case and in many others, what was most striking was Field's changing attitude toward the Chinese petitioners before him. It was absolutely hostile.

From 1883 to 1884, Justice Field decided in favor of only one Chinese petitioner who came before him. *In re Look Tin Sing*, though, was a groundbreaking decision. The case involved a "Chinese petitioner [belonging] to the Chinese race, but . . . born in Mendocino, in the state of California, in 1870."[78] The young man "claimed the right to [land] as a natural-born citizen of the United States."[79] Field gave a brief overview of citizenship rules in Great Britain and the United States, but relied most heavily on his own review of the Fourteenth Amendment. He concluded "it is enough that he was born here, whatever the status of his parents."[80] "Being a citizen, the law could not intend that he should ever look to the government of a foreign country for permission to return to the United States, and no citizen can be excluded from this country except in punishment for crime."[81]

Field's decision was important in many respects, notably as a precursor to the United States Supreme Court's decision in *United States v. Wong Kim Ark*, decided a year after Field had left the high court, two years before his death.[82] Wong Kim Ark was a laborer, the son of laborers. But in the present Chinese citizenship case, the Chinese immigrant was of a class that Field was not prone to exclude anyway: "The petitioner is the son of a merchant, and not a laborer, within the meaning of the [Exclusion] act."[83] For this son of a Chinese merchant, Field spared the invective he had routinely used against the many, many Chinese laborers he had excluded throughout that same year.

"They Do Not and Will Not Assimilate with Our People"

When Justice Field returned to Washington, D.C., in the fall of 1884, lawyers for Cheen Heong were waiting for him. The case of the absent Chinese laborer had divided the federal judiciary, and notwithstanding Field's attempt to settle the issue, a majority of the United States Supreme Court granted certiorari. Again, as in the federal circuit case, the primary question was whether the Exclusion Act applied to persons like Cheen Heong—Chinese laborers who, because of their absence abroad, were physically unable to obtain the residency certificate required for reentry to the United States under the Exclusion Act.[84] The case had a new name,

Chew Heong instead of Cheen Heong, but the petitioner and the facts were the same.

Writing for the majority in December of 1884, Justice Harlan held in favor of Chew Heong, reversing Field and also upholding the petitioner's right to provide the testimony of witnesses to establish prior residence. Harlan thought that any other result would be unfair: "What injustice could be more marked than, by legislative enactment, to recognize the existence of a right, by treaty, to come within the limits of the United States and, at the same time, to prescribe, as the only evidence permitted to establish it, the possession of a collector's certificate, that could not possibly be obtained by whom the right belongs?"[85] A clear majority concluded that Congress could not have intended such an unjust result.

Justice Field vehemently dissented in an opinion that was as long as Harlan's. First, as he had done before, Field phrased a limited role for the Court generally, but especially on these matters. The Court should not have "[imputed] bad faith" on the lower court finding for exclusion (perhaps meaning Field himself), nor on Congress for passing the Exclusion Act. He chastened the Court for interfering:

> [If] the legislative department sees fit for any reason to refuse, upon a subject within its control, compliance with the stipulations of the treaty, or to abrogate them entirely, it is not for this court or any other court to call in question the validity or wisdom of its action, and impute unworthy motives to it. It should be presumed that good and sufficient reasons controlled and justified its conduct.[86]

If the Chinese laborers or their government objected to Congress' action, "[they] may complain to the executive head of our government, and take such measures as may seem advisable for their interests."[87] Field argued that this was above all a political question best left to the political branches, and the judiciary should simply apply the law as it was intended: "The plain purport of the [Chinese Exclusion Act], as it seems to me, was to exclude all Chinese laborers except those who came at certain designated periods and continued their residence in the country, and, if they should leave and be desirous of returning, to require them to obtain a proper certificate of identification."[88] If this was unfair to persons like Chew Heong, "it is for Congress, not this court, to afford the remedy."[89]

Not stopping there, Justice Field repeated a number of "good and sufficient reasons" behind the Exclusion Act itself. He gave the Court a history of Chinese immigration to California: the Chinese were, at first, "industrious and docile, . . . generally peaceable, . . . valuable domestic servants," and "useful in constructing roads, draining marshes, cultivating fields, and generally, wherever outdoor labor was required."[90] However, in time, "they interfered in many ways with the industries and business of the State."[91] Without families to support and "content with small gains and simple fare," they made "successful competition with them . . . impossible, for our laborers are not content, and never should be, with a bare livelihood for their work."[92] Able to "underlive" whites, the Chinese "[degraded] labor, and [drove] our laborers from large fields of industry."[93] There was more, and even worse:

> Large numbers of them, more than one-half of all who have come to the United States, have been brought under what is termed the contract system; that is, a contract for their labor. In one sense, they come freely, because they come pursuant to a contract, but they are not the free immigrants whose coming the [Burlingame] treaty contemplates, and for whose protection the treaty provides. They are, for the time, the bond thralls of their contractor—his coolie slaves.[94]

This charge—that the majority of Chinese laborers were "coolie slaves"—resonated in a nation still recovering from the Civil War. That Field suggested another impending crisis—this time, between free labor and coolie slaves—only confirmed the popular contention that to protect white labor, as well as the still fragile Union, "The Chinese Must Go."[95] The solution was not to "free" the Chinese or to somehow grant them equal civil and political rights, as had been the attempt with former African slaves; rather, the plan was to exclude the Chinese from American society altogether, in a deliberate effort to *avoid* concerns about their future legal and political status here.

There were other reasons for a more strict reading of the certificate provision of the Exclusion Act. The Chinese were deceitful: "Our courts [on the Pacific Coast] will be crowded with applicants to land, who never before saw our shores, and yet will produce a multitude of witnesses to establish their formal residence, whose testimony cannot be refuted and yet cannot be rejected."[96] Field suggested that by leaving the certificate requirement only loosely enforced, Chinese laborers would falsify their way into the country. This would subvert the purpose of the Act, its legislative intent: "All the bitterness which has heretofore existed on the Pacific Coast on the subject of immigration of the Chinese laborers will be renewed and intensified."[97]

Furthermore, Field implied that the deceitfulness and bad faith of the Chinese laborers was also true for the government in China. As he had mentioned in his interview with the *Argonaut*, he argued that the original Burlingame Treaty "was one sided in the benefits it conferred as to residence and trade by the citizens or subjects of one country in the other, the condition of the people of China rendering any reciprocity in such benefits impossible."[98] Field implied that the Chinese in America were still more free to work and trade than the Americans in China. Accordingly, the Treaty should not have been granted such deference. Barbarians, as Field and Mill might agree, will not reciprocate.

Justice Field then turned to the character of the Chinese in America. He expressed new levels of exasperation:

> Notwithstanding [the] favorable provisions [of the Treaty], opening the whole of the country to them, and extending to them the privileges, immunities, and exemptions of citizens or subjects of the most favored nation, they have remained among us a separate people, retaining their original peculiarities of dress, manner, habits, and modes of living, which are as marked as their complexion and their language. They live by themselves; they constitute a distinct organization with the laws and customs which they brought from China. Our institutions have made no impression on them during the more than thirty years they have been in the country. . . . They do not and will not assimilate with our people; and their dying wish is that their bodies may be taken to China for burial.[99]

Insisting that the Chinese had remained a separate, unassimilated, and unassimilable people, Field sympathized with those who would exclude them:

> Thoughtful persons who were exempt from race prejudice saw . . . the certainty, at no distant day, that, from the unnumbered millions on the opposite shores of the Pacific, vast hordes would pour in upon us, overrunning our coast and controlling its institutions. A restriction upon further immigration was felt to be necessary to prevent the degradation of

white labor, and to preserve to ourselves the inestimable benefits of our Christian civilization.[100]

Here again, he said that the strangeness of the Chinese, combined with their numbers, constituted an invasion of "vast hordes," a threat to the "Christian civilization" that white Americans had carried with them on their march West. Field drew a picture of the Chinese as though they were complete outsiders of their own choice; if they should "overrun" and "control" the land, *whites* would become the outsiders. Coupled with the deceitfulness of Chinese laborers and their potential to exploit the legal system, Field hoped for a Congressional remedy against the majority's decision in the near future. None of these sentiments was new, but it was the first time that such anti-Chinese rhetoric appeared in such full bloom in the United States Reports. It was ironic and sad that it was Justice Field who had put them there. And if he had wanted a Congressional remedy for the evils of Chinese "mendacity" and Chinese immigration, he did not have to wait too long to get it.

5

"Beyond All Reason in Its Severity"

"A Feeling of Antipathy and Hatred . . . against the Subjects of the Emperor of China"

Although Stephen Field and many others may have agreed that the Chinese were undesirable as immigrants, there remained confusion over what ought to happen to the Chinese already residing within the United States. After the completion of the transcontinental railroad, as whites moved into California and other western states in greater numbers, many Chinese migrated in the opposite direction. They dispersed across the country for a number of reasons: state and local governments in the West passed more and more rules that harassed the Chinese constantly, and local law enforcement officials seemed as prone to incite violence against the Chinese as to protect them from harm. Fully aware that they were vulnerable in these ways, the Chinese settled and formed new communities in places as far away as Texas, Mississippi, Massachusetts, New York, and Pennsylvania.[1] Those who remained in California and in the West did not, however, remain passive in the face of obnoxious local ordinances and mob violence; again, they coordinated legal actions that pressed questions regarding the rights and position of the Chinese already in the United States, persons who were, despite the Exclusion Act, still under some federal protection both by treaty and by constitutional precedents.

Long before the Exclusion Act, anti-Chinese forces in the West attempted to stifle economic opportunities for Chinese immigrants with the intention of forcing them to leave the country. Threats of violence—often carried out by local officials—were made with the same purpose. Thus, in addition to the large numbers of Chinese turned away from the United States, the Chinese American community confronted both costly regulations and an increasingly dangerous public culture. As they asked the federal courts for relief, Field found himself again at odds with his fellow Justices, perhaps even with himself.

In 1886, the Supreme Court issued its famous decision in *Yick Wo v. Hopkins*, which struck down a series of laundry ordinances passed by the City of San Francisco. The case was a landmark decision because of the Court's analysis of what could constitute a violation of the Fourteenth Amendment.[2] Few knew, however, that the majority opinion by Justice Matthews drew heavily from earlier decisions written by Field in the Ninth Circuit. There was, of course, *Ah Fong*. And in one laundry case, *In re Quong Woo*, Field had also struck down an ordinance because to him it appeared simply to harass the Chinese, based only on "the miserable pretense that the business of a laundry . . . is against good morals or dangerous to the public health."[3] To Field, the City had been treating laundries, run primarily by Chinese immigrants, differently from other businesses, without any reason; saying that only racial animus could explain the ordinance, he held that it violated the Fourteenth Amendment. "A [Chinese alien's] right to follow any such occupation cannot be restrained by invalid legislation of any kind."[4] Before *Yick Wo*, Field had applied the Equal Protection Clause to strike down rules administered with "an evil eye" and "an unequal hand."

Yet, in the year prior to *Yick Wo*, Field had said in two other important laundry cases that the City's new laundry ordinances were not necessarily motivated by an "evil eye and an unequal hand." In one case, *Soon Hing v. Crowley*, in 1885, during the year that he was prone to exclude all Chinese laborers, Field said that the Chinese petitioner—suing against yet another laundry ordinance—relied heavily on "the supposed hostile motives of the supervisors passing it. . . . The petition alleges that it was adopted owing to a feeling of antipathy and hatred prevailing in the City and County of San Francisco against the subjects of the Emperor of China resident therein, and for the purpose of compelling those engaged in the laundry business to abandon their lawful vocation, and residence there, and not for any sanitary, police, or other legitimate purpose." Field was unmoved. "There is nothing, however, in the language of the ordinance, or in the record of its enactment, which in any respect tends to sustain this allegation."[5]

Yet the facts and evidence in *Soon Hing* and in *Yick Wo* were not substantially different, although in a strict technical sense, Matthew's decision in *Yick Wo* did not overrule Field's decision in *Soon Hing*. Still, Field's reasoning in *Soon Hing* suggested that he was not as sympathetic to poor Chinese laundrymen as he had once been, as in *Quong Woo*. Though he did not formally dissent in *Yick Wo*, Field was certainly not zealous in defending the economic rights of Chinese migrants, even though he knew that City officials had arrested hundreds of Chinese laundrymen for violating laundry ordinances since 1882.[6] Perhaps during that year, he was "struck with blindness" and "refused to see as a judge" what he saw as a man.

As a man, if one wanted to see antipathy and hatred toward the Chinese, one did not have to look very hard. Unfortunately, officials who used the law to harass the Chinese were quite prevalent in the mid-1880s. Indeed, public officials and even local judges appeared more sympathetic to white mobs than to the Chinese men murdered by white mobs, as Sucheng Chan and other historians have noted.[7] In 1871, for example, white rioters in Los Angeles killed nineteen Chinese laborers during one terrible week. In Chico, in that same year, white mobs tried to burn down the Chinatown there, killing four Chinese men in the process. Yet, in Los Angeles, "though eight men were convicted and sent to jail for the crimes, all were released a year later"; and in Chico, "though the suspects were convicted and sentenced, all were released on parole long before their sentences were up."[8] During the 1880s, if Chinese laborers weren't murdered, they were driven out of their homes, to be put on barges or on trains, leaving from places like Monterey or Watsonville. Coupled with the political and legal decisions against the Chinese, it must not have been entirely surprising to men like Field that by the mid-1880s, after formal exclusion, this violence and expulsion would escalate, take an even more insidious turn, become more organized and deliberate, and gain national attention.[9] By then, almost every town in California had an organized anti-Chinese club, and for their activities, "the fall and winter of 1885–86 . . . would prove to be a season of special ferocity."[10] In the following months, similar, coordinated acts of murder, arson, and expulsion erupted throughout the West—in larger towns like Denver, Portland, Marysville, San Jose, Folsom, Placerville, Redding, and Los Angeles, and in more obscure places like Snake River Canyon, Coal Creek, Black Diamond, Red Bluff, Puyallup, Gold Run, Lincoln, Wheatland, Dutch Flat, and Nicolaus.[11]

In the one federal case that dealt with protecting Chinese immigrants from mob violence, though, the Supreme Court refused to extend the Civil Rights Act of 1871, also known as the Ku Klux Klan Act, to punish white perpetrators. In a case about the organized expulsion of Chinese laborers from Nicolaus, California, the Court's decision in *Baldwin v. Franks* was a devastating blow to the Chinese, who had attempted to use the Civil Rights Act to invoke federal protection from mob violence, primarily because local officials were so unsympathetic to the Chinese.[12] In *Baldwin*, the Court concluded that with the Civil Rights Act of 1871, Congress had intended primarily "to enforce the political rights of citizens of the United States," not the rights of aliens. The Chinese petitioners were simply denied relief.[13]

Justice Field dissented in the case, arguing that the white rioters in *Baldwin* had violated the exclusive federal power to execute the treaty with China that still provided for the protection of Chinese living in the United States. "The purpose of the alleged conspirators was to permanently deprive the Chinese residing in Nicolaus—not any particular Chinese, but all of that class of persons—of the right of residence conferred by the treaty."[14] Though he had spoken and even lobbied for their formal exclusion, Field suggested that the exclusion of the "vast horde" did not necessarily mean leaving them to the mob. For Field, the treaty with China still bound the federal government to protect Chinese migrants. The majority's decision fell far short of that obligation: "The result . . . is that there is no national law which can be invoked for the protection of the subjects of China in their right to reside and do business in this country, notwithstanding the language of the treaty with that empire. . . . Such a result is to be deplored."[15]

Certainly, in March 1887, the state of American law must have looked deplorable to Chinese immigrants—the federal government protected their right to work in an "ordinary trade," in laundries, in what was perhaps the lowest, most menial occupation that a Chinese man could do. Yet it had done almost nothing to stop organized mobs threatening their very lives and destroying their property in virtually every town throughout the West. Still, for Field, an awareness of how awful and widespread this type of anti-Chinese violence and harassment had become did not seem to temper his own harsh rhetoric against the Chinese, nor did it give him reason to reconsider his support for Chinese exclusion. In fact, these developments may have *confirmed* his belief that the Chinese problem could only be fixed by eliminating the Chinese from American public life. Given that whites would always treat the Chinese harshly, Field seemed more convinced than ever that their presence would be a disaster. Alarmed that not even the federal government would protect the Chinese, Field became in turn a more vocal spokesman for Chinese exclusion.

"One Nation, One People, One Power"

On October 1, 1888, Congress amended the Chinese Exclusion Act by passing another law, the Scott Act, which annulled the controversial certificate provisions of the original Exclusion Act, and of the 1884 amendments. Now, irrespective of *when* a Chinese laborer came, or his prior residency in the United States, he was barred from entry.[16] Field had gotten his wish again: Congress had overruled the Court's decision in *Chew Heong* and had used Field's dissent as the template for the new law. According to Sucheng Chan, "The Scott Act, which went into effect immediately, abrogated the re-entry right of an estimated 20,000 Chinese laborers with certificates in their possession, including 600 who were en-route across the Pacific. These individuals were denied landing when they reached American shores."[17]

One such person, Chae Chan Ping, had lived in the United States before the Exclusion Act of 1882 was passed, but he was barred entry to San Francisco under the revised Act of 1888, only one week after its revision. In his arguments before the Court, Chae Chan Ping claimed that the Scott Act violated the terms of the Burlingame Treaty, and so should be struck down. In oral argument, his lawyers produced a valid residency certificate that specifically entitled him to return to the United States. Had he arrived just a few short months ago, he would have been admitted.

In *Chae Chan Ping v. United States*, regarded as *the* Chinese Exclusion Case, Justice Field reiterated many of the arguments he had made in *Chew Heong* and elsewhere: that the judiciary must defer to the political branches of government on these issues;[18] that the Chinese degraded labor, and forced hardships on white laborers;[19] that the Chinese laborers were essentially coolie slaves dangerous to fair competition and free labor;[20] that the Chinese were deceitful and had "loose notions . . . of the obligation of an oath";[21] that the government of China was also deceitful and acting in bad faith in carrying out the Burlingame Treaty;[22] that "it seemed impossible for [the Chinese] to assimilate with our people or to make any change in their habits or modes of living";[23] and "that their immigration was in numbers approaching the character of an invasion, and was a menace to our civilization."[24] In these many ways, the controlling opinion in *Chae Chan Ping* was simply a redeclaration of the dissent in *Chew Heong*, only this time Field spoke for a unanimous Court. In this opinion, however, Field underscored the central reason for upholding Chinese exclusion.

Justice Field noted that as early as 1857, from the time he had been appointed to the California Supreme Court, portions of the California electorate had pushed for exclusion. Now, thirty years later, Field said that "discontent was not confined to any political party, or to any class or nationality, but was well-nigh universal."[25] And "so urgent and constant were prayers of relief against existing and anticipated evils, both from public authorities of the Pacific Coast and from private individuals, that Congress was impelled to act on the subject."[26] He suggested here an account of the legislation that wasn't heavy-handed or remote from the people; the people specifically *called* for relief through "frequent and fair elections" of representatives supportive of their appeals. In Congress, their representatives used the legislative process to pass such laws.

Given this characterization of the origins of the Act, Field phrased a limited role for the Court in this area of law. "This court is not a censor of the morals of other departments of the government; it is not invested with any authority to pass judgment on the motives of their conduct. When once it is established that Congress possesses the power to pass an act, our province ends with its construction, and its application to cases as they are presented for determination."[27] Rather than claiming that the Court ought to protect certain groups *from* public opinion, or *from* the masses, the theory seemed to be that "public opinion" could "prevent abuses" better than the Court, and perhaps with more legitimacy. This opinion was "enlightened," the result of long experience. If the Court were to overrule the Exclusion Act, as the appellants had petitioned, it would do more than overrule Congress, it would overrule the will of the people: even more damaging to democracy, the Court would "make [law]."[28] The argument stood squarely against judicial activism, but it was also un-Madisonian—at its core, it relied heavily on the assumption that the public, even a local political majority, acting through the National Legislature, should have what it wanted even though members of the Court did not agree. Field had not been as sympathetic to local or state political processes that routinely produced legislation "unworthy of a brave and manly people," but here there was no hint of that, perhaps because it was not a local or state immigration rule under consideration, but a national one.

Justice Field then turned to the authority of Justice John Marshall to support the special role of *national* sovereignty in matters concerning immigration. Field warned against a weak, loose confederation of states instead of a single, united nation. Quoting Marshall, he said again: "These

States are constituent parts of the United States. They are members of one great empire."[29] Field suggested that after the Civil War, this idea was reaffirmed:

> The control of local matters being left to local authorities, and national matters being entrusted to the government of the Union, the problem of free institutions existing over a widely extended country, having different climates and varied interests, has been happily solved. For local interests the several States of the Union exist, but for national purposes, embracing our relations with foreign nations, we are but one people, one nation, one power.[30]

The crisis of the Civil War appeared everywhere in Field's opinion; the alliteration of "one people, one nation, one power" resonated both rhetorically and literally—it was as though, through his language, Field was as much *gathering* his countrymen toward a common bond rather than being already confident of its existence. In the Chinese Exclusion case, Field found at least one example for having a national government at all, and so he wrote forcefully in favor of it. In the exclusion of the racial other, Field and his fellow citizens would find an occasion for explaining why a national government should be necessary, and in the process, they would find also their own national identity reaffirmed as citizens of one great republic united against a common threat.

Protection from the racial other—the non-white and the non-Christian—was the primary objective. In the last part of his opinion, Field clearly stated that in the warm language of "we," in the appeal for national unity, the Chinese had no legitimate claim for membership: "These laborers are not citizens of the United States; they are aliens. That the government of the United States, through the action of the legislative department, can exclude aliens from its territory is a proposition which we do not think open to controversy."[31] In Field's view, the people—through their own government—had decided that "the presence of foreigners of a different race in this country, who will not assimilate with us, to be dangerous to its peace and security."[32] Field went so far as to suggest that the Chinese were like a military threat for which this exercise of national sovereignty was most appropriate: "It matters not in what form such aggression and encroachment come, whether from the foreign nation acting in its national character or from vast hordes of its people crowding in upon us."[33] Finally, "if there be any just ground of complaint on the part of China, it must be made to the political department of the government, which is alone competent to act upon the subject."[34] The Court would not intervene.

Field's opinion in the Chinese Exclusion case was, and remains, remarkable for a number of reasons—especially for this lengthy meditation on sovereignty, and what that concept truly meant in a democratic society. Strictly speaking, Congress was not excluding—the people were. The American people, using the government as their instrument, asserted *their* right not to accept certain persons to live among them. Field's connections between popular sovereignty and the democratic institutions expressing the popular will still resonate into our own day; they explain the tenacity of the doctrine that Congress should have plenary power over immigration without the Court's interference. Indeed, Justice Antonin Scalia relied on *The Chinese Exclusion Case* in 2001, eleven decades after it had been published, when he wrote that "an inadmissible alien at the border has no right to be in the United States." The terms of admissibility, Scalia insisted, has always remained with Congress.[35] The plenary powers doctrine in immigration law remains one of the most durable precedents in American public law.

"No Laborer of the Chinese Race Shall Be Permitted to Enter the United States"

In 1891 and 1892, several important developments occurred. Writing for majorities again, Justice Field decided against two Chinese petitioners who had appealed to the Court for relief against the Exclusion Acts because he believed that they were lying. But in the second of these cases, Justice David Brewer, who had been appointed to the Court in 1889, after *Chae Chan Ping*, emerged as an important dissenter against the prevailing tendency toward Chinese exclusion. Brewer was Field's nephew; Brewer's mother and her missionary husband were the ones who had taken the young Stephen Field to Europe when he was a boy. Like Field himself, Brewer took his early law training in David Dudley Field's New York office, but left for California a few years later, because, according to him, "I didn't want to grow up to be my uncle's nephew."[36] The Field family had by 1889 two members on the United States Supreme Court, but their differences at least with regard to the treatment of Chinese immigrants became obvious by 1891.[37]

For now, disputes over Chinese immigrants became matters of faith. In May 1891, the Court heard the case of Quock Ting, who had testified that he was a sixteen-year-old citizen of the United States, having been born in San Francisco. He claimed that he had lived in the city until he was ten years old, then traveled with his mother to China until his return to San Francisco in February 1888. He returned to San Francisco alone to rejoin his father. But it appeared that "although in the city, according to his statement, for ten years, he did not, upon his examination, show any knowledge of any places or streets therein, or of the English language. . . . Nor did he mention any circumstances, incident or occurrence, except being born in Dupont Street, upstairs, which would lead one to suppose that he had ever been in the city."[38] Even though the boy's father testified that "the petitioner was his boy, and that he was born 'at 1030 Dupont Street, upstairs,'" Field replied that "the testimony given by [the petitioner] amounted to very little; indeed, it was of no force or weight whatever."[39] Field himself must have known that as violence against Chinese immigrants intensified, living in an urban Chinatown like the one in San Francisco was more by necessity than by choice. Moreover, he knew, as any native of the city would, that as an isolated ethnic enclave, there was nothing unusual about the lack of English—"everywhere in the colony were signboards in Chinese characters, giving the stores and shops euphonious and poetic names," according to the historian Ronald Takaki.[40] Perhaps in the case of Quock Ting, Field did not object so much to the petitioner's testimony, but rather that it wasn't in English, and thus confirming that "our institutions have made no impression on them," and "they do not and will not assimilate with our people." Speaking as the lone dissenter in the case, Justice Brewer suggested just that: "No attempt was made to contradict either father or son, or impeach either, unless the ignorance of the English language is to be considered as impeachment."[41] "The government evidently rested on the assumption that, because the witnesses were Chinese persons, they were not to be believed. I do not agree with this."[42]

But Brewer probably knew that Chinese immigrants "did not always dutifully accede to the systematic efforts to control their presence in the United States." As Bill Ong Hing has noted, "Because of their relatively larger numbers, longer stays in the United States, and the hardship of family separation and anti-miscegenation laws, Chinese were given to undocumented migration more than any other group."[43] Increasingly, there were "paper merchants," someone who posed as a wealthy Chinese businessman exempt from the Exclusion Act; and there were "paper sons," someone not really related to his "father," who was (maybe) a native-born American citizen with whom he was "reuniting."[44] Still, without more solid evidence, Justice Brewer would have admitted Quock Ting.

In another major case, where a Chinese immigrant claimed to be a merchant although he did not have the proper papers or a residency certificate, Field simply denied his petition, following strictly the 1884 amendments to the Exclusion Act. His opinion was like a door closing: "The result of the legislation respecting the Chinese would seem to be this, that no laborers of that race shall hereafter be permitted to enter the United States, or even to return after having departed from the country, though they may have previously resided therein and have left with a view of returning." All others needed to prove "that they are not laborers."[45] Field suggested that credibility was no longer an issue when it came to Chinese exclusion. It was either a valid certificate or a steamer back to China. But even as he vehemently defended this cruel exclusion, Field encountered new legislation in 1892 that would test his faith in himself and in his jurisprudence of exclusion. The change in his tone would again be striking.

"It Is Beyond All Reason in Its Severity . . . It Is Cruel and Unusual"

In his criticisms of Justice Field and of the federal judiciary in 1880, General Miller of California had suggested "cutting out" the "Oriental gangrene," and of course such language implied removal, not just exclusion. In 1892, Congress passed the Geary Act, which required the remaining Chinese laborers in the United States to obtain yet another kind of certificate, this time to prove that they had been residing in the country legally since May 5, 1892. Those without a certificate could be held "by any customs official, collector of internal revenue or his deputies, United States marshal or his deputies, and taken before a United States judge." Unless they could prove that they were entitled to a certificate through the testimony of "at least one credible white witness," they would be subject to deportation.[46] Moreover, under section 4, "any such Chinese person, or person of Chinese descent, convicted and adjudged to be not lawfully entitled to be and remain in the United States, shall be imprisoned at hard labor for a period of not exceeding one year, and thereafter removed from the United States."[47] This was removal and punishment *before* removal, based on the assumption that most Chinese were lying, and that also, like a vast horde, they were indistinguishable from one another.[48]

Organized by Chinese groups across the country, large numbers of Chinese immigrants decided not to follow the new law as a collective act of civil disobedience. Feeling as though they had been "tagged and branded as a whole lot of cattle," Chinese organizations wanted to create a test case to overturn the Act, and such a case, *Fong Yue Ting v. United States*, appeared before the United States Supreme Court in 1893.[49]

Writing for the majority, Justice Horace Gray repeated many of the arguments made by Justice Field in *Chew Heong* and *Chae Chan Ping*. In fact, whole sections of Field's writings in those cases appeared in Gray's opinion. Gray relied on Field to support judicial deference on the matter of immigration, and to repeat the view that the Chinese degraded labor, were not to be trusted, remained unassimilated and unassimilable, and in general posed enough of a threat to the nation to justify exclusion.[50] Gray repeated the fact that "Chinese persons not born in this country have never been recognized as citizens of the United States, nor authorized to become so under the naturalization laws."[51]

But in addition, Gray claimed that deportation and exclusion were ultimately part of the same exercise of national sovereignty that Field had defended earlier. Moreover, he insisted that the deportation of Chinese immigrants under the Geary Act did not constitute "punishment" for which due process of law was required. First, "the right of a nation to expel or deport foreigners, who have not been naturalized or taken any steps towards becoming citizens of the country, rests upon the same grounds, and is as absolute and unqualified as the right to prohibit and prevent their entrance into the country."[52]

Perhaps because deportation was such a new issue to the American judiciary, Gray had to rely heavily on English and continental sources to make this point.[53] Despite the lack of American precedents on the issue, Gray was nevertheless very adamant and repetitive. Early portions of Gray's opinion served as precedents for its later portions.

Applying this logic to the Chinese, Gray concluded that because "they continue to be aliens, having taken no such steps towards becoming citizens, and incapable of becoming such, . . . [they] remain subject to the power of Congress to expel them, or to order them to be removed and deported from the country, whenever, in its judgment their removal is necessary or expedient for the public interest."[54] Gray repeated Field's claim that the Chinese were "unassimilable," and he implied that Congress had been generous in even providing for the residency certificates for such persons at all—should Congress decide to do so, *all* Chinese immigrants could conceivably be deported, with or without a certificate. If the public will was such, no judge or Court ought to interfere. Again, almost all of the central arguments were drawn from Field's opinions.

Turning to the nature of deportation itself, Gray wrote that "the order of deportation is not a punishment for crime."[55] "It is not a banishment" but simply "a method of enforcing the return to his own country of an alien who has not complied with the conditions upon the performance of which the government of the nation, acting within its constitutional authority and through the proper departments, has determined that his continuing to reside here shall depend." Never having had the right to reside in the country, such a person could be treated as though he was never there. "He has not, therefore, been deprived of life, liberty or property, without due process of law; and the provisions of the Constitution, securing the right of trial by jury, and prohibiting unreasonable searches and seizures, and cruel and unusual punishments, have no application."[56]

In addition, the power to expel "may be exercised entirely by executive officers."[57] While Gray did acknowledge that deporting someone might cause considerable hardship to the person deported, he insisted that this was a "political matter": "The judicial department cannot properly express an opinion upon the wisdom, the policy or the justice of the measures enacted by Congress in the exercise of the powers confided to it by the Constitution over the subject."[58]

Rather dramatically, Field dissented. In separate opinions indicating a very divided Court, Justices Field, Brewer, and Fuller insisted that deportation *was* punishment, or at the very least, a matter serious enough to trigger procedural protections. Field's dissent was particularly spirited and notable, given his constant, original support for Chinese exclusion.

First, Justice Field insisted that between deportation and exclusion, "there is a wide and essential difference."[59]

> The power of the government to exclude foreigners from this country, that is, to prevent them from entering it, whenever the public interests in its judgment require such exclusion, has been repeatedly asserted by the

legislative and executive departments of our government and never denied; but its power to deport from the country persons lawfully domiciled therein by its consent, and engaged in the ordinary pursuits of life, has never been asserted by the legislative or executive departments except for crime, or as an act of war in view of existing or anticipated hostilities.[60]

Justice Field said that to expel someone under the law, the government must have "reasonable grounds to suspect . . . treasonable or secret machinations against the government."[61] He himself had suggested as much in earlier cases, with regard to the "dangers" of Chinese immigration, but now he seemed as though he had changed his mind: "With respect to aliens who are not enemies, but members of nations in peace and amity with the United States, the power assumed by the act of Congress is denied to be constitutional."[62] In *Chew Heong* and *Chae Chan Ping*, Field had characterized the influx of Chinese immigrants as an "Oriental invasion," a "vast horde," "unnumbered millions," "coolie slaves," "a menace," and "a threat to the inestimable benefits of our Christian civilization." But here, he asserted that they had come in "peace and amity," and so did not deserve to be treated in such a manner.

Rather than insisting that it wasn't punishment, as Justice Gray had, Field insisted that it most certainly was. "If a banishment of this sort be not punishment, and among the severest of punishments, it would be difficult to imagine a doom to which the name can be applied."[63] Deportation was excessive punishment:

[It] is beyond all reason in its severity. It is out of all proportion to the alleged offense. It is cruel and unusual. As to its cruelty, nothing can exceed a forcible deportation from a country of one's residence, and the breaking up of all the relations of friendship, family, and business there contracted. The laborer may be seized at a distance from his home, family and his business, and taken before the judge for his condemnation, without permission to visit his home, see his family, or complete any unfinished business.[64]

"The offense" here was that a Chinese laborer had failed to procure a certificate of residence, or to prove by the testimony of "at least one credible white witness" that he had deserved one; the "cruel punishment" was that he could be held, punished, and deported without a trial. The language of proportionality between "crime" and "punishment," and the damning insistence that the punishment was "cruel and unusual," evoked Field's earlier opinion in *Ho Ah Kow*. The measure of humanity he had expressed regarding the severing of queues reappeared here: the government should not be able to "break up . . . all the relations of friendship, family, and business" contracted by the laborer—deny him "home," "family," "business." Again, where Field had once described the Chinese laborers in question as a faceless, "vast horde," as "unnumbered millions," he now described them as having worthwhile, meaningful human attachments, and more importantly, rights, like the one against cruel and unusual punishment, or the right to due process. They were persons again, not an abstract racial other, and their racial status ought to be irrelevant before the law.

Although Justice Gray had simply repeated some of Justice Field's own opinions to claim that Chinese immigrants were not citizens and could never be citizens, Justice Field argued that this alone did not mean that *all* of those immigrants were wholly without rights. Field acknowledged that even after the Exclusion Acts, the law was "constantly evaded." Chinese immigrants discovered "new means of ingress, . . . in spite of the vigilance of the police and customs officials."[65] "Their resemblance to each other rendered it difficult, and often impossible, to prevent the evasion of the law."[66] But Field insisted that while he accepted the motives behind the Geary Act, the process by which the Act determined who was and wasn't eligible to stay was entirely insufficient—legal immigrants could not be deported simply because a federal customs official, a collector of internal revenue, or a marshal suspected him of violating the immigration law. There was no trial per se, no process or protection. This was a "dangerous and despotic power, . . . a power which will authorize it to expel at pleasure, in time of peace, the whole body of friendly foreigners of any country domiciled herein by [the government's] permission." Field suggested that such unchecked power could potentially endanger "all persons in their liberty and property."[67] In *Chew Heong* and *Chae Chan Ping*, Justice Field had said that the judiciary should not impute "bad faith" on the part of government officials, nor question "the morals of other departments of the government," nor deny Congress "the right to its exercise . . . of those sovereign powers delegated by the Constitution." But Field hesitated: he himself appeared regretful of the doctrine he had shaped, the foundations for which he had largely created. More importantly, Field again *discounted* the significance of American citizenship by saying that "the guarantees of the Constitution" were intended for all persons irrespective of citizenship.

Overall, in *Fong Yue Ting*, Justice Field indicated yet another shift in his jurisprudence and disposition toward the Chinese. Once again, Field claimed that along with the homes, the families, friends, and business relations that they had had, the Chinese also had fundamental rights, such that "arbitrary and despotic power can no more be exercised over them with reference to their persons and property, than over the persons and property of native-born citizens." Although as noncitizens they could not vote or hold office, "As men having our common humanity, they are protected by all the guaranties of the Constitution. . . . To hold that they are subject to any different law or are less protected in any particular than other persons, is in my judgment to ignore the teachings of our history, the practice of our government, and the language of our Constitution."[68] Again, the legal significance of citizenship receded, a "common humanity" was enough to trigger rights and protection, and thus the government had gone too far. It was as though Field were reversing himself.

More than for his reputation, though, Field worried for the Chinese. In time, perhaps they could be "capitally punished without a jury or the other incidents to a fair trial."[69] Rather than claiming again that the Chinese needed to appeal to the "political branches" for remedies in this area of law, he took it on himself to criticize both the legislative and executive branches—in effect, to do what he had once said the judiciary was in no position to do—and to advocate the side of the Chinese laborers, perhaps against his former self and his own precedents. Field noted that the very immigrants he had characterized as having "loose notions of the obligation of an oath" should, under these deplorable circumstances, maybe have the right to jury trials in serious matters, and to juries composed partly of other aliens like themselves.[70] It is strange that Field came to this disjuncture: he did *not* insist that Chinese immigrants shouldn't serve on juries because they were deceitful; rather, he insisted that it should be their *right* to have their own juries when their peers were on trial and their rights threatened.

Altogether, the change in thinking is striking, almost complete. In *Chew Heong, Chae Chan Ping*, and other exclusion cases, Justice Field had carved a role for the legislative and executive branches that was extremely broad—virtually unlimited—in matters of immigration. But in *Fong Yue Ting*, Field worried whether that power would result in terrible government and a complete loss of that which held the whole American legal system together—the acknowledging of basic, universal rights, irrespective of ascriptive status, even immigration status. Perhaps reminded of the hostility faced by Chinese laborers, of how easily they would be deported by overzealous government officials, with very little due process if any, Field predicted the worst: the result would be "to establish a pure, simple, undisguised despotism and tyranny with respect to foreigners resident in the country by its consent." The Americans and their government *ought to be* distinguishable, ought to be *better* than "the Asiatic countries where personal caprice and not settled rules prevail." But the American government had acted despotically by allowing for the deportation of persons without sufficient due process even though "arbitrary and tyrannical power has no place in our system."[71] When faced with an offshoot of his own doctrine, Field found it "brutal and oppressive."[72] "The decision of the Court and the sanction it would give to legislation depriving resident aliens of the guaranties of the Constitution fills me with apprehensions."[73]

In a nation where immigration was one of the primary sources of growth and of expansion in the economy and society, Field's "apprehensions" extended beyond the Chinese and beyond the Chinese Exclusion Cases. "How far will this legislation go?" Would it endanger, for example, white ethnics, and make them just as vulnerable to arrest and deportation?

> Is it possible that Congress can, at its pleasure, in disregard of the guarantees of the Constitution, expel at any time the Irish, German, French, and English who may have taken up their residence here on the invitation of the government, while we are at peace with the countries from which they came, simply on the ground that they have not been naturalized?[74]

The same worries preoccupied his nephew, Justice Brewer, who wrote, in his own dissent: "The expulsion of a race may be within the inherent powers of a despotism. History, before the adoption of this Constitution, was not destitute of examples of the exercise of such a power; and its framers were familiar with history, and wisely as it seems to me, they gave to the government no general power to banish." Brewer suggested that Congress and the Court's majority only consented to this horrible policy against the Chinese "for no crime but that of their race and birthplace," so that they would "be driven from our territory."[75] Suggesting like his uncle that Congress had acted brutally and repressively, Brewer concluded: "In view of this enactment of the highest legislative body of the foremost Christian nation, may not the thoughtful Chinese disciple of Confucius fairly ask, 'Why do they send missionaries here?'"[76]

In 1893, the same year of the *Fong Yue Ting* decision, another series of expulsions took place against Chinese immigrants living in California. Once again, organized mobs forcefully and maliciously drove out the Chinese from Selma, Visalia, Bakersfield, Redlands, Fresno, and San Bernardino. Again, Field's apprehensions would be prophetic. The Chinese were indeed being "cut out."[77]

"It Is Hoped That the Poor Chinamen, Now before Us Seeking Relief from Cruel Oppression, Will Not Find Their Appeal to Our Republican Institutions and Laws a Vain and Idle Proceeding"

In his dissent in *Fong Yue Ting*, Justice Field implied that Justice Gray would have upheld his absurd version of national sovereignty even if "Congress . . . ordered executive officers to take Chinese laborers to the ocean and put them into a boat and set them adrift."[78] Justice Gray took the remark personally. "Gray was both offended and unnerved," according to Alan Westin. "Gray was so upset by Field's attack that he took back his majority opinion and modified the sentence quoted by Field. When Field learned of the change, he sent the Reporter a footnote to be added to his dissent, explaining that the sentence attacked had originally been in the opinion but had been withdrawn when criticized."[79] And so it went. A month later, in a letter to Attorney General Donald Dickensen, Field offered a few thoughts about what to do with *Fong Yue Ting*; at the very least, he wanted a rehearing, and if that failed, perhaps, he said, the Court could add additional members inclined to overrule it.[80] Yet here, when Field said that the American people would not "submit to such a doctrine" as expressed in Gray's opinion, he was perhaps not as astute of politics as he should have been. After all, the people themselves, acting through their representatives, had supported the law as well as the idea of Chinese exclusion, for a long, long time, as Field himself had once said.

But the Geary Act still bothered Justice Field when the last Chinese exclusion case appeared before him, one year before his retirement, during a time when he was not always attentive to court proceedings, "became noticeably feeble," and appeared to his colleagues occasionally in a "dull stupor."[81] In 1896, in *Wong Wing v. United States*, a collector of customs in Michigan arrested the plaintiff and three others. The plaintiffs were found without residency certificates, and prior to their deportation, they were sentenced to sixty days of hard labor, as provided in §4 of the Geary Act, to be served in a jail in Detroit.[82]

Justice George Shiras, who had been appointed to the Court in 1892, spoke for a majority on two central issues. First, Shiras noted that the Chinese Exclusion Acts separated two classes of persons, "those who came into the country with its consent," and "those who have come into the United States without their consent and in disregard of the laws. . . . Our previous decisions have settled that it is within the constitutional power of Congress to deport both of these classes, and to commit the enforcement of the law to executive officers."[83] Tired of habeas corpus petitions, the federal judiciary finally receded in these matters altogether, and as Lucy Salyer has observed, by this time the "Chinese could no longer use courts in the same manner to review the administrative decisions denying them entry."[84] Justice Field himself had presaged the shift in one of the early exclusion cases he had decided in Circuit Court in 1884.[85] For all intents and purposes, administrative hearings by executive officers *were* due process for Chinese immigrants and, often, for Chinese Americans.

The second issue in the case concerned the treatment of Chinese persons suspected of violating the Geary Act. At the time, Chinese immigrants were being held in "detention centers" for long periods of time pending the final adjudication of administrative or judicial proceedings, sometimes for a month, several months, a year, or more. Justice Shiras did not find this a "punishment" that was itself unconstitutional or in need of any greater due process: "Detention is a usual feature of every case of arrest on a criminal charge, even when an innocent person is wrongfully accused; but it is not imprisonment in a legal sense."[86] However, section 4 of the Geary Act was more of a problem. That section treated "unlawful residence" alone as an "infamous crime" punishable by "hard labor." But, "it is not consistent with the theory of our government that the legislature should, after having defined an offence as an infamous crime, find the fact of guilt and adjudge the punishment by one of its own agents." If it was such a crime, the infraction "should first be established by a judicial trial."[87] Thus, while the Court did not necessarily strike down the provision for hard labor in the Geary Act, it held that a judicial trial was necessary before such a punishment could be inflicted.[88]

Justice Field dissented from and concurred with the majority opinion. In the last two paragraphs of his opinion, he essentially repeated the two basic holdings of the decision issued by Shiras, but for most of his own opinion, Justice Field chastised the government and took the side of the Chinese plaintiffs. He scolded the government's lawyers:

> I dissent entirely from what seemed to me to be the harsh and illegal as-
> sertions, made by counsel of the Government, on the argument of this
> case, as to the right of the court to deny to the accused the full protec-
> tion of the law and constitution against every form of oppression and
> cruelty to them.[89]

He insisted again that the Chinese were persons who should be able to enjoy fundamental rights and protections despite their status as noncitizens.

> The contention that persons within the territorial jurisdiction of this re-
> public might be beyond the protection of the law was heard with pain
> on the argument at the bar—in face of the great constitutional amend-
> ment which declares that no State shall deny to any person within its ju-
> risdiction the equal protection of the laws.[90]

Although he himself had once insisted that Chinese immigrants "were not citizens," he again tried to mitigate the legal consequences of that fact: "It does not follow that, because the Government may expel aliens or exclude them from coming to this country, it can confine them at hard labor in a penitentiary before deportation or subject them to any harsh and cruel punishment."[91] On the provisions for hard labor, Field insisted that "if the imprisonment of a human being at hard labor in a peniten-tiary for any misconduct or offense is not punishment, it is difficult to un-derstand how anything short of the infliction of the death penalty for such misconduct or offense is punishment."[92] Altogether, Field's opinion im-plicitly expanded the scope of constitutional protections—the phrases, "harsh and cruel punishment," "servitude," "equal protection of the laws" each evoked constitutional principles that Chinese aliens could ap-peal to as integral parts of "the full protection of the law and constitution against every form of oppression and cruelty to them."

While he did not succeed in overturning *Fong Yue Ting* completely, he had a rehearing of sorts in *Wong Wing*. And although he had once hoped that Congress would hear the pleas for Chinese exclusion, "to preserve to ourselves the inestimable benefits of our Christian civilization," Justice Field ended his career with a different wish: "It is hoped that the poor Chinamen, now before us seeking relief from cruel oppression, will not find their appeal to our republican institutions and laws a vain and idle proceeding."[93] With that, Field ended his involvement in the Chinese exclusion cases.

Not long after this last case, Justice Stephen Field died in his home in Washington, D.C., on April 9, 1899. Several members of his family, including his nephew David Brewer, were with him during his final moments.[94]

Since his passing, Field's biographers and other students of his jurisprudence have credited him with developing a number of important intellectual strands in American public law, especially in his influential opinions regarding economic regulations and the right of persons to pursue a lawful profession free from unnecessary state interference. Charles McCurdy, Robert McCloskey, Howard Graham, and Carl Brent Swisher have all examined extensively Field's influence in this area of law.[95] But whatever success laissez-faire constitutionalism may have had in the decades immediately following Field's death, it did not survive the New Deal or the social welfare state.[96]

In contrast, Field's development and articulation of the plenary powers doctrine in immigration law have survived both. It still survives. The idea that Congress has plenary power to set the terms of immigration into the United States—as expressed in *The Chinese Exclusion Case*—has been reiterated by the Supreme Court and by lower federal courts in several leading cases, in every decade of the twentieth century, and even in contexts that don't directly touch on immigration.[97] The case has always stood for the notion that some issues are best dealt with through the political branches of government with minimal judicial review. The case has always stood for the idea that sometimes national sovereignty is a paramount virtue in the law. In one landmark case in 1967, regarding an immigration rule excluding persons who were homosexual, the Court said that "it has long been held that the Congress has plenary power to make rules for the admission of aliens and to exclude those who possess those characteristics which Congress has forbidden." In practice, Congress still does exclude persons for a variety of reasons, including poverty, illiteracy, political ideology, and sexual orientation. In theory, Congress could still exclude persons by race. This very possibility worried Justice Thurgood Marshall in 1985, when federal officials were accused of racial bias in their treatment of Haitian refugees.[98] And yet no federal court has ever dared to overturn this powerful precedent despite its obvious potential for abuse, as well as its tragic racist history, much to Marshall's dismay.

But in a fascinating way, Field's doubts about the treatment of immigrants and about the strange power of immigration rules have also appeared in every decade since his death. Relying heavily on Field's opinions in *Wong Wing*, in addition to other cases where he had decided in favor of the Chinese, the Supreme Court and the lower federal courts have often agonized over the treatment of immigrants before federal officials, just like Field himself. Indeed, Field's reasoning in *Wong Wing* has been by itself cited almost as frequently as *The Chinese Exclusion Case*, and often in ways favorable to immigrant plaintiffs who were mistreated by federal authorities and rules.[99] In one important case just decided in April 2003, the Supreme Court divided over the very meaning and significance of *Wong Wing* and its procedural safeguards for immigrants.[100] Oddly, the procedural safeguards spawned by the concerns in *Wong Wing* have often *substituted* for constitutional norms, as the legal scholar Hiroshi Motomura has argued.[101]

In addition and, perhaps more important, the general idea that the Fourteenth Amendment protects all persons and not just citizens was clearly rooted in Field's early opinions, and this doctrine has also survived into our own day. That all persons shall have the equal protection of the law—the central reasoning in *Ah Fong* and *Yick Wo*—remains a standard principle in American constitutional law. All first-year law students read *Yick Wo*, and one suspects that many law professors present the case in a celebratory way to show the wisdom and virtue of American constitutional law against racist and racially motivated legislation. The core of *Yick Wo* is found in Field's decision in *Ah Fong*. The core of that reasoning also appears in *Plyler v. Doe*, the case from Texas in 1982, and it continues to exist in a strange tension with the doctrine of national sovereignty, as we have seen. More than anyone, Stephen Field would have appreciated this set of contradictions, if only because he helped to delineate them.

PART III

Homeless Strangers

6

"They Will Disappear"

"They Will Disappear in a Short Time from Natural Causes"

Though the logic of exclusion would extend to other racial and ethnic groups, the Chinese Exclusion Acts and the judicial decisions upholding them had the most devastating effects on Asian immigration. This section attempts to measure some of this devastation. One obvious and immediate consequence of the Chinese Exclusion Acts was that the number of people of Chinese ancestry began to shrink. There would be no natural increase to replace the immigrant population. Unmarried Chinese women were routinely classified as prostitutes and thus barred by the Page Law of 1875; the wives of Chinese laborers in the United States were forbidden from rejoining their husbands under Justice Field's decision in *Ah Moy*; and Chinese men with wives in China could not go back to visit their families without forfeiting the chance to return to the United States altogether. Field had predicted in 1879 that the Chinese "will disappear in a short time from natural causes," and his prediction came true. From 1880 to 1920, about 16 million immigrants arrived from Europe; during the same period, only 700,000 new Asian immigrants entered, while the lonely bachelor society of Chinese men diminished, "from 105,465 in 1880 to 89,863 in 1900 to 61,639 in 1920."[1] The Chinese immigrant became "a homeless stranger."[2]

Moreover, despite Field's last hope that the Chinese in America would perhaps find some measure of justice and relief in American courts, the federal judiciary increasingly refused to intervene when Congress made deportation or exclusion proceedings even more summary, even more harsh. In the next chapter, we explore how immigration and naturalization decisions from the Supreme Court pushed Asian migrants farther and farther into the margins of American society in the early 20th century. And immigration rules were not the only set of laws to make life difficult. Rules governing property ownership, school segregation, marriage, and naturalization all functioned to keep Asians in American society beyond the protection of the law. As Lisa Lowe has argued, Asian Americans were regarded as "perpetual foreigners," such that, no matter the length of their residence or their willingness to assimilate into prevailing American norms, white majorities consistently refused to acknowledge or to recognize their rights or their desire for citizenship. State and federal governments used race and immigration status as disabling categories against Asians until well into the mid-20th century.

The following section also presents the variety of ways in which Asian immigrants dealt with discriminatory rules that drew clear lines between them and American citizens. Relegated to a distinct minority status through exclusion rules, Asian immigrants tried to cope as best they could. Shut out of the Lockean commonwealth, discriminatory rules harassed them everywhere, so everywhere they tried to avoid the impact of such rules. This involved some common strategies to alter or to subsume their identities: for example, many Chinese migrants lied about their true identity to gain admission into the United States, and they invented family relationships to take advantage of loopholes in the exclusion laws. Japanese immigrants also subsumed their true selves: they used their children's identity when their own proved disabling. Wanting to marry, many Filipino immigrants either lied about their racial background, or crossed state boundaries to avoid hostile state rules. In the two landmark naturalization cases in the early 1920s, *Ozawa v. United States*, and *United States v. Thind*, the two protagonists suggested that they were really white after all, or they at least shared some of the premises of white supremacist thought. Faced with a legal regime in which immigration status and racial identity were *not* treated as arbitrary characteristics, Asian immigrants hid, subsumed, or denied these aspects of their selves. They disappeared before the law.

In time, though, the devastating consequences associated with racial identity became more fraught with peril, even as American citizenship became more accessible. During and after World War II, the fate of those labeled "enemy aliens" was horrible indeed, first for Japanese Americans and then for Chinese Americans. The former faced internment, the latter the threat of widespread deportation. In each instance, American citizenship required ever more insistent claims of belonging, and the expression of an ever more strident American patriotism. For many young Japanese Americans, fighting internment involved proving assimilation, and for still others, a desire for American citizenship meant a willingness to fight the enemies of the United States. For large numbers of Chinese immigrants caught in midst of the Cold War, American citizenship could be possible if they informed on one another: by pointing out the leftists and Communists among them, Chinese immigrants with suspicious immigration histories could have the American citizenship that they had always wanted. In this way, American public law shaped desires for belonging such that they produced thousands of acts of betrayal. That story occupies the next chapter.

This chapter discusses the full flowering of immigration law in the fifty years following Field's death. American law preserved and strengthened the distinction between citizens and "aliens ineligible for citizenship." The logic of this distinction relied on the premise that the political community could circumscribe who could and could not belong, the federal power akin to "the federative power of commonwealth" defended by Locke and other liberal theorists. Thematically, this section attempts to show the consequences of such a long and sustained deprivation of membership, as well as the formal strategies developed in response to this legal regime. The experiences of the Asian American protagonists reflect ultimately the tremendous emotional and psychological toll inflicted on persons told that they could not belong. Conceptually, their efforts in many instances helped to *further* the distance between citizens and strangers, even as they would ultimately challenge the rationality of using race or immigration status as meaningful grounds for exclusion.

"Stopped at the Limit of Our Jurisdiction and Kept There"

In the immediate years following Justice Field's death, the United States Supreme Court solidified the plenary powers doctrine in immigration law. Having embraced the idea of popular sovereignty in matters of immigration and formal membership, the Court issued a string of decisions saying that due process for immigrants would be whatever procedures Congress would provide, no matter how summary or seemingly unfair. Against the Chinese, then the Japanese, then all Asians, and finally against several other groups of immigrants, including those from southern and eastern Europe, the Court remained unsympathetic. And extrapolating from the Chinese cases, the Court held that Congress could exclude whole classes of immigrants from the United States. Gifted jurists, including Justice Oliver Wendell Holmes, gave these harsh new doctrines their most memorable justifications.

In cases like *United States v. Sing Tuck* (1904) and *United States v. Ju Toy* (1905), Justice Holmes situated immigrants beyond constitutional protection. In the first case, Justice Holmes expressed his suspicions of Chinese landing in the United States. The case concerned thirty-two persons of Chinese descent who had attempted to enter the United States from Canada; when detained, five claimed American citizenship and filed habeas corpus petitions with the federal courts.[3] In one sense, the case was in no way different than many other cases during this period, where Chinese petitioners had asked for the intervention of the federal courts after they had been detained by executive officers.[4] And as in those cases, Justice Holmes, speaking for a clear majority, upheld the right of executive officials to determine whether a person could land in the United States without "interference" from the federal courts.

The decision in *Sing Tuck* reinforced what was developing into a standard immigration procedure: according to a series of special rules intended to provide some level of due process, an immigration official had the right to determine whether a petitioner could land; in the event of an adverse finding, the petitioner then had to appeal to higher executive officials first, up to the Secretary of Commerce and Labor; and only after such appeals were exhausted could he petition the federal courts.[5] Perhaps the strangeness of this new "administrative law" required annual justifications, as case after case divided the lower courts.[6]

In *Sing Tuck*, though, more striking than the decision itself was Justice Holmes' language toward Chinese petitioners: "Here the issue, if there is one, is pure matter of fact, a claim of citizenship under circumstances and in a form naturally raising a suspicion of fraud."[7] Like Field in his darker moments, Holmes made clear that he had little faith in the veracity of the Chinese: they "naturally raised suspicion of fraud." Justice Brewer, dissenting as he had in many similar cases, insisted that this denial of equal protection and due process was unconstitutional: "The most notorious outlaw in the land, when charged by the United States with a crime, is, by constitutional enactment, given compulsory process for obtaining witnesses in his favor and the assistance of counsel for his defense, but the Chinamen—although by birth a citizen of the United States—is thus denied counsel and the right of obtaining witnesses." Brewer observed that, in effect, the federal immigration law was becoming "extra-constitutional," with a series of special, relatively summary set of procedures for noncitizens, as well as those *suspected* of being non-citizens (those who may in fact *be* citizens). Rather dryly, Holmes remained unmoved: "A mere allegation of citizenship is not enough. But, before the courts can be called on, the preliminary sifting process provided by the statutes must be gone through with."[8] As though following his leadership, lower federal courts began rejecting habeas corpus appeals in record numbers, according to legal historian Lucy Salyer.[9]

Yet the development of an immigration law so heavily weighted against those making claims to land raised such controversy among the federal courts that the issue appeared again a year later, in *United States v. Ju Toy*. There, the essential facts were the same. Landing in San Francisco and detained by executive officers, Ju Toy alleged native-born American citizenship. He demanded a full hearing in federal court to prove the veracity of his claim, not just a summary procedure before "immigration officers appointed to deal with objectionable aliens."[10] In fact, other persons like him—prior to the ruling in *Sing Tuck*—had had some success in forcing federal courts to intervene when they had been similarly detained.[11] As in many of those cases, Ju Toy actually won in the lower courts, after proving successfully that he was a citizen. On appeal, the thrust of the government's argument lay not in Ju Toy's actual status, but in an objection that the lower federal court had heard his case at all.

In his majority opinion, Holmes articulated no new arguments in his decision in favor of the government. For him, the matter was well settled and unambiguous, despite the number of older precedents in favor of Ju Toy, and despite the lower court finding that he was an American citizen. "In view of the cases which we have cited it seems no longer open to discuss the question propounded as a new one. Therefore, we do not analyze the nature of the right of a person presenting himself at the frontier for admission. . . . But it is not improper to add a few words." The words were brief, but quite devastating: "The petitioner, although physically present within our boundaries, is to be regarded as if he had been stopped at the limit of our jurisdiction and kept there while his right to enter was under debate."[12] Ju Toy found himself suddenly deportable on a matter of procedure. With the government, Holmes agreed that the federal courts should not have intervened at all. Indeed, during the time he sat on the Court, Holmes voted to allow the federal courts to intervene in summary immigration proceedings only in cases where executive officials behaved particularly and obviously badly.[13]

But the decision in *Ju Toy* was important also for the legal fiction that Holmes had articulated. Even though an immigrant may dwell on the territory of the United States, American constitutional law and many of its fundamental protections did not apply to him. It was as though persons like Ju Toy existed in a kind of bubble—both here in the United States, literally, but not here legally—"stopped at the limit of our jurisdiction and kept there while his right to enter was under debate." Since so many Chinese migrants entered under claims of citizenship that were heavily contested by immigration officials, the concept in *Ju Toy* made many Asian immigrants perpetual strangers, here and not here, subject to the harsh new rules governing exclusion and deportation but without the fundamental constitutional protections typically invoked to press evidentiary claims. Holmes and other Justices would repeat the metaphor again, sometimes in cases not involving Chinese litigants, but the legal fiction was particularly apt in capturing the status of Asians in America.[14] Though here physically in the United States, they were perpetual strangers, persons for whom American constitutional law would always treat as foreign. No matter the length of their residence, so long as their true status was "under debate," they were "foreigners within, . . . located outside the cultural and racial boundaries of the nation," to borrow phrases from Lisa Lowe.[15]

Curiously, this doctrine was the reverse of the doctrine of extraterritoriality, under which Asian governments could not punish foreign subjects for crime. The concept of extraterritoriality was most often invoked as a form of protection against Chinese law by Westerners disdainful of Asian legal norms: in 1844, for example, the United States and China concluded the Treaty of Wanghia, and Article 21 of that treaty said that "Americans committing crimes in China could be tried and punished only by the consuls or other duly empowered American officials 'according to the laws of the United States.'"[16] The French concluded a similar agreement a year later. Many Chinese scholars and officials regarded the practice of extraterritoriality as an affront to Chinese power, which had been in decline since the conclusion of the Opium Wars in China. Punished by the British for their attempts to destroy the traffic in opium, the Chinese Imperial government agreed to a number of humiliating treaties that effectively cocooned Western subjects from Chinese law. Thus, in Asia, legal doctrines protected Westerners from purportedly barbaric rules; in America, however, Chinese subjects had no protections from "enlightened" American rules, including the Constitution. Asians were cocooned against American legal norms, even as Westerners were allegedly protected from Asian ones.

"Any Alien That Enters the Country Unlawfully May Be Summarily Deported"

In large part because of China's decline, however, American immigration laws did not discourage the most desperate Chinese migrants. As China crumbled in the face of Western and then Japanese encroachment, and as famines and civil strife swept the country, many Chinese migrants tried everything in their attempts to leave a dying empire. Aware that simply having an immigrant's status was enough to engender suspicion and abuse, many Chinese simply lied about who they truly were.

Given the harsh consequences stemming from distinctions between immigrant and citizen, it was no wonder that this strategy would become so popular in the years following Exclusion. Prior to the Chinese Exclusion Act, Chinese migrants facing discrimination in the United States often pressed for their rights as immigrants—on the grounds that immigrants were protected by federal treaties and by constitutional amendments specifying "persons," not just citizens, as within the scope of fundamental safeguards. Yet as the early immigration law and Supreme Court decisions made clear, immigrants could no longer count on their status as immigrants to enjoy the full range of protections that American citizens possessed. Faced with an immigration law that drew harsh boundaries between aliens and citizens, many Chinese simply tried to pass themselves off as citizens. For the Chinese, the widespread strategy of deliberate misidentification arose in large part *because of* the increasing harshness of immigration law itself.

After 1892, Chinese immigrants to America—faced with exclusionary laws designed specifically to keep them out—lied. In his influential history, *Strangers from a Different Shore*, Ronald Takaki recounts how many Chinese immigrants misrepresented their immigration status on landing in American territory, almost immediately after the Chinese Exclusion Act of 1882. The earthquake and fire of 1906 in San Francisco also destroyed government records of births and deaths, and so, taking advantage of the American government's lack of proof, numerous Chinese immigrants lied and cheated their way into the country. They coached one another, falsified documents, bought identities, made up whole new ones, and otherwise misrepresented themselves on a grand scale, so much so that almost an entire generation of Chinese immigrants consisted of "paper sons," native-born Americans only by deceit and forgery. According to Takaki, "Exactly how many men falsely claimed citizenship as 'paper sons' will never be known, but it was later calculated that if every claim to natural-born citizenship were valid, every Chinese woman living in San Francisco before 1906 would have had to have borne eight hundred children." In a recent history on the exclusion period, Erika Lee pointed out that illicit entry into the United States was also rather sophisticated and transnational, not to mention expensive, through third countries and circuitous routes north and south, with more than a few Chinese "passing" as Mexicans, Cubans, or even African Americans. In most instances like these, Chinese migrants simply misrepresented who they were.[17]

Such frequent episodes exemplified the act of "passing" with a distinctively Asian American flavor. With some notable, creative exceptions, Chinese immigrants did not lie about their "race" per se—they never claimed to be "white"—but they did lie about their immigration status, relying on rulings like *Wong Kim Ark* to take advantage of immigration and naturalization rules that were racist, but perhaps not racist enough. In 1898, in a 5–4 decision, the Supreme Court ruled in that case that all persons born within the territory of the United States ought to be regarded as American citizens under the Fourteenth Amendment. The irony for the Chinese and other Asians was that the primary beneficiaries of the rule appeared to have been persons who had falsely claimed native birth, not actually those who were in fact native born.[18]

From a broader perspective, these acts of transgression and lying appear as subversions of the primary intent of white supremacists during the period. Labor unions, anti-Chinese organizations, and opportunistic politicians did not want Chinese laborers to land in the United States. By phrasing Chinese laborers as "unassimilable," and worse, as "heathens" and "barbarians," they had successfully lobbied for an immigration law that was the first of its kind in American history, a federal immigration rule that targeted one specific racial group for exclusion. In the face of such an openly racist and white-supremacist rule, Asian immigrants misrepresented who they were on a rather spectacular scale. They formally claimed American identities to protect themselves when their true identities could not.

But certainly, the mendacity of the Chinese clearly contravened and subverted the "will of the American people." The Chinese were the first illegal immigrants, based on race under the terms of the federal law. The many acts of lying to get into the United States may have confirmed one of the primary complaints against the Chinese, that they did not understand the "obligation of an oath." Indeed, after the Exclusion Act, dozens of cases in American immigration law were about the identity and alleged misrepresentation of Chinese litigants. These cases came to dominate American immigration law for the next thirty years.

After 1910, the federal courts expressed frustration over the seemingly endless, willful misrepresentations. Holmes himself condoned ever more summary proceedings against immigrants alleging citizenship, often merely stating harsh rules that Congress had enacted without attempting to justify them. In one case, upholding summary procedures passed by Congress in 1912, Holmes said: "By the language of the act any alien that enters the country unlawfully may be summarily deported by order of the Secretary of Commerce and Labor at any time within three years."[19] His justifications consisted of citations to earlier precedents.

Holmes was not alone in his frustration. His brothers on the Court, Justices Hughes, McKenna, McReynolds, and Sanford, each took turns writing in favor of the government's power to exclude and deport, based on the findings of executive officials charged with sorting through claims of Chinese American citizenship.[20] For roughly twenty years, the Supreme Court rarely ever decided in favor of Chinese petitioners, only doing so when there was substantial evidence of egregious abuse, as when immigration officials in one case excluded the testimony of three "important white witnesses, . . . all men of standing [in Monterey]."[21]

It was during this time that Congress ordered the construction of permanent government buildings that would together serve as a central facility for immigration detention and interrogation on the West Coast. Originally funded in 1904, the federal facilities on Angel Island in San Francisco Bay were opened in 1910, originally described by the government's own agents as "wretchedly filthy," overcrowded, vermin infested, and otherwise inadequate. The historian Roger Daniels reported that immigration officials referred to the hospital as "an outrage to civilization."[22] Daniels estimated that roughly 100,000 persons passed through Angel Island until 1940, when "a disastrous but happily nonfatal fire destroyed the administration building and many of the records."[23] Ronald

Takaki estimated that roughly 50,000 Chinese persons passed through Angel Island before it was closed; most had undergone intense interrogations designed to catch them in a lie.[24] Today, Angel Island is a National Park, and what remains of the detention facilities serves as a museum, part of which includes some original Chinese poetry carved into the wooden walls, lamenting the "laws harsh as tigers."[25] But by 1930, Chinatown was actually growing as a residential and commercial center, a key part of San Francisco's eclectic identity and a place that even the City touted in its tourist brochures. Judging by the numbers of Chinese admitted, most had "lied" successfully, as a generation of real-life sons and daughters of Chinese paper sons was born in the United States.

"Aliens Ineligible for Citizenship"

The Chinese were not the only Asian immigrants to rely on deceit to survive in the United States. A few years after large numbers of Japanese migrants arrived in California, the exclusion of Japanese migrants had been accomplished through the Gentlemen's Agreement of 1908, a treaty between the United States and Japan that limited the further migration of Japanese laborers to the United States. The Japanese imperial government agreed to stop the emigration of laborers in exchange for federal protection for Japanese men already in the United States, as well as the right of those same men to reunite with their families, particularly their present or future spouses.[26] President Theodore Roosevelt presided over the delicate treaty negotiations personally, keeping in mind the new, powerful role of Japan in East Asia after the Meiji Restoration. Earlier, in 1904, it was an angry Roosevelt who had reprimanded the City of San Francisco for segregating Japanese children into schools established for the Chinese.

Lawmakers in California made no distinctions in their hatred for Asian migrants. Since 1885, acting on the request of urban school districts, especially San Francisco, the State of California passed blunt, race-conscious rules: school districts could open separate schools for "children of filthy or vicious habits, or children suffering from contagious or infectious diseases, and also to establish separate schools for children of Mongolian or Chinese descent. When such separate schools are established Chinese or Mongolian children must not be admitted into any other schools."[27] The subsequent controversy over the segregation of Japanese children had inspired the federal response culminating in the new treaty, and Roosevelt was reluctant to offend the Japanese further. There was a simple reason for Roosevelt's diplomacy: Japan was becoming an empire, modeling itself on other European powers and reorganizing its entire society and military to become a major world power. The Japanese Empire would win a series of wars, against the Chinese and then against the Russians, that would signal its arrival as *the* military power in East Asia.[28]

The provisions of the Gentlemen's Agreement reflected to some extent the special status of the Japanese Empire in the eyes of American policy makers. By allowing for the emigration of the spouses of Japanese laborers, the United States permitted Japanese men to have legally what Chinese men could have only illegally: families. Until the general Immigration Act of 1924, which would bar the further migration of all "aliens ineligible for citizenship," including the Japanese, large numbers of Japanese women steadily migrated to the United States, many as "picture brides."[29] The presence of these women fundamentally changed the structure of the early Japanese American community, particularly on the West Coast, where Japanese immigrants would settle in the greatest numbers outside of Hawaii.

As Japanese Americans began to form families, they entered the ever more lucrative agricultural economy of California. They began leasing agricultural lands in large numbers, as Chinese immigrant men had done before; but unlike the Chinese, Japanese Americans eventually purchased agricultural lands, and in some cases they created very successful agricultural corporations. From small farms, to truck farming, and then toward agricultural businesses, Japanese American farmers and distributors became some of the most important figures in the California economy.[30]

But like the Chinese, their entry into a core sector of the economy engendered resentment. Again, as with the Chinese, the political impetus to restrict the economic participation of the Japanese came from poorer whites. Within five years of the Gentlemen's Agreement, labor unions and civic organizations successfully lobbied legislators in the State of California so that they passed the first of the infamous Alien Land Laws, which barred "aliens ineligible for citizenship" from owning or leasing land.[31] Like many other rules in American law, these rules obviously dealt with race, but without mentioning race or racial categories anywhere in the language of the statute. Clearly, though, the proponents of the rule had race in mind, as was evidenced by the comments of politicians like the State's Attorney General: the rule was passed against the Japanese "to limit their presence by curtailing their privileges which they may enjoy here; for they will not come in large numbers and long abide with us if they may not acquire land."[32] Another advocate insisted that the law was necessary because "the Japanese are unassimilable and more dangerous as residents in this country than any other of the people ineligible under our laws."[33] These arguments were again premised on the notion that economic goods and opportunities should be restricted to full members, or at least to persons capable of becoming full members. Thus, the passage of these rules served as an occasion both to take advantage of and then to reinforce the fact that Asians could not become American citizens.

At first, Japanese immigrant farmers simply evaded the rule. As several legal scholars have shown, these farmers took advantage of a number of different loopholes to evade the law—they held their lands under the names of their American-citizen children, either in trust or as a bequest; they set up "dummy corporations" or fake agricultural companies which they controlled even though they held a minority interest; or they simply "borrowed" the identities of their children, or the names of willing, cooperative whites, who would hold the land in their name while having an understanding that the property belonged to the "alien ineligible for citizenship."[34] In this way, Japanese immigrants evaded the laws in larger numbers with substantial success. In fact, by 1920, Japanese Americans leased and owned *more* land than they had in 1913.[35]

These strategies triggered a backlash. After widespread discussion of this "problem," voters in California passed an amended version of the Alien Land Law in 1920 through a statewide referendum. This version of the law closed the most popular loopholes and provided for "escheat" actions by the state that would dispossess of their land any parties who knowingly violated the rule. This new version of the rule completely raised the stakes for land ownership among Japanese immigrants. It was also an incredibly popular referendum, passing by a wide margin.[36] Moreover, it would inspire many imitations. By 1943, versions of the Alien Land Law had spread to other states, including Texas, Nebraska, Montana, Idaho, Washington, Minnesota, Missouri, Oregon, New Mexico, Arizona, Louisiana, Wyoming, Arkansas, and Utah.[37]

Proponents of the referendum supported it, though, precisely because Japanese immigrants exploited so well the loopholes in the original law. Subsuming one's identity, and either taking on or borrowing the identities of others, were strategies that deliberately contravened the purpose of these restrictive property rules, as much as misstating the place of birth or a family relationship contravened immigration restrictions. Rather than being passive victims of the law, or rather than challenging the law directly, Japanese Americans simply went around the rules. According to the historian Paul Spickard, the new rule passed in 1920 "proved equally unenforceable. . . . The Issei responded to all these legal stratagems with energy and creativity. They hired lawyers and contested discriminatory laws through several levels of appeal, found legal ways to circumvent the law's intent, and defended themselves to the public in books and magazines."[38] Evasion, not always confrontation, proved an effective form of resistance to racially discriminatory rules.

"The Marriage in Question Took Place in New Mexico"

For some Asian immigrants, the right to marry a person of one's choice proved as compelling as the right to migrate and the right to own land. In 1930, in his study of Filipino immigration, Bruno Lasker insisted that the trouble with these immigrants was that they were, unlike the Chinese or Japanese, rather successful at passing as Europeans. The "earlier arrivals" were "not laborers but students." They were overwhelmingly men; by 1940, there were roughly 100,000 Filipino immigrants in the United States, most settling in California.[39] They appeared to many as though they were Western. "They often resembled Spanish-Americans, whose language they spoke, rather than Japanese or Chinese." Furthermore, "they were neat and clean, with a leaning toward good if occasionally too showy clothes, musical, considerate, eager to please, good dancers. All of them were under twenty-five years old, many of them good-looking." "They were romantic and cheerful," and so "girls liked them. . . . Mature women liked them. Everyone liked them."[40] In terms of religion and culture, they seemed already assimilated: having been colonized by Spain prior to the arrival of the Americans, most native Filipinos were already Catholic; after the arrival of the Americans, many received an education from young American teachers. As one observer stated with some irony, "Our school system in the [Philippine] Islands is causing a growing number of Filipinos to be more or less proficient in speaking English." And "American teachers in the Islands have taught him that 'all men are created equal.'" In part, this was the crux of the problem, according to a scholarly observer from the Midwest: "The difference between the Filipino problem and the Oriental problem lies in the attitude of the Filipino. He will not take his place as the Oriental races have done."[41] For a racial pariah in a white supremacist society, "taking his place" would involve, of course, keeping away from white women.[42]

But according to several accounts, white men apparently resented more than anything the intimate interracial contact that did occur between Filipino men and white women.[43] For example, in his study of the anti-Filipino riots in Watsonville, California, in January 1930, Emory Bogardus reported that when a Filipino club "imported nine white dance hall girls, and set up a taxi dance hall for the Filipino members, . . . incensed white young men in Watsonville" went on a murderous rampage, killing one Filipino laborer and injuring many others. Prior to the riot, the Northern Monterey Chamber of Commerce cited the threat of miscegenation as one of the primary reasons for barring Filipino immigration.[44] Much like the Chinese, Filipino immigrants were phrased as a threat to law and order, but in addition to the familiar charges that they lowered wages or degraded labor, they were widely regarded as threats to prevailing racial and gender mores. Several commentators insisted that the Filipinos were to blame: "While the great majority of immigrant Filipinos are most careful not to give offence, the rowdier element too often loudly proclaims their interest in white American girls and their insistence on freedom to associate with whomever they like."[45]

Nor did it matter that when they did meet with white women, and occasionally married them, Filipino men seemed to associate mostly with working-class women. According to one researcher writing in 1938, "The American girls . . . tend to be either children of immigrants, girls from the East or Midwest, or girls from the lower classes, and in general girls with no strong family ties. Many Filipinos appear to be married to taxi-dancers, fellow women employees in hotels, restaurants, hospitals and private homes, and relatively few are married to better types of American women."[46] Another speculated that in places like Southern California, where many Filipino immigrants resided, there was a "superabundant supply of marriageable girls available to Filipinos."[47] Most of the girls were new to the region, young, and vulnerable, and perhaps easy prey for Filipino men who had "vices almost entirely based on sexual passion," according to David Barrows, the eminent professor of sociology at the University of California.[48]

Some did not blame the immigrant men. Bruno Lasker, for example, wrote that opportunistic white women just as easily preyed on lonely Filipino men in more casual relationships. "In a western university town, the chief of police said, concerning the dance-hall problem, that a unique situation had arisen from the aggressive pursuit of Filipino patrons by immoral women frequenting these places. And a similar opinion was expressed by the dance-hall supervisor in a middle-western city."[49] Popular dance halls were closed to protect naive *Filipino men* from predatory *white women,* even as Filipino men were often characterized either as savages who did everything deliberately to "capture the admiring glances of American girls," or by "flaunting [themselves] with any white woman who will go out with [them]."[50] Sometimes, according to one scholar, cultural gaps between Filipino men and white women led to miscommunication: "The relatively free behavior of American girls is . . . a frequent course of misunderstanding. They do and say things that are done and said only by girls in the Islands who wish to encourage boys."[51]

Whoever was to blame, whatever the reason, unions of these immigrant men and white women often elicited harsh formal and legal responses, precisely because of the purported "impropriety" of such relationships, however initiated. Many such relationships eventually did lead to marriage, touching off considerable debate about whether these unions were desirable for American society, or even for the good of either of the two spouses. One commentator insisted that "the Filipinos themselves disapprove intermarriage with American girls."[52] Another stated that "the *Pinoy* who can date a white girl achieves considerable intra-group social success as a result." Moreover, "It has been observed that when the Filipino does set up a stable family life, mixed or not, he tends to appreciate it greatly and to be the envy of his unmarried fellows."[53] Yet another, Benicio Catapusan, a Filipino American graduate student at the University of Southern California, described these marriages generally as a kind of unmitigated disaster for both parties, in an article entitled "Filipino Intermarriage Problems."[54] In his Master's thesis, Catapusan outlined again the horrible problems faced by the children of such unions, and said that "children born of such unfortunate matings are better not born, if they are going to suffer and not be able to enjoy life."[55] Clearly, there were compelling stories of discrimination and hostility toward Filipino married couples and their children, and a few are recounted in well-known biographical and autobiographical volumes in Filipino American history. Carlos Bulosan, in his book, *America Is in the Heart,* wrote of several horrific episodes.[56]

But prior to 1933, even in California, which had the highest concentration of Filipinos in the continental United States and where hostility toward Filipino immigrants was perhaps the most intense, the legal status of Filipino-white marriages was somewhat ambiguous. In an article published in 1932, Nellie Foster listed five cases where the legality of Filipino-white marriages was at issue.[57] In four of these cases, state judges attempted to determine whether "Malays" were synonymous with, or sufficiently analogous to, "Mongolians," to determine whether Filipinos were subject to the existing miscegenation statute in California which barred "Mongolians" from marrying whites. In two instances, "Malays" were determined to be "Mongolians"; in two other cases involving petitions for annulment, the courts denied the petitions on the grounds that marriages between "Malays" and whites were not necessarily forbidden.[58] In the fifth case, concerning the marriage of Gavino Visco and Ruth Salas, the presiding judge ordered the Los Angeles County clerk to issue a license to Mr. Visco on the grounds that his future wife was a Mexican Indian. "It [was] reported, however, that the judge stated he would not have decided in favor of Mr. Visco had Miss Salas been a white person."[59]

Visco's case drew an immediate response from a major Filipino organization based in Los Angeles. Members of the Filipino Home Club raised funds to hire attorneys on behalf of Visco's cause because they felt that Filipinos were being "arbitrarily" classified as "Mongolians." Indeed, in an open letter to all Filipinos, the Home Club insisted that "the fundamental issue involved in [Visco's] case is, that Filipinos are not Mongolians." The Home Club suggested that being classified as "Mongolians" would be a terrible insult to all Filipinos—the Club insisted that they all join forces to prevent this result.[60]

The conflicting views about the legality of such unions were settled in 1933, when the State of California amended its miscegenation statute in response to a successful lawsuit by a Filipino man, Salvador Roldan. The Los Angeles County clerk had denied him a license to marry "a woman of Caucasian descent," on the grounds that marriages between "Mongolians" and whites were illegal. Roldan replied that he was "Malay," "'an Illocano, born in the Philippine Islands of Filipino progenitors in whose blood was co-mingled a strain of Spanish,' and not a Mongolian."[61] As in many other cases concerning racial categories and their exact boundaries, the Court struggled to find a definitive answer to whether Malays were Mongolians, or whether they were a separate racial group altogether. Based on a reading of prevailing anthropological standards (which yielded a conclusive answer of sorts) and a legislative history of the miscegenation rule (which had been motivated primarily by animus against the Chinese), the Court concluded that Malays were probably distinct from Mongolians, and that Malays were most likely "not in the thoughts of any" California legislators when they were most recently amending the state's miscegenation rules in 1905. However, "if the common thought of to-day is different from what it was at such time, the matter is one that addresses itself to the legislature and not to the courts."[62] Within three months of the decision in *Roldan*, the Legislature added "Malays" to the list of races prohibited from marrying whites.

But many couples took great pains to evade the formal prohibitions. Two strategies appeared most frequently: Filipino men misrepresented their racial identity when they married white women; and Filipino-white couples would cross state lines to avoid miscegenation laws in their own state. The facts of one specific case, *People v. Godines* (1936), suggested both types of strategies. Here, the protagonist, Ms. Godines, had originally sued to annul her marriage to a Filipino man "on the ground that she had been induced to marry him by the fraudulent representation that he was of Spanish Castilian descent." Apparently, for her, the revelation of his true self made him repellant: "There followed the statement that he had informed her immediately after the marriage of his real racial heritage and that the parties had then separated and had lived apart ever since."[63] Husband and wife disputed this last point. "The defendant and her witnesses denied that there had been cohabitation. In the main the state's evidence consisted of contrary testimony by the Filipino himself."[64] But based on his testimony, and also a letter sent from her to him "while the marriage was still in effect," submitted into evidence and "full of admissions inconsistent with [her] defense," the state had convicted her of perjury and she was also denied an annulment. The Appeals Court in the present case concluded, though, that neither his testimony nor the letter should have been used against her over her objections, because the "husband" should not have been allowed to testify without his "wife's" consent. [65] The Court ordered for her a new trial.

For our purposes, whether the two parties did or did not cohabitate after his revelation is not as important as the two other indisputable facts about the case. The Filipino man conceded that he had misrepresented his racial identity prior to their marriage. He had attempted to pass as a "Spanish Castilian" for whatever reason, perhaps to woo his beloved or perhaps to evade the miscegenation rule after *Roldan*. Moreover, "the marriage in question took place in New Mexico, where it was valid and hence of itself the ethnological status of the parties was not a ground of annulment."[66] The couple had also traveled across state lines, for reasons that were not clearly stated but perhaps with the purpose of evading, again, the new miscegenation rule.

This particular strategy was not uncommon, according to Constance Panunzio, a researcher writing in 1942: "While decreased immigration and increased repatriation have partly reduced their sex disparity, Filipinos still occasionally marry whites. They go to Oregon, New Mexico, Utah, and Idaho, which do not have laws proscribing such marriages." Many Filipino-white couples in Southern California, perhaps like Mr. and Ms. Godines, "[preferred] New Mexico because that state does not even have a law proscribing Mongolian-white marriages, and because it is easily accessible to persons residing in Los Angeles."[67] Other first-person accounts of Filipino immigrant men reported the same strategy: one man reported that he and his fiancée went to Utah, still another related the story of marrying his spouse outside the United States entirely, in Vancouver.[68]

Although the full extent to which Filipino immigrant men and white women legally married was and is difficult to measure, there was certainly evidence that such marriages were not uncommon in spite of miscegenation rules. Close to 80 percent of Filipino men were unmarried in 1930, and in light of the gender imbalance between Filipino men and Filipino women, it wasn't surprising that a substantial number of married Filipino men had non-Filipino spouses.[69] The rate of marriage to white women seemed to vary widely by region, although all accounts suggested a rather high rate compared to other groups: in Los Angeles, Filipino men, more than any other racial group, were likely to marry white women; roughly half of all married Filipino men in 1930 had white spouses.[70] In another study of interracial marriage, "[during] a 22 month-period, [from] January 1, 1940 to October 31, 1941, in which a count was made of all the marriages in Washington, D.C., according to race, it was discovered that for every Filipino male who married a Filipino female, 13 Filipino males married non-Filipino females." Between 1940 and 1947, 209 Filipino men and white women were married in Washington, D.C., as opposed to just nine marriages between Filipino men and black women, or twenty-six marriages between whites and blacks.[71]

The high rate of Filipino-white marriages occurred in spite of the fact that formal racial animus against Filipinos did exist across the country, even on the East Coast. By 1940, Virginia and Maryland, for example, both had miscegenation statutes that specifically included "Malays." Indeed, animus against Filipino-white marriages was fairly widespread, such that by 1960, Arizona, California, Georgia, Nevada, South Dakota, Utah, and Wyoming also had passed rules forbidding marriages between whites and "Malays."[72] But despite open hostility and these resulting legal barriers, by 1940, a majority of children born to Filipino immigrants were of mixed race, and most Filipino men who had married interracially had married white women.[73]

For the white spouses of Filipino and Asian immigrant men, interracial marriage inspired much more than the simple-minded hostility of their neighbors. In fact, in 1907, Congress had passed the Expatriation Act, which resurrected a form of derivative citizenship for married women. Under this Act, a woman entering marriage took on the legal status of her husband: if her husband was an alien ineligible for citizenship, she would be regarded as such, too; if she herself was an American citizen, she lost her citizenship when she married a foreign man. This rule also applied to Asian women born in the United States—if they married an Asian immigrant man who was obviously ineligible for American citizenship, they essentially lost the American citizenship they had gained at birth. The essence of this rule was retained in the Cable Act of 1922, and stayed a part of American law until 1931. Even when it was repealed, it was only after Congress was assured that state rules barring miscegenation were both extensive and effective, at least in deterring the marriages of white women and aliens ineligible for citizenship. It is enough to say that hostility against mixed-race couples was national in scope throughout the early 20th century, and that white women marrying Asians could be severely punished for it.[74] They, too, could be erased by law.

Legal Disabilities and Functional Lies

Cases like *Sing Tuck* and *Ju Toy* placed Asian migrants beyond the protection of American law, and having sensed their vulnerability to entirely new sets of rules disabling them on the grounds of immigration status or race, Asian immigrants adapted to these harsh realities. They were certainly not passive in the face of so much hostility. Altogether, the varied experiences of Chinese immigrants after exclusion, of Japanese farmers after the Alien Land Laws, and of Filipino men after miscegenation rules, are all suggestive of a common theme: in order to have what was prohibited, Asian immigrants simply evaded the law. By deliberately misrepresenting who they truly were, they attempted to avoid the will of hostile white majorities. It often worked.

In most of these instances, the types of misrepresentation amounted to "functional lying," or misrepresentations that were accomplished solely for practical purposes. In circumstances that did not require an Asian immigrant to prove loyalty to the United States or to declare allegiance, Asian immigrants lied about basic, mundane facts—the place of their birth, for example, or the true owner of a piece of land. Despite the expense and burden of traveling to another state, Filipino immigrants and their spouses did so to achieve a practical end—to get legally married. Many Filipino men also lied about their ancestry, sometimes to their own spouses. But in these instances, no one asked for formal declarations of allegiance to the United States (which were, of course, a moot issue for Asians) or for proof of assimilation into American norms. None were required to evade successfully some types of rules.

In other instances, however, when Asian immigrants were pressed to state what they *were* really thinking, their replies tended to be sincere, often disturbingly so. The sheer pervasiveness and popularity of white supremacist rules required many Asian immigrants to do more than misrepresent themselves for functional ends. In order to become citizens, and in order to bear some of the classic burdens of republican citizenship, Asian litigants provided striking, public declarations of their self-identity. In the next chapter, as we review the landmark naturalization cases of the early 1920s and the internment cases during World War II, we see that Asian litigants often phrased their claims of belonging in ways that challenged arguments of their unassimilability. Yet at the same time, these alternative strategies created distances among themselves as well as between Asians and other pariah racial groups, especially African Americans. Sadly, as the Cold War approached, this theme of turning against other groups would veer toward turning in one another.

7

"Loyalty Is a Matter
of the Heart and Mind"

"Free White Persons"

Largely in response to the spate of race-based disabilities that they faced, especially the Alien Land Law of 1920, Asian immigrants made direct attacks against naturalization rules that restricted American citizenship to "free white persons." On these occasions, however, Asian protagonists often claimed to be white themselves in an effort to "pass" as loyal, assimilated Americans. Unlike lying about citizenship status to gain entry, or using dishonest legal arrangements to hold land, this new form of passing confronted race-based barriers to citizenship directly. They challenged the idea that some racial groups simply could not integrate into the commonwealth. Yet in many of the leading cases, the arguments put forward by Asian immigrants implicitly *embraced* white supremacist assumptions rather than rejecting them.

In the most important lines of decisions issued by the Court in 1922 and 1923, Justices George Sutherland and Pierce Butler would issue opinions that were devastating to the political, economic, and legal position of Asian immigrants in America.[1] In the first line of cases, testing the meaning of the Naturalization Act of 1790, Justice Sutherland, himself a naturalized American from England, ruled that only "whites" and persons of African nativity could become naturalized citizens and that Asians were excluded because they were obviously neither. In the two famous cases he authored, *Ozawa v. United States*, and *United States v. Thind*, Sutherland struggled with definitions of "white" and "race."[2] Ian Haney-Lopez and other legal scholars have explored at length the consequences of these decisions for the "legal construction of race," for the ways in which key legal institutions like the Supreme Court interpreted and enforced race-based discriminations. In determining where formal racial barriers should be, "law constructs race."[3]

But what was as striking as Sutherland's response was the legal strategy employed by the litigants and their attorneys. The two protagonists in these leading cases openly provoked a debate about the relationship between race and citizenship. Takao Ozawa insisted that he was an American in every way; according to historian Yuji Ichioka, "[he] was a paragon of an assimilated Japanese immigrant, a living refutation of the allegation of Japanese unassimilability."[4] He could not have been a better candidate for such a test case when the Japanese American Citizens League offered to help him during his federal appeals cases. Ozawa refused to speak his native Japanese, stated that his wife and children dressed as Americans and spoke English even at home, and that all of them were Americans at heart. He noted in the record of his case that he had refused to register the birth of his children with the Japanese consulate as was customary among Japanese immigrants in America. Unlike many immigrants, Ozawa was an educated man, having graduated from Berkeley High School and having attended the University of California, the only impediment to his degree being the great earthquake in San Francisco. In his initial legal effort for American citizenship, Ozawa did not rely on any help from the Japanese government or from Japanese American civic organizations; indeed, he did everything to distance himself from both. He eventually received help from Japanese American organizations, but only when the case reached the federal appellate level. Prior to that, it had been a "private battle." His arguments to the Court were heart-breaking for the way they expressed a desire to belong to the United States: "In name, I am not an American, but at heart I am a true American."[5] Given the distance he had placed between himself and his Japanese identity, Ozawa suggested that if the United States would not grant him membership, he would belong nowhere.

David Withington, one of Ozawa's lead attorneys in the federal appellate courts, made several race-based arguments on behalf of his client. Withington claimed most of all that persons of Japanese ancestry were both "free" and "white," and should thus pass the test for naturalization that had been in place since the Naturalization Act of 1790. "The Japanese are a free people . . . their direct root stock, like that of the Polynesian, is of the white race and . . . while Mongolian and Malay types are found amongst the Japanese, the Caucasian or white type is as prevalent." The Japanese were certainly not black because they had no African descent. Withington said that marriage patterns suggested less hostility toward Japanese than blacks. "Naturally, a Japanese prefers to marry a Japanese, not only on account of race prejudice, but for other obvious reasons; but they do intermarry with whites, and the almost uniform testimony is that they have happy families and vigorous progeny, pre-eminently American. Section 2169 authorizes the naturalization of black men, but half the states forbid marriage between whites and blacks." Withington pointed out that these states had yet to prohibit marriages between whites and Japanese, and that some southern legislators in Congress had said openly that Japanese were clearly preferable to blacks.[6] Another attorney for Ozawa, George Wickersham, repeated these arguments before the Supreme Court, stating that the term "white" meant "not black." "'White' we have already sufficiently defined, and shown that the words 'free white persons' had in 1875 acquired signification in American statute law as expressing a superior class as against a lower class, or, to speak explicitly, a class called 'white' as against a class called 'black'; the white man against the Negro."[7]

The legal strategy also relied on a distancing between the Japanese and other Asians, particularly the Chinese. For example, the lawyers argued that while the Chinese "did not come to establish homes," and "[imported the women] as slaves for immoral purposes," the Japanese were committed to their families, as one could see from their low crime rates and low divorce rates in Hawaii. Indeed, large portions of both appellate briefs disparaged the Chinese at length, implying that the repeated denials of the Chinese petitions for naturalization were correct.[8] And then this: "Other authorities have sought to account for the mental alertness of the Japanese, a quality of mind in which they differ from other Asiatics and resemble the Europeans and the inhabitants of North America above the Mexican line. The Japanese are commonly called 'the Yankees of the Orient,' and they show no marks of the degeneracy common in the mixture of non-assimilable races."[9] As "Yankees," the Japanese were free and white and deserving of American citizenship based on these racial characteristics. In short, "the Japanese are assimilable."[10] His lawyers further insisted that Japanese men like Ozawa were physically "whiter" than many of the Eastern and Southern Europeans who had gained naturalized American citizenship.[11] One can almost imagine Ozawa's lawyers encouraging their client to display himself before black-robed judges for visual inspection, as some light-skinned African Americans did before southern courts for the same purpose.[12] As much as light-skinned African

Americans distanced themselves from darker-skinned African Americans, so too Ozawa's lawyers distanced their client from other Asians as well as African Americans.

The Supreme Court rejected these arguments. "White" did not mean color: "To adopt the color test alone would result in a confused overlapping of races and a gradual merging of one into the other, without any practical line of separation." The Court opted for what it knew to be a temporary solution: "The determination that the words 'white person' are synonymous with the words 'a person of the Caucasian race' simplifies the problem, although it does not entirely dispose of it." Since the Japanese were not Caucasian, they were not white, but a more comprehensive definition of race had yet to be proposed. Sutherland said that subsequent cases, as they "arise from time to time," would help clarify the issue.[13]

"In the Same Manner as the American Regards the Negro"

Almost immediately after the *Ozawa* decision, the Supreme Court was pressed again in another naturalization case, *Thind v. United States* (1923). Here, the litigant also claimed that he was "white" according to the definition in *Ozawa*: Bhagat Thind was a "high caste Hindu, of full Indian blood," who claimed that anthropologically, and thus "racially," he was a "Caucasian." Guided by *Ozawa*, a lower federal court had sided with Thind before the federal government had appealed that decision. Again, the legal arguments by the attorneys on behalf of Thind were instructive: "The foregoing scientific authorities show that the people residing in many of the states of India, particularly in the north and northwest, including the Punjab, belong to the Aryan race." Thind himself was a Punjabi Sikh, and as such, he insisted on ancestral and linguistic ties to Europe as a fellow Aryan. His lawyers phrased his claim for whiteness in language that the court could understand: "The high-caste Hindu regards the aboriginal Indian Mongoloid in the same manner as the American regards the Negro, speaking from a matrimonial standpoint." Here again was an argument based on a similar concern for miscegenation.

Whereas Ozawa presented himself as assimilating into "white" norms, Thind's lawyers attempted to elicit empathy from the Court by showing that their client shared the same type of revulsion for "inferior races" as most whites. Altogether, as in *Ozawa*, the strategy of this case involved a double rejection—a distancing between "high-caste Hindus" (who ought to be eligible for naturalization) and "aboriginal Indian Mongoloids" (who, like other "Mongoloids," especially the Chinese, should not be eligible); and a distancing between certain higher classes of Asians and African Americans. A large part of Thind's argument rested obviously on creating a distance from blackness in order to make a persuasive claim for whiteness.[14] In this way, Thind and his lawyers intended for this strategy to win him and other "high-caste" South Asians the right to naturalize as American citizens, even as the race-consciousness blatant in such an approach tended to reinforce notions of "Aryan" supremacy.

Again, in reply, Justice Sutherland said that a high-caste Brahmin from India was anthropologically "Caucasian," but not really "white." The case proved enormously difficult, as Sutherland was frustrated that science could provide no conclusive answer for race: "The various authorities are in irreconcilable disagreement as to what constitutes a proper racial division."[15] And so, in *Thind*, Sutherland relied less on science, and more on a "common sense" definition of whiteness:

What we now hold is that the words "free white persons" are words of common speech, to be interpreted in accordance with the understanding of the common man, synonymous with the word "Caucasian" only as that word is popularly understood. As so understood and used, whatever may be the speculations of the ethnologist, it does not include the body of people to whom the appellee belongs. It is a matter of familiar observation and knowledge that the physical group characteristics of the Hindus render them readily distinguishable from the various groups of persons in this country commonly recognized as white.

Sutherland then listed the groups "commonly recognized as white," and gave a broad justification for why they ought to be included:

The children of English, French, German, Italian, Scandinavian, and other European parentage, quickly merge into the mass of our population and lose the distinctive hallmarks of their European origin. On the other hand, it cannot be doubted that the children born in this country of Hindu parents would retain indefinitely the clear evidence of their ancestry. It is very far from our thought to suggest the slightest question of racial superiority or inferiority. What we suggest is merely racial difference, and it is of such character and extent that the great body of

our people instinctively recognizes it and rejects the thought of assimilation.[16]

Unlike Justice Sutherland himself, who quickly merged into the mass
of the American population and lost at least enough of his European heritage, Asians—even the highly assimilated ones like Ozawa, or high-caste
ones like Thind—would never be similarly accepted. They would always
"wear" what the sociologist Robert Park would call a "racial uniform."
As such, in clear, simple language, Justice Sutherland marked how it
was that all Asian immigrants were different from all European immigrants: the former inspired an "instinctive recognition" and a "rejection
of assimilation" that justified legal barriers to full membership. Finally,
Sutherland relied on the existence of several congressional statutes passed
since 1917, which created a "barred zone" throughout Asia and the
Pacific where immigration restrictions were particularly severe.[17] Sutherland thus followed a line of reasoning similar to, and different from, John
Stuart Mill's: half-savages from Europe could successfully transition into
American civilization, but the savages from Asia could not.
In both *Ozawa* and *Thind*, Sutherland crafted decisions that appeared
on their face to draw from democratic traditions. The standard for determining who was or wasn't eligible for naturalization rested with "the
understanding of the common man," not the decisions of judges or the
determination of learned experts. In their separate efforts to pass as
white, the litigants made claims not just based on claims of physical appearance or ancestry, but also on claims of sharing something that all
whites seemed to have in common—a revulsion of "lower races," especially Africans. This was, after all, the essence of white supremacy, and
the litigants implied that they shared that very basic premise. But Sutherland replied that "the great body of our people," by forever noticing the
difference between themselves and men like Thind and Ozawa, actually
reviled them, too, notwithstanding Sutherland's point that the decision
did not imply racial inferiority. The theory was that the majority of whites
would reject Asians as full members, either individually or through their
democratic institutions; most of them had already done so, and would
continue to do so. This was true despite the fact that several important
politicians, most notably Theodore Roosevelt, had long favored supporting the naturalization of Japanese immigrants. Indeed, questions of Asian
American citizenship had been contested among white elites for several
decades.[18] But by framing this specific resolution as a result of a hypo-

thetical consensus, even in the face of disagreement among elites, the Court's majority phrased yet another race-based restriction as though it rested on democratic institutions and processes, implying that the majority would and should ultimately have its way.

For persons like Thind, the decision was devastating, as it "un-did" several important instances where Asian Indians had in fact acquired American citizenship.[19] The economic consequences of these decisions were particularly terrible for South Asians. For Japanese immigrants, who collectively had had the greatest financial stake in California's agricultural lands, the naturalization cases were especially damaging. Having been told with finality that American citizenship would be untenable, Japanese immigrants tried another strategy, attaching their fortunes to the rights of whites and again subsuming their own identities and rights in the process. This strategy would fail as well, as the Court relied on Lockean notions of self-defense and national sovereignty to circumscribe economic opportunities for ineligible aliens.

"The Safety and Power of the State Itself"

In four separate decisions, all issued in November 1923, Justice Pierce Butler affirmed the constitutionality of the Alien Land Laws that had been passed by California voters in 1920. Interestingly, the cases had been brought by white farmers wishing to sell or lease land to Japanese immigrants: Mr. and Mrs. Terrace, of *Terrace v. Thompson*, wanted to have as a tenant farmer a Mr. Nakatsuka in Washington State; Mr. Porterfield, of *Porterfield v. Webb*, wanted to lease agricultural land to a Mr. Mizuno in Los Angeles; Mr. O'Brien, of *Webb v. O'Brien*, wanted to enter into a cropping contract with a Mr. Inouye in Santa Clara; and Mr. Frick, of *Frick v. Webb*, wanted to sell his interests in a Merced farming company to a Mr. Satow.[20] The most interesting aspect of these cases may be what they all lacked: Asian litigants pressing for their rights. Having been denied the right to naturalize and represent themselves as Americans and deeply conscious of their precarious rights as perpetual immigrants, Asian immigrants harmed by the Alien Land Law thus relied on the cooperation of whites who were in such cases sympathetic, opportunistic, or both. Behind these challenges to the Alien Land Laws were white landowners claiming that these rules unduly infringed on *their* right to do what they wished with their own private property; these lands did not properly "belong" to the state, unlike wild game or state jobs, which could be restricted by the states to American citizens only.[21]

Justice Butler replied that while these agricultural lands were private property, the states could distinguish between various types of persons using agricultural lands. Land ownership was different, he said, because control over land had long been related to public allegiance and to national defense: "It is not an opportunity to earn a living in common occupations of the community, but it is the privilege of owning or controlling agricultural land within the State. The quality and allegiance of those who own, occupy, and use the farm lands within its borders are matters of highest importance and affect the safety and power of the State itself."[22] Butler suggested that contracting or leasing lands was also a matter of national security: "Conceivably, by the use of such contracts, the population living on and cultivating the farm lands might come to be made up largely of ineligible aliens. The allegiance of the farmers to the state directly affects its strength and safety."[23] Butler's arguments reflected those made by the proponents of the Alien Land Laws in California, all of which tied control over agricultural production to political control over the state.[24] After Butler concluded that Asian immigrants could never declare an intent to become American citizens, he said that the states had wide discretion to control agricultural lands: "It may forbid indirect as well as direct ownership and control of agricultural land by ineligible aliens."[25] Thus, although all aliens in the United States could own and control land, "aliens *racially* ineligible to naturalization"— Asians—could not.

Butler's logic placed Asian immigrants in an unusual position. It pointed to a much deeper problem. Land ownership could be restricted to those capable of formally expressing loyalty to the United States; acquiring American citizenship—taking the oath and forswearing allegiance to all other nations—was the primary way of ascertaining that loyalty. But Asians were incapable of doing this on racial grounds, such that even if they wanted to express loyalty to the United States, they were forbidden from doing so. Thus, they could not own or lease land, according to Butler, because control over land and concerns over national security were inextricably linked. It wasn't so much that Asian immigrants weren't American citizens or capable of American citizenship per se; it was, rather, that their inability to express loyalty always rendered their loyalty to be suspect.

Their loyalties would always be questioned under these conditions. Americans and their government would never know the true loyalties of these persons, even though this was because the majority of Americans and their government had decided that Asians were racially ineligible to express this loyalty in the first place. In this strange, circular logic, because Asians would be incapable of swearing allegiance to the United States, they could be restricted from controlling this form of property. The bar against naturalization and the restrictions against property ownership—all laced with questions of loyalty and allegiance—rendered Asian immigrants as perpetual, foreign threats.[26] This presented a severe political problem for several subsequent generations of Asian immigrants.

The economic impact of these decisions was far more immediate for Asians engaged in farming, as total land holdings and leasing arrangements declined for the next two decades. As in years past, many Asian immigrants continued to "own" or "lease" lands under precarious arrangements, often with the cooperation of whites who lent their names to Asian farmers for a fee—in essence, selling the value of their whiteness as though it were property.[27] In some instances, when Asians were cheated from their lands in such arrangements, they retaliated violently, as in the case of an Asian Indian man who had murdered his dishonest white partners in 1925.[28] But most either tried to live with the rules through suspect or illegal arrangements. First-generation Japanese immigrants passed on agricultural lands to their American-born children, although many of these young Japanese Americans would eventually give up farming altogether in response to white hostility.

Finally, one important facet of these decisions was the assertion of popular sovereignty over the rights of private property. After all, the plaintiff's theory was that the Alien Land Laws infringed on the rights of legitimate landowners, namely whites, to do what they wished with their own land. Butler's decision, however, affirmed that majorities could impose restrictions on the use of private property insofar as there was a rational connection between a particular form of property and national security. Because land ownership and the use of agricultural lands implicated the "safety and power of the state itself," majorities could restrict severely the rights of individual owners to sell, lease, or make contracts with persons whose loyalties were suspect, or at least inconclusive. Majorities could forbid individual, self-interested parties from colluding with ineligible aliens, and even if there were economic losses, these were less important than presumably broader, more vital national security inter-ests.[29] Thus, like the naturalization cases, these decisions were written in a tone that again appeared supportive of more noble democratic principles and processes. They supported the will of white majorities against selfish, politically insensitive whites.

The real victims were of course Asian immigrants. Throughout the 1920s and 1930s, they were in this way increasingly held at the frustrated margins of American society, as a special category of American immigrants. In 1925, the Supreme Court reaffirmed the constitutionality of California's Alien Land Law in yet another case, *Cockrill v. California*, where again the Asian protagonist did not appear to press for his own rights. In 1927, the Supreme Court upheld state rules segregating Asian children in public schools, and throughout the 1930s various state legislatures—following California's lead—would reaffirm rules against miscegenation between whites and Asians.[30] All of these rules underscored the distance between Asian and white, capturing the prejudices, resentment, and racial hatred shared by "common men" in America.

The rejection of Asians as citizens corresponded with their rejection as eligible migrants to the United States. The Tydings-McDuffie Act of 1934 promised independence for the Philippines but at the same time placed restrictions on Filipino migration. It was the last of a long line of new exclusion rules directed against Asians, as the principle of exclusion against Asians was extended again and again until 1965. Exclusion meant rejection, as Sutherland pointed out in *Thind*:

> It is not without significance . . . that Congress, by the Act of February 5, 1917 . . . has now excluded from admission into this country all natives of Asia within designated limits of latitudes and longitude, including the whole of India. This not only constitutes conclusive evidence of the congressional attitude of opposition to Asiatic immigration generally, but is persuasive of a similar attitude toward Asiatic naturalization as well, since it is not likely that Congress would be willing to accept as citizens a class of persons whom it rejects as immigrants.[31]

Sutherland's reference was to the Immigration Act of 1917, which created an Asiatic Barred Zone, the "latitudes and longitudes" of which included all of South Asia, Southeast Asia, and the Far East. Japan was not included in the law, but Japanese migration had been curtailed by treaty nine years earlier, through the Gentleman's Agreement. After World War I, fearing another wave of poor migrants from southern and eastern Europe, Congress enacted the Quota Law of 1921, and then the Immigration Act of 1924, which severely restricted migration to the United States in general. The laws barred all migrants "ineligible to citizenship," aimed primarily at Asians.

Passed with the support of anti-Asian forces from the West, anti-immigrant, anti-Catholic, and anti-Semitic groups from the Midwest and the East, along with progressive eugenicists throughout the country, the numerical and percentage limits of the Quota Law and the national-origins system of the Act of 1924 would remain in force until after World War II. During this period, when migration to the United States was severely curtailed, various organs of government attempted to assimilate immigrants aggressively, such that they would become "100 percent American." Asians—rendered unassimilable—were complete pariahs. "Immigration restriction marked both the climax and the conclusion of an era of nationalistic legislation," an era that had great popular support.[32]

Indeed, these pieces of legislation passed almost unanimously. The Quota Law passed by a margin of 78 to 1 in the Senate. Labor unions, anti-immigrant groups, leaders of industry, major national scholars, including several prominent scientists and anthropologists, political conservatives, the Ku Klux Klan, progressives, and two presidents supported the immigration restrictions of 1921 and 1924. Representative Albert Johnson, the chairman of the House Committee on Immigration, became a prominent national politician because of his successful efforts to steer through the Act of 1924. While Johnson and his allies moved to limit, by quotas tied to census statistics, the numbers of southern and eastern European migrants, he wanted a complete bar to Asian migrants, particularly the Japanese.[33] The effort was designed to maintain the racial balance of the United States, except, of course, for Asians, whose numbers would surely decline as their migration was completely barred. No serious opposition could withstand the popularity of race-based exclusion: in these acts, "Congress was expressing the spirit of the nation," according to the historian John Higham.[34] And so, from 1920 to 1940, roughly 130,000 Asians came to the United States, mostly as spouses of American servicemen, or under other family reunification provisions in the law. During that same period, over 2.8 million persons migrated from

Europe.[35] Immigration rules largely succeeded in keeping Asians a distinct and insular minority within the United States. By World War II, Asians comprised less than one percent of the American population.

"Loyalty Is a Matter of the Heart and Mind"

The fact that Asians couldn't swear loyalty to the United States remained a source of great suspicion as to their true loyalties, at least for many whites. As the Japanese Empire in particular ascended to become itself a brutal, colonizing power in Asia, as well as an increasing threat to American interests, the position of Japanese immigrants in particular would prove increasingly precarious. When they were incarcerated within months of the bombing of Pearl Harbor, the constitutional questions raised by Japanese Americans would fall again on the Supreme Court. But as their cases came before the high court, Japanese litigants again asserted strong moral claims of belonging, based largely on their assimilation into American life.

The line of cases, from *Hirabayashi v. United States* to *Ex Parte Endo*, has received a great deal of commentary, but most of that commentary has tended to focus on the decisions of the Supreme Court.[36] Less attention has been paid to the way in which the litigants presented themselves, or in one case, the way in which he was discovered. Indeed, all of the litigants challenged the evacuation and internment orders with evidence of their assimilation into mainstream American life. They insisted that they were in fact not "Japanese," but "Americans." Against the assumption that they were racially incapable of loyalty to the United States, they presented themselves as willing citizens.

Their strategy was not easy given the strength of the racist assumptions against them. Within four months of the formal declaration of war, civilians of Japanese ancestry in the United States were treated as hated enemy aliens. They were evacuated and interned as early as 1942, although the most important Japanese internment cases occurred during the middle of the war, from the summer of 1943 and the winter of 1944. The protagonists in the early cases were successful young Japanese American men, native-born American citizens from Washington and Oregon. While some of the more liberal members of the Supreme Court expressed reservations about using racial ancestry as a proxy for loyalty, the Court upheld the military's treatment of Japanese immigrants and Japanese American civilians. In *Hirabayashi v. United States* and *Yasui v. United States*, the Court considered constitutional challenges arising from President Franklin Roosevelt's infamous Executive Order 9066, which was issued in February 1942 and confirmed by Congress a month later. Under these orders, military authorities had organized the evacuation of all persons of Japanese ancestry from the West Coast. For the Court, however, the constitutional question in 1943 was whether persons violating such military orders could be punished lawfully, even when they showed no individual signs of disloyalty or treachery against the American government.

Both Gordon Hirabayashi and Minoru Yasui were native-born citizens. Indeed, much like Takao Ozawa, Hirabayashi and Yasui were models of assimilated Japanese Americans. Hirabayashi was educated in public schools in the State of Washington, and he was a senior at the University of Washington when he was arrested. His parents had converted to Christianity prior to their emigration from Japan, and as a Quaker, Hirabayashi obtained conscientious objector status before the war had begun. In other ways, Hirabayashi was quite assimilated: he was "a YMCA member, [and] a Boy Scout leader."[37] Similarly, Yasui had earned both his undergraduate and law degrees from the University of Oregon, and he was a member of the Oregon bar, as well as the Japanese American Citizens League. Yasui had also achieved the rank of second lieutenant in the Army Reserve. In fact, after the Americans had declared war, Yasui volunteered immediately to serve in the army. For a time, he commanded a company at Fort Vancouver but was soon dismissed because of his ancestry. But despite the discrimination he had faced as a Japanese American, "like many other JACL Nisei, Yasui did not question the legality of instituting a curfew for the Issei [first-generation Japanese immigrants], nor of putting them in concentration camps."[38] He did object, however, to his government treating American citizens like him in the same manner, and like Homer Plessy a generation ago, Yasui actively sought to be part of a test case challenging such racial discrimination.[39] In both cases, Hirabayashi and Yasui presented themselves as conscientious American citizens pressing for the protection of their civil rights.

The third case involved a rather different protagonist. Fred Korematsu was a welder and a second-generation Japanese American from northern California. Before and after the exclusion order, he tried to remain undetected by civilian or military authorities. According to the historian Paul Spickard, Korematsu had taken some drastic measures:

[Korematsu] was a welder in San Leandro, California, and was engaged to Ida Boitano, a White woman who worked in a biscuit factory. Before the exclusion order, he decided to move to Arizona and marry his beloved. He contacted a shady San Francisco surgeon and had plastic surgery on his nose and eyelids in an attempt to look less Japanese. When the exclusion order came, Fred Korematsu was still in San Leandro, trying to pass himself off as a Spanish-Hawaiian named "Clyde Sarah." Someone informed police he was a Nisei, and he was arrested in 30 May. While he sat in the Tanforan Assembly Center awaiting trial, he received a letter from Boitano saying she wanted no further contact with him.[40]

Without doubt, Korematsu's case before the Supreme Court remained one of the most important, if not the most important, case of the four cases challenging the federal government's internment order. It split the Court in a 5–4 vote, and even the majority opinion written in favor of the government would subsequently be cited by civil rights advocates attempting to strike down race-based classifications.[41] Yet, as we see, Fred Korematsu certainly did not envision himself a civil rights pioneer prior to the outset of his infamous case. When his Japanese ancestry marked him as an enemy alien, and when his American citizenship afforded no protection against a race-based exclusion order, he attempted to pass as another kind of American, as someone who was not of Japanese ancestry at all. He had opted for invisibility before the law.

The only person to win a case against the government during the internment period was someone that the government itself conceded was a loyal American citizen. Like Hirabayashi and Yasui, Mitsuye Endo was a second-generation Japanese American.[42] The facts of her case were very different, in that she had already been detained in an "assembly center" for over two years, during which time the government's own examiners had determined that she was loyal to the United States. They nevertheless refused to release her unconditionally, on the grounds that she would return to her home in Sacramento, an area still off limits to persons of Japanese ancestry. The Supreme Court opinions written in her favor, by Justices Douglas and Murphy, underscored her loyalty to the United States, and concluded that "loyalty is a matter of the heart and mind, not of race, creed, or color."[43]

Government policies toward persons of Japanese ancestry, though, did not tend to reflect that idea. Rather, government agencies charged with managing Japanese American internment began with the presumption of disloyalty that individual Japanese Americans and Japanese immigrants had to overcome. The oddest method to determine loyalty might have been the government questionnaires employed at the internment camps. According to Ronald Takaki, "The questionnaires had two purposes: 1) to enable camp authorities to process individual internees for work furloughs as well as for resettlement outside of the restricted zones, and 2) to register the Nisei for the draft."[44] Those who responded agreeably to these tests of loyalty were released or drafted; those who declined to respond, or responded suspiciously, were sent to special internment camps, some convicted and sentenced for conspiracy against the government. Roughly three hundred Nisei refused to be drafted and were sentenced to prison terms in federal penitentiaries.[45] As Eric Muller has pointed out, these men spent time in "jails within jails."[46]

The clear majority of second-generation Japanese Americans did declare loyalty to the nation that had interned them and their families. They had responded positively to one of the queries on the infamous government questionnaire: "Question 27 asked draft-age males: 'Are you willing to serve in the armed forces of the United States in combat duty, wherever ordered?'" Eventually, 33,000 men of Japanese ancestry served in the United States military during World War II, stationed in both the Pacific and European theaters. Of course, in both classical and modern republic theory, the willingness to risk one's life and to fight the enemies of the state marked one of the highest duties of citizenship. In that regard, young Japanese American men gave ample proof of their desire for American citizenship. Soldiers of the 442nd Regimental Combat Team "suffered 9,486 casualties, including six hundred killed." They became the most decorated unit during the war, perhaps the most decorated in American history: "They had earned 18,143 individual decorations—including one Congressional Medal of Honor, forty-seven Distinguished Service Crosses, 350 Silver Stars, 810 Bronze Stars, and more than thirty-six hundred Purple Hearts. They had given their lives and limbs to prove their loyalty."[47]

At the end of their military service, Japanese immigrants who had served were granted American citizenship, as were Filipinos, Koreans, Chinese, and other Asians. This ended a series of precedents established before the war, when the federal courts routinely denied Asian servicemen the opportunity to become naturalized Americans solely on the grounds of their Asian identities.[48] In 1952, Congress passed the McCarran-Walter Act, which entirely reframed and reorganized immigration rules, and which provided for naturalization privileges irrespective of race or ancestry. The sacrifice of Japanese servicemen and other Asian soldiers proved a compelling political example, according to Ronald Takaki: "Actively lobbying for its passage, the [Japanese American Citizens League] stressed how the law would recognize the parents of the Nisei soldiers who had distinguished themselves during World War II, and how it would acknowledge the worthiness of the Issei to become citizens."[49] In this way, widespread military service during the war helped all Asians pass into American citizenship.

"Tearing Families Apart"

But in the period immediately following the war, matters of loyalty surfaced again with the rise of McCarthyism in the United States. Asian immigrants and Asian Americans were forced once again to explain their loyalties. The group targeted most intensely during this period was the group discussed at the beginning of this section—Chinese Americans. As China "fell" to the Communists in 1949, Chinese Americans moved from being perceived as allied with Americans, as they had been during the war, to being labeled suspected enemy aliens. The pressures of suspicion tore apart the Chinese American community. In San Francisco's Chinatown, for example, when Chinese American associations gathered to celebrate the victory of the Chinese Communists, anti-Communist Chinese Americans and others sympathetic to the Chinese Nationalists violently broke up their gathering. Circumstances worsened when Chinese Communist troops entered the war in Korea in 1950, against American troops. That same year, Congress passed the McCarran Internal Security Act, which authorized the attorney general to incarcerate Communists during national emergencies.[50]

In response, leading Chinese American organizations, including the Chinese Six Companies, declared their opposition to Communism, and expressed Chinese American loyalty to the United States.

> The Anti-Communist League sent letters to American politicians urging them not to recognize the Communist government in China, assuring them of the support of American Chinese for the regime of Chiang, and, as one Chinatown newspaper editor recalled, "succeeded in convincing

the American public that Chinatown was one hundred percent in support of Chiang Kai-Shek."[51]

In addition, leftist groups in Chinatowns throughout the United States faced increasing scrutiny, both by anti-Communist Chinese American organizations, and by federal authorities.[52]

Indeed, as Xiaojian Zhao has pointed out, federal authorities moved to identify and deport leftist Chinese Americans. The Immigration and Naturalization Service worked with the Federal Bureau of Investigation to produce an elaborate system of informants from within the Chinese American community.[53] Given the immigration history of many Chinese migrants, the entire community was particularly susceptible to this form of surveillance. Unlike Japanese immigrants, most of whom had migrated legally and could thus take advantage of the more liberal naturalization rules in the McCarran-Walter Act, Chinese migrants were much more likely to have checkered immigration histories. As another historian, Mae Ngai, has noted, "Once the paper trail started in the early twentieth century, Chinese Americans using paper names had no choice but to perpetuate the false lineage in order to bring their true family members into the United States."[54] Victor Nee wrote that "since the use of false immigration papers was still common in Chinatown during the forties and fifties, the threat of deportation by the Immigration Office was constantly used to intimidate leftists or their relatives who had entered with false papers."[55]

Federal authorities also carried out a "Confession Program," whereby persons found presumptively eligible for deportation could "confess" their illegal status or their leftist sympathies in exchange for amnesty and legal residency. As part of this deal, the informant had to divulge the identities of all other persons he or she had suspected of being sympathetic to Communism, including relatives, friends, and coworkers. The program produced a feeling of mutual paranoia in the Chinese American community, as it was the first time that many Chinese immigrants had been afforded such a clear opportunity for legal status.

These policies were devastating for many Chinese Americans, even though for many others within the same community they afforded the only avenue for naturalized citizenship. The Confession Program in the mid-1950s "led to mistrust among family members, tearing some families apart," according to Zhao. The mistrust extended to major civil organizations within the Chinese American community, including the Chinese

Six Companies, the Chinese Hand Laundry Alliance, and the Chinese American Citizens Alliance. "The fear of prosecution haunted Chinese Americans who had never violated any laws other than those related to immigration." Although some Chinese American families and community groups banded together and resisted this terrifying new surveillance, "13,895 Chinese participated in the program, leading to the exposure of 22,083 persons," which represented roughly a quarter of all Chinese persons living in the United States. Eventually, even the Chinese Six Companies—the civic organization with one of the longest histories in American Chinatowns—agreed to cooperate with the government's orders in spite of its initial protests.

At the level of individual households, "many families divided over whether or not to confess, sometimes quite bitterly." In her study of the Confession Program, Mae Ngai estimated, though, that "the vast majority of the 30,000 people who were involved in the Confession Program did, in fact, become legally resident aliens or naturalized citizens. . . . The Program thus benefited a large segment of the Chinese American population."[56] Widespread deportations were not common, but those who were deported were primarily "leftists," persons involved in the labor movement or in progressive political organizations, or persons more likely to sympathize with the Communist government in China rather than the Nationalist government in Taiwan.[57]

With the exception of two extensive scholarly treatments, by Mae Ngai and by Xiaojian Zhao, there has been little written on the Confession Program or on the Internal Security Act of 1952, at least as it pertained to Chinese Americans. But the paucity of scholarly research does not diminish the importance and tragedy of this episode in American history, for it underscores one of the primary themes of American naturalization law.

This is because in the fiction of naturalization, one is "reborn." The word "naturalization" shares the same Latin root as words such as "nativity" and "natal," all denoting the concept of birth. When one is naturalized, one is "reborn" into the political community in which one wishes to become a member. It is the liberal nation-state's equivalent of a baptism, where one is reborn as a Christian, or of a marriage, where one is literally and spiritually reborn with one's spouse, both becoming one person. Legal processes governing naturalization typically preserve the fiction that all citizens share attachments with one another that are somehow organic and even prepolitical. They also suggest that only prepolitical, "natural" attachments form the bases for political associations.[58] In a democracy, where in theory sovereignty resides among the citizens, naturalization means joining in the exercise of power for the good of the whole. One joins the whole. At the beginning of both the Cold War and the Civil Rights Movement, Chinese American citizenship—the collective rebirth of Chinese immigrants in America—became possible not just through expressions of loyalty and allegiance—matters of the heart and mind—but through thousands of acts of betrayal. For members of that community, joining the whole meant splitting apart. The drawing of boundaries can impose such terrible costs.

8

"Outside the Pale of Law"

"Full Participation in the Community"

On November 8, 1994, a clear majority of California voters approved Proposition 187.[1] Under the more controversial provisions of the new law, the estimated 1.6 million undocumented aliens in California would be denied public education and all nonemergency medical care.[2] In addition, all social service and health-care facilities would be required to report to the state Attorney General and to the Immigration and Naturalization Service those "suspected of being present in the United States in violation of federal immigration laws."[3] Presumably, the INS would then initiate deportation proceedings for those found to be present illegally.[4] Not surprisingly, Proposition 187 inspired a visceral public discourse, and because both proponents and opponents of the measure discussed the several themes that have been central to this study, particularly those related to sovereignty and civil rights, we turn now to reexamine that debate. If nothing else, this debate is suggestive of the fact that problems of sovereignty and belonging will likely remain perennial features of American public life.

That the issue of illegal immigration would emerge again in the late 20th century, as it had in the late 19th, revealed perhaps how familiar and recurring the problem had become. Although television images of Mexican immigrants running across the southern border had displaced the images of Chinese men disembarking from ships, the rhetorical appeals from the Governor's office were much the same: these aliens threatened the public safety and treasury, they were invading the state, and the federal government needed to do something about it. Governor Pete Wilson insisted this time that this was not a racial issue—all of California's citizens, Asian Americans, Latinos, African Americans, and whites were similarly harmed by the presence of this foreign, illegal population. By 1994, of course, the Governor knew that he could not appeal simply to white voters: the Immigration Act of 1965 resulted in substantial numbers of immigrants from Mexico, Latin America, and Asia, many of whom settled in California. Asians composed roughly 10 percent of California's population; Latinos, roughly 15 percent. This particular debate also occurred well after the Civil Rights revolution of the 1960s and 1970s, such that significant numbers of people of color were now active in California's politics, even though the vast majority of Asians and Latinos were but one generation removed from their new migrations to the United States.

Yet as we shall see, participants in this debate—including people of color—often spoke of "rights" in a way that denied the possibility for undocumented aliens to have rights at all. When citizens spoke, they did so in a way that implicitly linked rights to citizenship—in other words, they assumed that without citizenship, persons were not entitled to rights or rights-based claims. Ironically, the debate about Proposition 187 pointed to the continuation of a "civil rights vision," as that debate reduced undocumented aliens to "nonpersons" without a legitimate place in society. California citizens talked, instead, about how useless or useful undocumented aliens were and about how society should best manage them as a resource. The debate raised serious questions about the limits of a civil rights discourse, and about its potential to divide people of color against themselves. The arguments for and against Proposition 187 were revealing because they showed how questions of belonging and membership still tend to be perplexing and persistent. They also suggested how those so recently included into the community of American citizens often take part in practices of exclusion, as if they too feel the enduring moral and political appeal of liberal commitments to closed, bounded communities.

"A Massive and Unlawful Migration of Foreign Nationals"

The political movement for Proposition 187 began in the early months of 1994, when Governor Pete Wilson prepared a series of lawsuits against the federal government to obtain reimbursement for "educating illegal immigrants in California public schools," and "for the cost of providing health services and incarcerating undocumented immigrants."[5] In speeches that shaped the subsequent debate, Wilson argued that California was forced to pay for the "net cost" of undocumented aliens—which he estimated at some $2.3 billion per year—because the federal government had failed to secure the nation's borders.[6] Wilson demanded $10 billion from the federal government to defend against "an invasion . . . [a] massive and unlawful migration of foreign nationals," many of whom arrived in California specifically to take advantage of social services and public education.[7] If, as Justice Field had suggested, immigration rules were the exclusive domain of the federal government, Wilson now suggested that that government was failing spectacularly to do its job.

Wilson claimed that even if undocumented aliens did not migrate primarily to benefit from state programs, the provision of services to undocumented aliens constituted a significant cost to legal residents of California. In either case, by cutting benefits to undocumented aliens, Californians could eliminate an incentive to migrate and retrieve scarce resources at a time when the state was fiscally vulnerable.[8] In a speech in Orange County, Wilson said: "We are unable to provide services to our own legal residents. . . . Now that is terribly unfair, and I say we should end those services to illegal immigrants. We are rewarding people for violating U.S. law."[9]

Other proponents also feared that undocumented workers were taking, or would take, jobs from legal residents.[10] Although some economists said that undocumented aliens did not compete with legal residents in the labor market, and even though some organized proponents of the measure did not argue to that effect, proponents often cited the fear of competition for jobs in supporting Proposition 187.[11] Among people of color, the resentment toward undocumented immigrants was especially acute. Kevin Ross, an Inglewood deputy district attorney and political action chairman of the NAACP chapter in Los Angeles, noted that "forty percent of African American youth are unemployed. When the assertion is made that illegal immigrants do the jobs others wouldn't do in the first place, the black community is offended."[12]

For some supporters of Proposition 187, the issue of whether undocumented immigrants use or take resources seemed irrelevant. Many simply saw the issue as one of law enforcement, or lack thereof. The very presence of undocumented aliens indicated the failure of their government to control their borders. For example, Michael Huffington, the California Republican candidate for United States Senate during the same election, supported Proposition 187 because it was "time to send a message to illegal immigrants who disregard our laws." Huffington called the initiative a "first step toward finally enforcing our immigration laws."[13] Building on these themes, proponents of Proposition 187 described how the measure would be used as a tool to regain control over the system.[14] Citizens responded to that argument; a Mexican American woman in Los Angeles said, "I'm against all those girls coming over here [to have children] so they can get a check, free [food] stamps, medical and everything."[15] Another Mexican American woman resented the fact that there were cars bearing Mexican license plates at her community college.[16]

Proponents claimed that some of the unfairness could be traced to the federal government, which caused the problem through lax enforcement of immigration laws, court decisions that mandated state spending on undocumented aliens, and general neglect of California's illegal alien problems.[17] Whatever the merits of Proposition 187, proponents agreed that a vote in favor of it would "send a message that even the White House will understand."[18] Thus, Proposition 187 was an occasion for the electorate to "send a visceral 'we're fed up' message to the [federal] government about the need to tighten both the border and the public's spending on undocumented immigrants."[19] Ultimately, though some proponents saw Proposition 187 as divisive, contrary to federal statutes, and flatly unconstitutional, they favored the measure solely because it was "California's wake-up call."[20] Commentators like George Will took the measure's unconstitutionality as a major strength: Proposition 187 would "force the Supreme Court to rethink" *Plyler*.[21]

Finally, proponents spoke of Proposition 187 as though it were a vent for deep-seated hostility toward undocumented aliens and their foreign cultures.[22] This was apparent in the responses to the mass demonstration held in opposition to Proposition 187 in Los Angeles three weeks before the election. The display of foreign flags, the speeches delivered in Spanish, and the enormous size of the crowd made some feel that "American values are being overrun by an uncontrolled influx of Third World citizens."[23] "To proponents of Proposition 187 . . . the march was an outrageous display of Mexican nationalism that bolsters the case for reducing immigration. 'Any time they're flying Mexican flags, it helps us.'"[24] Perhaps like John Stuart Mill, who wondered whether a multicultural nation-state could survive, and who proposed an aggressive assimilation of the "savages" within "civilized" societies, these proponents seemed angry with immigrants who appeared uninterested in crawling out from underneath their ethnic enclaves. These persons seemed instead to be proud and happy of those characteristics that marked them as different from mainstream, white Americans.

"Hard-Working Gardeners and Nannies"

Proposition 187 engendered what appeared to be a formidable opposition, both among liberals as well as a few influential conservatives. Major newspapers published editorials against it, including the *Los Angeles Times*, the *San Francisco Chronicle*, the *Christian Science Monitor*, the *Chicago Tribune*, and the *New York Times*.[25] Two new groups, Taxpayers Against Proposition 187 and Californians United Against Proposition 187, organized grassroots opposition to the measure.[26] Both groups obtained support from a long list of organizations, including the California Medical Association, the League of Women Voters, and the California Catholic Conference.[27] Although early on in the debate opponents conceded that illegal immigration was a problem for California, they nonetheless opposed the measure primarily on policy grounds, because "the measure is a poorly drafted solution to the problem" and because "it will neither save money nor stop illegal immigration but will introduce other problems that will affect everybody, not just undocumented immigrants."[28]

Opponents said the rule would be ineffective. They emphasized how the initiative would not stop illegal aliens from either coming to California or voluntarily leaving. It was as though some Americans were conceding that the problem had become a regular facet of American life that would not end simply by ending social services. The root of the problem lay in the profoundly different structures of opportunity between the United States and the rest of the world. An influential economist, Deborah Cobb-Clark, said, for example, that "if you compare the opportunities in the United States and the opportunities in their home countries, the U.S. is still going to be a better deal."[29] And "no matter how harsh benefit policies become, the lure of California's jobs and wages are likely to keep attracting Mexicans, Central Americans, and others over the border and keep most of the 1.5 million illegal aliens now estimated to be in the state from voluntarily returning home."[30]

Opponents claimed that Proposition 187 would not reduce California's immediate financial burdens for two reasons: it would be too costly to implement, and it would jeopardize federal money slated for California. The Legislative Analysts Office estimated "hidden" administrative costs of up to $100 million in the first year alone because Proposition 187 required virtually all local agencies to somehow discover and report undocumented aliens.[31] Editorials warned that the measure would create "considerable administrative disarray," and that it "would add to the state's already nightmarish bureaucracy."[32] Because at least one aspect of Proposition 187 was unconstitutional, and because its reporting requirements constituted a prima facie violation of federal law, opponents warned that California schools would lose federal money if it passed.[33] President Clinton's Chief of Staff, Leon Panetta, predicted that "[Proposition 187] will produce chaos. School districts [and hospitals] will not know how much they will receive from the federal government."[34]

Critics warned of additional, long-term costs. For example, Howard Chang, an Asian American law professor at the University of Southern California, wrote: "[Proposition 187] would create an underclass of illiterate and impoverished residents . . . that would create new risks to public health and new breeding grounds for crime, and thereby threaten the welfare of all Californians."[35] On the issue of health care, for instance, the California Medical Association predicted that "undocumented patients with tuberculosis would tend to delay seeking care for more than two months, infecting an average of ten people each."[36]

On the field of education, Robert Dornan, a former Republican congressman from Orange County, California, and a firm supporter of Proposition 187, expressed some concern about the effect of the law on undocumented children. Noting that "idle hands are the devil's workshop," he asked, "What do you accomplish by putting kids on the street where they can get into mischief?"[37] One politically progressive group warned that "the damage to innocent children will be incalculable in its profound harm to them and to this state's economic and social future. . . . Without public education for immigrant children and adults, high rates of illiteracy in English will prevent their full participation in the community and fuller participation in the work force."[38] Again, in these arguments, it was as though many Americans did not expect this population of persons to leave the state—the relevant problem was rather to find the terms under which they would stay.

Opponents further suggested that even if undocumented aliens could be eliminated from American society, the goal would be undesirable because it would entail the loss of a politically and economically important group. Politically, Latinos represent the fastest-growing group of voters in California.[39] Recalling how Republicans lost "the last generation of immigrants from Italy, Ireland, and Central Europe," and noting that "the vast majority of immigrants hold principles which the Republican

Party warmly embraces," former Education Secretary William Bennett and former United States Representative Jack Kemp asked, "Can anyone calculate the political cost of again turning away immigrants this time . . . Asians, Hispanics, and others?"[40] Similarly, conservative and liberal critics underscored the economic importance of undocumented aliens. Government agencies and private research groups estimated that there were over one million immigrants with some form of false identity documentation currently employed in California. Thus, Proposition 187 turns "hundreds of thousands of our hard-working, tax-paying, minimum-wage gardeners and nannies into prison inmates at a cost of tens of billions of dollars [and] hardly seems a sensible means of solving our state's budget problems."[41] Undocumented aliens were also important in areas other than domestic labor.[42] As one Latino community activist warned, "Just imagine what would happen to the garment industry. . . . It's sweat labor. Who would take those jobs?"[43] Harry Kubo, the president of the Nisei Farm League, estimated that "year-round, 50 percent [of Fresno County's farm laborers] are illegals."[44] Manuel Cunha, the Farm League's Executive Director, queried, "Who is going to pick the fruit in the fields?"[45] Another farmer chastised Governor Wilson for supporting Proposition 187, stating that "the work force that's being targeted is our work force. And we'd be crazy to come out against our work force."[46] Many farmers simply declared that they would ignore Proposition 187 if it should pass.[47]

Moreover, some opponents feared that Proposition 187 would politically and economically alienate Mexico, which was becoming an increasingly important trading partner since the passage of the North America Free Trade Agreement (NAFTA).[48] A Mexican official in the foreign minister's office commented that "it's confusing to people that the U.S. is building iron fences after so much talk of us becoming partners."[49] Protesters in Mexico were less diplomatic. Some urged boycotts, some protested along the United States-Mexico border, others had trashed a McDonald's franchise in Mexico City.[50] In light of these incidents, business persons worried that with the passage of Proposition 187, California would lose trade with Mexico to less hostile states like Texas or Arizona.[51]

Critics also cited a number of ethical considerations in opposing Proposition 187. Regarding education, opponents claimed that Proposition 187 "[makes] kids victims because adults haven't enforced existing laws."[52] Undocumented children who came to the United States with their parents did not come of their own volition. As in *Plyler*, the new law unjustly "[imposed] its discriminatory burden on the basis of a legal characteristic over which children can have little control."[53]

Critics commented that the enforcement of the new rule would lead to discrimination against citizens, particularly people of color, and thereby cause an increase in racial tensions among Americans. Proposition 187 ordered public officials to report those "reasonably suspected" of being undocumented to the INS, and "because 'reasonably suspect' is not defined, anyone who is foreign looking and speaks with an accent could be affected."[54] William Bennett and Jack Kemp argued that "[Proposition 187] is also a mandate for ethnic discrimination. Does anyone seriously doubt that Latino children named Rodriguez would be more likely to 'appear' to be illegal than Anglo children named, say, Jones?"[55] Latino commentators charged that "the racism underlying the measure targets Latinos," that Proposition 187 was "a direct attack on everyone of Latino heritage," and that this was especially dangerous in a society "already racially divided."[56] Prominent African American figures warned that Proposition 187 threatened to "Balkanize . . . the already polarized arena of racial politics."[57] Instead of subsuming or ignoring racial differences, the measure would call racial identities into question, such that the subsequent attention to race would become politically volatile.

Opponents of Proposition 187 also claimed that the law required citizens to act as law enforcement officials, and thus engendered "Big Brotherism run amok."[58] Attorney General Janet Reno complained that "it does not make sense to turn schoolteachers and nurses into Border Patrol agents."[59] For people of color, such discretion appeared especially prone to abuse: "One does not need a crystal ball to see how distinctions would be made. . . . The power to determine who is suspect is put in the hands of any person at a school or health facility."[60] For these reasons, many pledged not to comply with the reporting requirements; even some supporters said they would not report people suspected of being illegal.[61] Local police organizations hinted that they would not comply because "police departments around the country . . . recognized that undocumented immigrants often [would] fail to report criminal activity to the police and refuse to serve as witnesses for fear of coming to the attention of the INS."[62] Physicians' and teachers' groups insisted that they too "would not be used as agents for the INS."[63]

"Rightless Persons"

Despite these arguments, Proposition 187 passed by an overwhelming margin.[64] In exit polls California voters cited illegal immigration as *the* issue in that election. "Proposition 187 . . . polarized the electorate along racial lines, winning big among white voters while losing in every other ethnic group."[65] Having won the race for reelection, Governor Wilson wrote to President Clinton asking for his "full cooperation and assistance" in implementing the initiative, and Republicans in Washington, D.C., announced plans for a federal bill to eliminate benefits to all noncitizens, including legal residents.[66] Republicans noted that although Latinos in California rejected Proposition 187 as a group, 22 percent of Latinos still supported it. Almost half of all Asian American and African American voters had supported the measure.[67] Indeed, the issue not only divided Californians along racial lines, it also divided people of color against themselves.

One of the most striking features of the debate around Proposition 187 was the almost total absence of undocumented aliens who spoke for themselves, even though they had the most to lose. Undocumented aliens did not write editorials or appear in public, either in support of or in opposition to the measure. If they spoke at all, they usually remained anonymous, nameless, and untraceable. Moreover, there were no organizations that represented undocumented aliens directly. Although some organizations purported to speak for them, no organization spoke as them. Because their mere presence "by definition is breaking the law," revealing any presence was an occasion for detention, or eventually, deportation.[68] Thus, undocumented aliens were, in this discussion and in society generally, without a right to speak, without a right to assemble. The debate revealed that unlike those formally accused of wrongdoing, undocumented aliens did not so much "have a right to remain silent," but rather needed to remain silent in order to remain at all.[69] Ironically, "the more visible [undocumented aliens] became, the more difficult it [was] to beat [Proposition 187]."[70]

The debate also showed that undocumented aliens also had no right to privacy. The details of Proposition 187 make this clear. The measure required local agencies to report undocumented aliens however they were discovered. Under the rule, local agencies needed to report any information that could reveal illegal status, regardless of whether such information directly pertained to immigration. On its face, Proposition

187 violated both the spirit and letter of the Family Educational Records and Privacy Act, which provides persons protection for confidential information.[71] But rather than claim that Proposition 187 infringed on the privacy rights of undocumented aliens, opponents focused on how Proposition 187 would violate the privacy of citizens. Opponents complained that in the enforcement of Proposition 187 and similar laws "[a] police-state mentality will be created in which everyone carries citizenship papers and anyone who can't prove his or her citizen status is in jeopardy of being reported."[72] One voter remarked, "I would be extremely offended to have to give proof of my legal residence in this country"; another stated, "It's an unnecessary invasion of our personal privacy."[73] Although Proposition 187 explicitly denies privacy rights to the undocumented, opponents spoke as if only citizens had such rights anyway, stating that Proposition 187 would primarily entail "invasions" of citizens' privacy. If undocumented aliens had rights to privacy, they weren't invoked at all in this debate.

Proponents and opponents alike also spoke of access to health care and public education as claims "to society's resources," not as rights-based claims. Proponents knew that public education and health care may or may not be "rights" to which all persons were entitled.[74] In *Plyler*, the Supreme Court did not defend the "rights" of undocumented children to receive a public education.[75] Rather, the Court described education as being more important than "merely some governmental 'benefit.'"[76] The Supreme Court has been contradictory on this issue. In *Brown v. Board of Education*, for example, where the Court confronted access to public education for African American children, the Court had stated that "such an opportunity [as public education], where the state has undertaken to provide it, is a right which must be available to all on equal terms."[77] But in a later case, *San Antonio Independent v. Rodriguez*, the Court upheld the notion that education is not a fundamental right deserving equal protection.[78] Nevertheless, if education was a "right" in 1954 for American citizens, it clearly was not a "right" for undocumented children in 1982. Indeed, even following *Plyler*, if a state like California could prove "some substantial state interest" in denying California's undocumented aliens a public education, the Court would presumably hold such a denial constitutional. Because undocumented children can make no rights claims under *Plyler*, their "interests" could well be sacrificed to the interests of the citizens of the state.

Opponents of Proposition 187 predicted civil strife in the wake of its passage. Because the enforcement of Proposition 187 would mean reporting those "suspected" of being undocumented, opponents stressed the spillover effects of the law to people of color. A Korean American newspaper editorial stated, "Prop. 187 will lead to discrimination against Asian Pacific Americans and other groups who look or sound foreign."[79] Two African American commentators wrote that Proposition 187 would "subject Latinos and Asians—but not Europeans—to suspicion and stigmas."[80] These opponents of Proposition 187 emphasized the potential discrimination that *citizens* might suffer, primarily because distinguishing between "real" undocumented aliens and those who only looked like them was not an easy task. Opponents argued that "the most dangerous and racist implications of Proposition 187 are that all Latinos will be targets and considered suspects just because of how they look. [Moreover], it doesn't outline carefully how a person will be identified."[81] The arguments concerning health care were no different. One editorial spoke of how "illegal immigrants with diseases such as tuberculosis and AIDS, even chicken pox and smallpox, would not qualify for medical treatment, endangering every California resident by subjecting them to a new wave of communicable diseases."[82] The upshot of this argument was that the measure would turn illegal aliens into even more dangerous vectors, ultimately threatening the health of American citizens.

Although opponents of Proposition 187 expressed concern that the measure would inflame racial tensions among citizens, lead to discrimination against Latinos, or cause an increase in disease among citizens, they remained silent about the discrimination, ostracism, and sickness undocumented aliens themselves would endure if Proposition 187 was enacted. They opposed Proposition 187 not on the grounds that it would violate the "rights" of undocumented aliens, engender discrimination against them, or make them more vulnerable to disease. Rather, they spoke as though such matters were irrelevant issues, or at least not as relevant as the constitutional rights of citizens of color, the discrimination that citizens faced, or the awful diseases that citizens could contract.[83] Citizens had rights and concerns that needed to be protected; aliens had no meaningful rights at all.

Strangely, in the context of Proposition 187 and immigration law generally, the only way for undocumented aliens to be treated like legal residents would be by committing a crime. A commentator noted that undocumented aliens who were imprisoned would receive preventative medical care: "Even the worst thugs housed in our prisons get vaccinations."[84] Throughout the criminal justice system, undocumented aliens could have the same procedural rights as legal residents who had committed similar crimes; the more serious the offense, the more likely the criminal procedures would be the same.[85] Undocumented aliens could also acquire legal rights if they remained undetected—"outside the pale of law"—long enough to become eligible for naturalization. In 1986, for example, the Immigration Reform and Control Act (IRCA) ordered the INS to legalize "eligible undocumented aliens," which included persons who had resided in this country for five or more years.[86] Between 1987 and 1989, some 1.7 million people (960,000 of whom were from California) applied for legal status.[87] What was odd about the IRCA's legalization provisions was that they seemed to "reward law-breaking"; the undocumented aliens who were eligible for legalization were, after all, those most successful in evading immigration laws.[88] As Hannah Arendt observed in another context, "The entire hierarchy of values which is present in civilized countries was reversed" for undocumented aliens—those who broke the immigration laws or could manage to avoid the effects of such laws for longer periods had the best chance of eventually enjoying the protection of naturalization.[89]

The possibility for naturalization proved to be the key to understanding much of the opposition to the measure. If opponents of Proposition 187 ever admitted that law-abiding, undocumented aliens had rights, they did so only in the context of discussing how the undocumented could become potential citizens. William Bennett and Jack Kemp emphasized that undocumented aliens could be an important group of potential voters; Howard Chang discussed ways in which immigrant children could be integrated into our society and our workforce as future citizens.[90] Noncriminal undocumented aliens apparently had no rights worth mentioning, but if they became citizens, they "could enjoy the full protection of legal institutions." Unless they were "completely assimilated and divorced from their origins," they had neither rights claims nor claims to society's resources.[91] Citizens spoke as though undocumented aliens, having no substantial connection to this nation and without a legitimate place in American society, were owed nothing, not even the most minimal provisions. In the face of being considered "rightless persons," undocumented aliens confronted a perilous fate—the only remedy would be to join the political community, and thereby become a person capable of making rights claims.

"Someone Who Loves Your Children"

Although proponents and opponents both spoke as if undocumented aliens had no rights in society—at least not as undocumented aliens— they did not agree about what to do with undocumented aliens. There were several options: do nothing; engineer a mass deportation or voluntary out-migration of illegals; eliminate social services and other "costs" associated with having such persons within the state's borders; or assimilate them into American society. In choosing among these options, undocumented aliens had no right to speak, no right to an education, no right to privacy, and no right to any social resources. If a "right is something that can be demanded or insisted upon without embarrassment or shame," undocumented aliens had none that commanded the attention of citizens.[92] Perhaps because they were treated as though they had no rights, Proposition 187's proponents and opponents alike often discussed undocumented aliens as resources to be managed. Aliens were either to be expelled because they were useless, retained because they were useful, or improved and assimilated because they could be useful. The debate around Proposition 187 became, in many respects, a discussion among citizens about the present and future *utility* of undocumented aliens to citizens. The debate often devolved into a discussion over the proper management of human resources.

Some proponents of Proposition 187 claimed that undocumented aliens were a net drain on society, and thus had no use. Undocumented aliens were hired while "people who were born here can't find jobs."[93] Ron Prince, chairman of Save Our State, argued that "presently we are denigrating the quality of services" because of undocumented aliens.[94] Harold Ezell, a coauthor of Proposition 187 and former commissioner of the INS, asked, "How many illegals can we educate, medicate, compensate, and incarcerate before California goes bankrupt?"[95] Some proponents were more blunt. One voter wrote: "For the past couple of decades, people have been pouring into this nation . . . to have their babies and overpopulate and overburden our state and federal services. We really need Proposition 187 to stop the flaunting of our laws and overburdening of our systems."[96] Still another voter said that undocumented aliens "contributed nothing" to society.[97] Because undocumented aliens were useless, even harmful to legal residents, they needed to be expelled, or at least excluded from social services, as was the intent of Proposition 187. After its passage, Governor Wilson moved quickly to begin implementation of the measure by issuing an executive order to discontinue public benefits to undocumented aliens.[98]

Some Californians, however, preferred the present system. A Korean American businessman urged other Korean Americans to remember that their businesses—from sweatshops to supermarkets—relied heavily on undocumented aliens for cheap labor.[99] Former GOP gubernatorial candidate Ron Unz championed their skills as gardeners and nannies.[100] Both California candidates for the United States Senate—Michael Huffington and Diane Feinstein—had employed at least one undocumented alien as a housekeeper or child-care provider.[101] Indeed, Arianna Huffington praised the qualities of their undocumented nanny: "She was a magical Mary Poppins, and I feel the children have been privileged to know her. . . . It's not easy to find someone who loves your children. You can find people to take care of them, but not to love them."[102] Undocumented aliens had also picked fruit and vegetables so well that even Governor Pete Wilson himself once thought them an indispensable asset. When Wilson was a United States senator in 1986, during the passage of the IRCA, he said: "I deplore the [Immigration and Naturalization Service] raids on farms in [California] in the roundup of illegal aliens. Our economy needs such workers."[103] Although Wilson had changed his mind since then, many farmers had not. Asian American farm groups opposed the measure. One Asian American farmer said, "Let's hope 187 is tied up in the courts for a long time, because if they stop [undocumented aliens] from coming over, you can kiss this valley good-bye."[104] Although most employers of farm workers formally remained neutral on Proposition 187, many did so because they believed the law was irrelevant or unenforceable.[105] "Agricultural employers are inclined to follow [immigration laws], but not if it means losing their crops," according to one labor expert.[106]

For William Bennett, Jack Kemp, and William Buckley, undocumented aliens could become tremendous assets to the Republican Party. Conservative opponents of Proposition 187 spoke against the measure because it would alienate, eliminate, degrade, or underdevelop undocumented aliens as political assets.[107] Latinos quickly underscored the argument that Republican support of Proposition 187 would hurt the GOP: "Throughout the next decade, well over one million new Latino voters will enter the California electorate. . . . Political memories are long lasting in ethnic communities."[108] Latino groups reminded Republicans that undocumented aliens were a type of resource, a potential threat to the GOP. For conservative strategists like Bennett, Kemp, and Buckley, these persons needed to be absorbed into the party, mostly because it was highly unlikely that most of them would ever leave. If anything, these commentators shared a profound pessimism about ever completely removing unwanted immigrants from the American political landscape.

Because they would be here indefinitely, probably permanently, leaving undocumented aliens without social services or public education would hurt citizens and undocumented aliens alike. Both proponents and opponents of Proposition 187 worried that undocumented aliens would "imperil the health of Californians."[109] Undocumented children would "learn the lessons of the streets—gangbanging, violence, and crime."[110] By failing to educate these children, legal residents would miss an opportunity: "High rates of illiteracy in English will prevent their full participation in the community and fuller participation in the work force."[111] Additionally, if, as the Court had said in *Plyler*, "education provides the basic tools by which individuals might lead socially productive lives to the benefit of us all," then it made no sense to keep these persons away from the normalizing institutions of American society.[112] By making sure that undocumented aliens were healthy and educated, society could make them more productive units of labor. Proposition 187 represented, in this way, a deliberate squandering of potential resources, the loss of opportunities.

Of course, other opponents—some farmers, business owners, and senators—did not seem to care much for improvements in the population of undocumented aliens overall. They feared simply that undocumented immigrants would be unavailable to work, to cut grass, and to love their children.[113]

And even as citizens talked of ways to use undocumented aliens, they themselves insisted on not being used. Teachers and physicians, even policemen, did not want to be used as INS agents.[114] Fearful of losing federal money, citizens did not want to be used as political hostages if Proposition 187 passed. Some taxpayers did not want to pay for undocumented aliens, and so they supported Proposition 187.[115] Others did not want to pay for a sicker, more criminal undocumented alien population if Proposition 187 passed, so they opposed it.[116] No one who spoke in this debate wanted their own person or property to be used in the same way undocumented aliens were.

Unable to defend the "rights" of undocumented aliens, citizens debated the aliens' usefulness. Proponents of Proposition 187 often denied that undocumented aliens had any positive value to society, saying that undocumented aliens were about as valuable to society as a plague. Opponents countered that under the provisions of Proposition 187, undocumented aliens would become just that harmful. Either way, a major part of the debate around Proposition 187 concerned the questions of the net costs of undocumented aliens to society and the best way to eliminate or to reduce such costs. Both sides treated undocumented aliens not as "ends in themselves," as persons with rights, with an intrinsic worth independent of their usefulness in a market economy, but rather as a "human resource," to be expelled, retained, or improved, depending on how the community of citizens—including citizens of color—assessed their present or future utility. In a profound way, the use of a civil rights discourse implicitly entailed the utter disregard for the dignity and worth of those who were not de jure members of civil society.

"They Are Likely to Remain"

The experiences of undocumented immigrants here and now help us reflect on the strangeness of American law. First of all, their plight reveals the extent to which liberal states retain legal structures that discriminate on characteristics that are arbitrary from a moral point of view. The entire system of law—in the way it assigns presumptive membership, and then denies nonmembers meaningful rights—continues to mask privileges and create disabilities that appear normal, just, and based on common sense. Many citizens emphasized the fact that the illegal immigrants were not members; very few, though, gave any argument as to why citizenship alone should trigger such profound inequalities in rights and opportunities. To put the matter more bluntly, very few conceded that their own status as members was, at least for many, a tremendous advantage gained by having done nothing. Yet, as Proposition 187 was composed of a set of draconian rules that clearly delimited the boundaries between citizens and noncitizens, California voters supported the rule by a wide margin, indicating perhaps the continuing moral and political appeal of that classic, liberal vision of a closed political community. Obviously, many people of color—some just recently naturalized—also found this vision appealing, even if it came at the expense of other people of color. The greatest irony here might be that the civil rights paradigm intended to help people of color often hurt the most vulnerable among them, as people of color who were American citizens voted for a measure directly harming people of color who weren't.

In considering the plight of undocumented aliens, one can hardly think of a group of persons in a more precarious position, socially and politically. And the idea that political rules ought to be designed in a way that accounts for the least well-off in society has perhaps its most eloquent expression in the work of liberal theorists. Using insights from their work, if American voters could for a moment use their collective imagination to put themselves in the same position as undocumented persons, or as persons living in desperate, impoverished conditions somewhere else in the world, would they continue to support a system of rules that provided for rights and privileges contingent solely on membership in a commonwealth? The Rawlsian original position allows persons to know various aspects of their world, even as it denies them other types of knowledge. That perspective points to yet another irony—many, many commentators conceded that illegal immigrants were, and always would be, in our midst. Again, if American citizens could assume a perspective where *they* might be the "rightless" pariahs created by immigration rules, it hardly seems a stretch to think that they might not support those rules as zealously, if at all.

It is as though the constant oscillations between the principle of sovereignty and the principle against ascriptive status can have no firm resolution, at least not politically. We have lived in the midst of this tension, ever since the birth of federal immigration rules. We still live in the midst of this tension, so long as these rules exist. It will, no doubt, continue to produce contradictory laws and policies.

For example, in the years since its passage, Proposition 187 died in the federal courts, as numerous groups challenged its constitutionality and as a new governor, Gray Davis, refused to press the suit any further on behalf of the state. In a strange twist, exactly one month after September 11, 2001, the state that had passed such a harsh rule in 1994 passed a very different one that allowed undocumented students to pay in-state tuition for state universities and community colleges, just like every other Californian.[117] The law was very similar to the one that had passed in Texas just four months earlier, signed by a Republican governor. The California version conceded a truth: "There are high school pupils who have attended elementary and secondary schools in this state for most of their lives and who are likely to remain, but are precluded from obtaining an affordable college education because they are required to pay nonresident tuition rates."[118] Thus, while it is still illegal for persons to cross into the United States without the nation's consent, those who remain in states like California and Texas can now get an inexpensive college education. The principle behind *Plyler* has remained remarkably resilient.

But so too has the principle of sovereignty in the name of self-defense. In the wake of September 11, especially after the passage of the Patriot Act of 2002, the entire system of border enforcement and immigration control have fundamentally changed. The Immigration and Naturalization Service no longer exists, its demise premised on its gross incompetence. Border enforcement has been separated from Naturalization Services, although both now function under the newly created Department of Homeland Security. National security, personal security, and the security of major cities from terrorist attacks—these have framed issues of immigration and belonging as intensely as ever in the past few months. In addition, under the terms for removing and interrogating foreign terrorists, the Department of Justice and the Attorney General have moved to incarcerate large numbers of noncitizens, many of Middle Eastern and Asian origin. In Cuba, at the American military installations in Guantanamo Bay, as well as in immigration detention facilities throughout the United States, the American government has incarcerated many noncitizen permanent residents, in addition to persons captured abroad, in Afghanistan, Pakistan, and other parts of the Arab world. Some of these detainees have remained under detention for periods similar to the time spent by Japanese American internees during World War II.[119]

And yet frightened as never before, many Americans have popularly supported these new laws and policies, and public officials have defended them as though they were essential to the very survival of the country. It is as though the nation is again alone in the world, one body in a state of nature, facing incredibly dangerous states and peoples, some even defined as "evil." It would seem highly implausible that in this era the citizens of the United States would give up the notion of national sovereignty, or the right to act forcefully in the world, even unilaterally if necessary, to deal with these threats both internationally and domestically. In the midst of danger, many still rush toward Leviathans.

Notes

1. Tex. Educ. Code Ann. §21.031 (1981). For a brief but useful summary of recent state responses to undocumented aliens in education, including the case in Texas, see Lora Grandrath, *Illegal Immigrants and Public Education: Is There a Right to the 3 R's?* 30 VAL. U. L. REV. 749 (1996).

2. Plyler v. Doe, 457 U.S. 202, 205 (1982).

3. Id., at 210.

4. Id., at 213, where Brennan quotes Field from Wong Wing v. United States, 163 U.S. 228 (1896).

5. Id., at 218–219.

6. Id., at 220, quoting Trimble v. Gordon, 430 U.S. 762, 770.

7. Id.

8. Id.

9. Id., at 222.

10. Id., at 221. See San Antonio School District v. Rodriguez, 411 U.S. 1 (1973); Meyer v. Nebraska, 262 U.S. 390 (1923); Ambach v. Norwick, 441 U.S. 68 (1979); and Wisconsin v. Yoder, 406 U.S. 205 (1972). That education is not a "fundamental right" has a direct bearing on Equal Protection analysis, at least during *Plyler*. A government denial of a "fundamental right"—a right specifically mentioned in the Constitution or a right articulated as "fundamental" within the Court's own precedents—requires the courts to apply a "strict" level of scrutiny to the grounds of the denial. The courts would search for a "compelling justification" for why the right was or should be denied, and unless they found one, the denial would be rendered unconstitutional under the Equal Protection Clause of the Fourteenth Amendment.

11. Brown v. Board of Education, 347 U.S. 483, 493 (1954). The quote continues: "Today it is a principal instrument in awakening the child to cultural values, in preparing him for later professional training, and in helping him to adjust normally to his environment. In these days, it is doubtful that any child may reasonably be expected to succeed in life if he is denied the opportunity of an education. Such an opportunity, where the state has undertaken to provide it, is a right which must be made available to all on equal terms."

12. 457 U.S., at 222.

13. Id., at 223–224. Moreover, "the stigma of illiteracy will mark them for the rest of their lives. By denying these children a basic education, we deny them the ability to live within the structure of our civic institutions. . . . In determining the rationality of [the state's rule], we may appropriately take into account its costs to the Nation and to the innocent children who are its victims. In light of these countervailing costs, the discrimination contained in [the Texas rule] can hardly be considered rational."

14. Id., at 226. Brennan's reference was clearly to the Immigration Reform and Control Act of 1986 (IRCA). This federal law punished American employers who knowingly hired illegal immigrants, but it also "legalized" large numbers of illegal immigrants who had resided in the United States for a number of years. Provided that such persons could prove extended residency in the United States, they were eligible for permanent residency as a form of relief.

15. Id., at 230. This reasoning has led several influential scholars to conclude that the Equal Protection Clause and other important constitutional safeguards stand for an "anti-caste" principle in American law. In other words, Anglo-American legal principles either mitigate against, or should mitigate against, the development and continuation of a permanent caste in liberal democracies like the United States. For a statement of this position, see Cass Sunstein, *The Anti-Caste Principle*, 94 MICH. L. REV. 2410 (1994).

16. 457 U.S., at 252–253.

17. Id., at 253–254. Burger cited from Brennan's majority opinion, at 221.

18. Id., at 254.

NOTES TO CHAPTER 2

1. See generally, First Treatise, and ROBERT FILMER, PATRIARCHIA, in JOHN LOCKE, TWO TREATISES OF GOVERNMENT (Thomas Cook, ed., 1947), hereafter Filmer. Hereafter, references to "First Treatise" and "Second Treatise" refer to Locke's TWO TREATISES OF GOVERNMENT.

2. See Filmer, ch. 1, §§4–6; Locke, First Treatise, §§16–20, and also, Second Treatise, §§75–76, discussed later. A thorough review of this debate, as well as a full discussion of the theory of equality developed by Locke, is presented in JE-REMY WALDRON, GOD, LOCKE, AND EQUALITY: CHRISTIAN FOUNDATIONS IN LOCKE'S POLITICAL THOUGHT (2003). According to Waldron, contemporary theorists have underestimated or ignored the importance of Christianity to Locke's political philosophy. Waldron suggests a corrective: "I want to ask, not only whether we can discern the influence of Christian teaching in Locke's normative doctrine of the 'equality of men in virtue of their shared species-member-

ship,' but also whether one can even make sense of a position like Locke's—and a substantive position like Locke's does seem to be what we want so far as basic equality is concerned—apart from the specifically biblical and Christian teaching that he associated with it." WALDRON, 13, and quoting from JOHN DUNN, THE POLITICAL THOUGHT OF JOHN LOCKE: AN HISTORICAL ACCOUNT OF THE ARGUMENT OF "THE TWO TREATISES OF GOVERNMENT" (1969).

3. Filmer, ch. 1, §10: "If we compare the natural rights of a father with those of a king, we find them all one, without any difference at all but only in the latitude or extent of them: as the father over one family, so the king, as father over many families, extends his care to preserve, feed, clothe, instruct, and defend the whole commonwealth. His war, his peace, his courts of justice, and all his acts of sovereignty, tend only to preserve and distribute to every subordinate and inferior father, and to their children, their rights and privileges, so that all the duties of a king are summed up in a universal fatherly care of his people."

On the absolute sovereignty of the monarch, see ch. 3, §1: "Hitherto I have endeavoured to show the natural institution of regal authority, and to free it from subjection to an arbitrary election of the people. It is necessary also to inquire whether human laws have a superiority over princes, because those that maintain the acquisition of royal jurisdiction from the people do subject the exercise of it to positive laws. But in this they also err; for as kingly power is by the law of God, so it hath no inferior law to limit it."

4. First Treatise, §4.

5. Id., §29. In §13, Locke explained further: "Every man had a right to the creatures by the same title Adam had, viz, by the right every one had to take care of, and provide for, their subsistence; and thus men had a right in common, Adam's children in common with him."

6. Second Treatise, §76. See generally, Second Treatise, §§74–76, and also, Jeremy Waldron, *John Locke: Social Contract versus Political Anthropology*, 51 REV. OF POLITICS 3 (1989).

7. First Treatise, §55: "But grant that the parents made their children, gave them life and being, and that hence there followed as absolute power. This would give the father but a joint dominion with the mother over them; for nobody can deny but that the woman hath an equal share, if not the greater as nourishing the child a long time in her own body out of her own substance."

8. Id., §53. Locke writes: "But is there any so bold that thus far arrogate to himself the incomprehensible works of the Almighty Who alone did at first and continues still to make a living soul? . . . [God] alone can breathe in the breath of life. If nay one thinks himself an artist at this, let him number up the parts of his child's body which he hath made, tell me their uses and operations, and when the living and rational soul began to inhabit this curious structure, when sense began, and how this engine which he has framed thinks and reasons."

9. Second Treatise, §118: "He is under his father's tuition and authority till he comes to age of discretion; and then he is a freeman, at liberty what government he will put himself under, what body politic he will unite himself to; for if an Englishman's son, born in France, be at liberty, and may do so, it is evident there is no tie upon him by his father's being a subject of this kingdom, nor is he bound up by any compact of his ancestors."

10. Filmer, II, §§3 and 4.

11. First Treatise, §47: "God . . . give not, that I see, authority to Adam over Eve, or to men over their wives, but only foretells what should be the woman's lot, how by his providence he would order it so that she should be subject to her husband, as we see that generally the laws of mankind and customs of nations have ordered it so, and there is, I grant, a foundation in nature for it." Locke did not elaborate on what this "foundation" might be. Feminist theorists have noted that Locke and other early liberal theorists did denigrate women by suggesting that they were not the moral or intellectual equals of men, but were suspiciously vague about exactly how women were not equal. For this, see CAROL PATEMAN, THE SEXUAL CONTRACT (1988).

12. Id., §48.

13. Id., §67.

14. See, for example, David Hume, *Of the Social Contract*, in HUME'S ETHICAL WRITINGS (Alasdair MacIntyre, ed., 1965); A. JOHN SIMMONS, THE LOCKEAN THEORY OF RIGHTS (1992); and A. JOHN SIMMONS, JUSTIFICATION AND LEGITIMACY: ESSAYS ON RIGHTS AND OBLIGATIONS (2001). Hume is rather colorful in his comments: "Were you to preach, in most parts of the world, that political connexions are founded altogether on voluntary consent or a mutual promise, the magistrate would soon imprison you, as seditious, for loosening the ties of obedience; if your friends did not before shut you up as delirious, for advancing such absurdities." HUME'S ETHICAL THEORIES, 258–259.

15. Second Treatise, §§49–51.

16. *An Essay on the Poor Laws*, in JOHN LOCKE, POLITICAL ESSAYS 180 (Mark Goldie, ed., 1997).

17. Id., at 186–194.

18. Consider the following excerpt from the First Treatise, §42: "As justice gives to every man a title to the product of his honest industry and the fair acquisitions of his ancestors descended to him, so charity gives every man a title to so much out of another's plenty as will keep him from extreme want where he has no means to subsist otherwise. And a man can no more justly make use of another's necessity to force him to become his vassal by withholding what relief God requires him to afford to the wants of his brother, than he that has more strength can seize upon a weaker, master him to his obedience, and with a dagger at his throat, offer him death or slavery."

19. Second Treatise, §190. Emphasis added.

20. Id., §72.

21. Id., §182: "The right of conquest extends only to the lives of those who joined in the war, not to their estates, but only in order to make reparations for the damages received and the charges of the war, and that, too, with the reservation of the right of the innocent wife and children." See also, §§175–182. The following passage, from §182, reiterates the same idea: "But because the miscarriages of the father are no faults of the children, and they may be rational and peaceable, notwithstanding the brutishness and injustice of the father, the father, by his miscarriages and violence, can forfeit his own life, but involves not his children in his guilt or destruction. His goods, which nature that willeth the preservation of all mankind as much as is possible hath made to belong to the children to keep them from perishing, do still continue to belong to the children; for supposing them not to have joined in the war, either through infancy, absence, or choice, they have done nothing to forfeit them; nor has the conqueror any right to take them away, by the bare title of having subdued him that by force attempted his destruction, though, perhaps, he may have some right to them to repair the damages he has sustained by the war and by the defense of his own right."

22. Second Treatise, §183.

23. See HENRY MAINE, ANCIENT LAW 74–76 (1861, 1963, 1972).

24. First Treatise, §93.

25. See D. J. O'CONNOR, JOHN LOCKE (1952).

26. Second Treatise, §97.

27. John Stuart Mill, *The Subjection of Women*, in COLLECTED WORKS (1963, 1982), vol. 21, 265.

28. Id., at 273. Note, again, similar passages in MAINE, *supra* note 23, 165, 168: "The movement of the progressive societies has been uniform in one respect. Through all its course it has been distinguished by the gradual dissolution of family dependency and the growth of individual obligation in its place. The individual is steadily substituted for the Family, as the unit of which civil laws take account. . . . If then we employ Status, agreeably with the usage of the best writers, to signify these conditions only, and avoid applying the term to such conditions as are the immediate or remote result of agreement, we may say that the movement of the progressive societies has hitherto been a movement from Status to Contract."

29. *Subjection, supra* note 27, 274.

30. Id., at 325.

31. JOHN STUART MILL, PRINCIPLES OF POLITICAL ECONOMY, in COLLECTED WORKS, vol. 2, 759–760.

32. Indeed, for Mill, women, particularly if they were married, had a lot in common with slaves. See Mary Lyndon Shanley, "The Subjection of Women," at

401: "Mill frequently made an analogy between the situation of married women and that of chattel slaves. He thought that the position of married women resembled that of slaves in several ways: the social and economic system gave women little alternative except to marry; once married, the legal personality of the woman was subsumed in that of her husband; and the abuses of human dignity permitted by custom and law within marriage were egregious."

33. John Stuart Mill, *The Negro Question*, in COLLECTED WORKS, vol. 6, 92.

34. PRINCIPLES OF POLITICAL ECONOMY, *supra* note 31, 250. Whether Roman slavery was so "open" to manumission and social advancement by slaves can surely be doubted.

35. John Stuart Mill, *The Contest in America*, in COLLECTED WORKS, vol. 21, 141.

36. John Stuart Mill, *Considerations on Representative Government* in JOHN STUART MILL, ON LIBERTY AND OTHER ESSAYS 345 (1991). Hereafter, references to this essay shall appear as "Considerations."

37. John Stuart Mill, *Chapters on Socialism*, in COLLECTED WORKS, vol. 21, 713.

38. PRINCIPLES OF POLITICAL ECONOMY, *supra* note 31, 209, 218.

39. Id., at 208.

40. *Socialism*, *supra* note 37, 714. He continued: "Even the idle, reckless, and ill-conducted poor, those who are said with most justice to have themselves to blame for their condition, often undergo much more and much severer labour, not only than those who are born to pecuniary independence, than almost any of the more highly remunerated of those who earn their subsistence; and even the inadequate self-control exercised by the industrious poor costs them more sacrifice and more effort than is almost ever required from the favoured members of society."

41. Id., at 714.

42. Id.

43. Id.

44. Id., at 715.

45. *The Subjection of Women*, *supra* note 27, 325. Mill continued: "Human beings do not grow up from childhood in the possession of unearned distinctions, without pluming themselves upon them. Those for whom privileges are not acquired by their merit, and which they feel to be disproportioned to it, inspire with additional humility, are always the few, and the best few. The rest are only inspired with pride, and the worst sort of pride, that which values itself upon accidental advantages, not of its own achieving."

46. Considerations, at 299.

47. PRINCIPLES OF POLITICAL ECONOMY, *supra* note 31, 754. The passage continues: "I do not affirm that what has always been must always be, or

that human improvement has no tendency to correct the intensely selfish feelings engendered by power; but though the evil may be lessened, it cannot be eradicated, until the power itself is withdrawn." Consider also the following passage from a student of Mill, C. L. Ten, "Democracy, Socialism, and the Working Classes," at 394: "Just as Mill is impatient with the revolutionary socialists who wish to transform society radically and immediately, so too he is impatient with the defenders of the existing social order who are complacent about its virtue and who misrepresent the socialist alternative to it."

48. Consider, for example, this excerpt from PRINCIPLES OF POLITICAL ECONOMY, *supra* note 31, 208: "If the institution of private property necessarily carried with it as a consequence, that the produce of labour should be apportioned as we now see it, almost in inverse ratio to the labour—the largest portions to those who have never worked at all, the next largest to those whose work is almost nominal, and so in a descending scale, the remuneration dwindling as the work grows harder and more disagreeable, until the most fatiguing and exhausting bodily labour cannot count with certainty on being able to earn even the necessities of life; if this or communism were the alternative, all the difficulties, great or small, of Communism would be but dust in the balance." For more on this, see Jonathon Riley, "Mill's Political Economy."

49. PRINCIPLES OF POLITICAL ECONOMY, *supra* note 31, 221, 224. The difference between "bequeathing" and "inheriting" lies with the manifest intent of the giver. A "bequest" is a conscience declaration, made prior to death, to leave something for a beneficiary after the giver has died. "Inheritance" does not require any such conscious act. Persons can inherit, according to law or custom, even when the giver dies intestate.

50. Id., at 224.

51. For example, in id., at 749–750, Mill wrote: "[W]e may suppose this better distribution of property attained, by the joint effect of the prudence and frugality of individuals, and of a system of legislation favoring equality of fortunes, so far as it is concerned with the just claim of the individual to the fruits, whether great or small, of his or her own industry. We may suppose, for instance, a limitation of the sum which any one person may acquire by gift or inheritance to the amount sufficient to constitute a modern independence. Under this two-fold influence society would exhibit these leading features: a well-paid and affluent body of laborers; no enormous fortunes, except what were earned and accumulated during a single lifetime; but a much larger body of persons than at present, not only exempt from the coarser toils, but with sufficient leisure, both physical and mental, from mechanical details, to cultivate freely the graces of life, and afford examples of them to the classes less favorably circumstances for their growth."

52. Considerations, at 335.

53. Considerations, at 336–337: "The 'local' or 'middle class' examination

for the degree of Associate, so laudably and public-spiritedly established by the Universities of Oxford and Cambridge, any similar ones which may be instituted by other competent bodies (provided they are fairly open to all comers), afford a ground on which plurality of votes might with great advantage be accorded to those who have passed the test."

54. Considerations, at 337–338.

55. Consider a passage from J. H. Burns, "J. S. Mill and Democracy, 1829–1861," in MILL: A COLLECTION OF CRITICAL ESSAYS (J. B. Schneewind, ed., 1969), 280–328, on 327: "Democracy in the last resort fails by Mill's standards because it rests counter to all that he had believed and preached for thirty years—the assumption that men are equal in the moral and intellectual qualities required by the exercise of political power."

56. JOHN RAWLS, A THEORY OF JUSTICE 7 (1971), hereafter, "Theory." Again, in Theory, at 54, Rawls says, "The primary subjects of the principles of social justice is the basic structure of society, the arrangement of major social institutions into one scheme of cooperation."

57. Any summary of Rawls' work is fraught with peril. Several distinguished commentators themselves cannot agree on what Rawls said or intended, and it is virtually impossible for anyone to come to a comprehensive, "accurate" summary of this original and challenging work. The summary presented here clearly must be taken in that light, and is by no means intended to be definitive.

58. See Theory, at 12.

59. See Theory, at 120 and 137, and see also, JOHN RAWLS, POLITICAL LIBERALISM 25–30 (1995). Hereafter, references to POLITICAL LIBERALISM will appear as PL.

60. Theory, at 139.

61. Id., at 120.

62. Id., at 12.

63. Id., at 137. Literally, persons in the original position have knowledge of different types of persons and comprehensive doctrines that exist in society, but they themselves do not "know" what type of person they may be outside the original position, nor do they know to which of the several competing comprehensive doctrines they may possibly subscribe as individuals. Consider an analogous passage from PL, at 25: "To model this conviction in the original position, the parties are not allowed to know the social position of those they represent, or the particular comprehensive doctrine of the person each represents. The same idea is extended to information about people's race and ethnic group, sex and gender, and their various native endowments such as strength and intelligence, all within the normal range. We express these limits figuratively by saying the parties are behind a veil of ignorance."

64. Theory, at 137.

65. Critics of the original position have been less flattering of its usefulness.

Some have argued that it is psychologically impossible to think that persons can actually deliberate behind the veil of ignorance as Rawls describes it, while others disagree that the same conditions lead reasonable persons to the two principles of justice. For a review of these critiques, see READING RAWLS: CRITICAL STUDIES OF RAWLS' "A THEORY OF JUSTICE" (Norman Daniels, ed., 1989), especially the articles by Gerald Dworkin, David Lyons, Ronald Dworkin, and Benjamin Barber.

66. Theory, at 26–32; 148–170.

67. Id., at 28.

68. Id., at 15.

69. Id., at 149.

70. Id., at 60.

71. Id., at 83. In a number of places, the two principles are modified, or are articulated in slightly, but substantially, different ways. For example, later in Theory, on 250, the first principle appears thus: "Each person is to have an equal right to the most extensive total system of equal basic liberties compatible with a similar system of liberty for all." In PL, at 5–6, the two principles appear this way: "Each person has an equal claim to a fully adequate scheme of equal basic rights and liberties, which scheme is compatible with the same scheme for all; and in this scheme the equal political liberties, and only those liberties, are to be guaranteed their fair value. . . . Social and economic inequalities are to satisfy two conditions: first, they are to be attached to positions and offices open to all under conditions of fair equality of opportunity; and second, they are to be to the greatest benefit of the least advantaged members of society." And again, at 291: "Each person has an equal right to a fully adequate scheme of equal basic liberties which is compatible with a similar scheme of liberties for all. Social and economic inequalities are to satisfy two conditions. First, they must be attached to offices and positions open to all under conditions of fair equality of opportunity; and second, they must be to the greatest benefit of the least advantaged members of society."

72. Theory, at 20. The Rawlsian concept of a "reflective equilibrium" captures this sense of revising abstract principles after considering particular applications of those same principles in particular cases or circumstances. See Theory, at 49, and PL, at 8.

73. Id., at 61: "These principles are to be arranged in a serial order with the first principle prior to the second. This ordering means that a departure from the institutions of equal liberty required by the first principle cannot be justified by, or compensated for, greater social and economic advantages. The distribution of wealth and income, and the hierarchies of authority, must be consistent with both the liberties of equal citizenship and equality of opportunity."

74. Id., at 176: "In this respect the two principles of justice have a definite advantage. Not only do the parties protect their basic rights but they insure

themselves against the worst eventualities. They run no chance of having to acquiesce in a loss of freedom over the course of their life for the sake of a greater good enjoyed by others, an undertaking that in actual circumstances they might not be able to keep." Later, on this same point, in Theory, at 255, Rawls wrote: "[Persons] must decide . . . which principles when consciously followed and acted upon in everyday life will best manifest this freedom in their community, and most fully reveal their independence from natural contingencies and social accidents."

75. Id., at 73.

76. Id., at 179. Rawls borrowed heavily from Kant, as he indicated throughout Theory. See, for example, at 253–254.

77. Id., at 243.

78. Rawls himself argued that it wasn't fear that drove persons to commit to the two principles of justice, but rather their rationality, which, when combined with the parameters of the original position, functioned much like "benevolence." Without actually meaning to, persons in the original position would end up caring for the least well-off. See Theory, at 143–148.

79. Id., at 15.

80. Although social theorists now routinely argue that something like "race" is a "social construct," a rather fluid idea subject to reinterpretations by political movements and other types of social, political, and legal contestations, they readily acknowledge that "racial labels" are often inflicted on persons, usually without their consent. See, for example, MICHAEL OMI AND HOWARD WINANT, RADICAL FORMATION IN THE UNITED STATES (1994).

81. Theory, at 102. He continued: "But it does not follow that one should eliminate these distinctions. There is another way to deal with them. The basic structure can be arranged so that these contingencies work for the good of the least fortunate. Thus we are led to the difference principle if we wish to set up the social system so that no one gains or loses from his arbitrary place in the distribution of natural assets or his initial position in society without giving or receiving compensating advantages in return."

82. Id., at 100–101. That a person's talents ought to be regarded as a "common asset" has drawn powerful criticism, most notably from Nozick, who argues that treating persons' talents that way violates their individual worth and dignity by treating what is *theirs* as though *others* had a legitimate claim to it. See Nozick's famous Wilt Chamberlain example, in ROBERT NOZICK, ANARCHY, STATE AND UTOPIA (1974), arguing that Mr. Chamberlain had every right to make money from his talents as a basketball player, even if a large part of his talents were "God given," and even if, in other societies and other times, his ability to play basketball would not be remunerative. In any event, Nozick insists that to treat Mr. Chamberlain's talents as a "common asset" violates Mr. Chamberlain's dignity as a person; it amounts to a kind of socialist theft.

In another vein, recent commentaries in political philosophy have suggested that Rawls' theory leads inevitably to a kind of "luck egalitarianism," which, according to an account provided by Samuel Scheffler, "denies that a person's natural talent, creativity, intelligence, innovative skill, or entrepreneurial ability can be the basis for legitimate inequalities." Samuel Scheffler, *What is Egalitarianism?* 31 PHIL. & PUB. AFF. 5, 6 (2003). Scheffler is himself not a luck egalitarian, nor does he think that Rawls would endorse this position. Yet, "luck egalitarianism" is but a powerful example of the variety of works attempting to deal with the implications of Rawls' theory for various questions of inequality caused by circumstances, personal characteristics, and especially personal choices. For a review of these types of debates, see Jonathon Wolff, *Fairness, Respect, and the Egalitarian Ethos*, 27 PHIL.& PUB. AFF. 97 (1998); Elizabeth Anderson, *What Is the Point of Equality?* 109 ETHICS 287 (1999); and RONALD DWORKIN, SOVEREIGN VIRTUES: THE THEORY AND PRACTICE OF EQUALITY (2000).

83. Consider the following passage from Loren Lomansky, *Toward a Liberal Theory of National Borders*, in BOUNDARIES AND JUSTICE (David Miller and Sohail Hashmi, eds., 2001), 57: "A baby born a few miles north of the Rio Grande will, by virtue of this natal location, enjoy prospects substantially different from and very likely much superior to those of someone born a few miles south. She will be the beneficiary of a more commodious arena of economic activity to which she will be permitted easy access because of the citizenship this accident of birth confers. Similarly, the political institutions under which she will live are more democratic and more responsive to her interests than those available to the other child. Should she find herself in conditions of exigency, she will enjoy support from a welfare apparatus which, if not munificent, nonetheless substantially surpasses that available to her southern peer. How eminently shrewd a decision to be born where life prospects are good!"

84. Second Treatise, §191. And merely dwelling in a commonwealth, and being subject to its laws, did not make a person not already a member into one: "And thus we see that foreigners, by living all their lives under another government and enjoying the privileges and protection of it, though they are bound, even in conscience, to submit to its administration as far forth as any denizen, yet do not thereby come to be subjects or members of that commonwealth."

85. Id., §122.

86. Id., §122. Once a public act of allegiance was performed, though, the act was considered binding: "He that has once, by actual agreement and any express declaration, given his consent to be of any commonwealth is perpetually and indispensably obliged to be and remain unalterably a subject to it, and can never be again in the liberty of the state of nature, unless by any calamity the government he was under comes to be dissolved, or else by some public act cuts him off from being any longer a member of it." Second Treatise, §121. For other forms

of political obligation that accrue due to ownership of property, or acts of "tacit consent," see Second Treatise, §§120 and 121.

87. Considerations, at 431.

88. Id., at 432.

89. Id. Consider another passage: "The absorption of the conquerors in the less-advanced people would be an evil: they must be governed as subjects, and the state of things is either a benefit or a misfortune, according as the subjugated people have or have not reached the state in which it is an injury not to be under a free government, and according as the conquerors do or do not use their superiority in a manner calculated to fit the conquered for a higher stage of improvement." Id., at 432–433.

90. Rawls explained, in Theory, at 8: "The conditions for the law of nations may require different principles arrived at in a different way. I shall be satisfied if it is possible to formulate a reasonable conception of justice for the basic structure of society conceived for the time being as a closed system isolated from other societies." In PL, at 40, Rawls explained again: "It is complete in that it is self-sufficient and has a place for all the main purposes of human life. It is also closed, as I have said, in that entry into it is only by birth and exit from it is only by death." Rawls continued: "For the moment we leave aside entirely relations with other societies and postpone all questions of justice between peoples until a conception of justice for a well-ordered society is on hand. Thus, we are not seen as joining society at the age of reason, as we might join an association, but as being born into society where we will lead a complete life."

Elsewhere, in PL, at 136, the idea emerged again: "To us it seems that we have simply materialized, as it were, from nowhere at this position in this social world with all its advantages and disadvantages, according to our good or bad fortune. I say from nowhere because we have no prior or nonpublic identity: we have not come from somewhere else into this social world. Political society is closed: we come to be within it and we do not, and indeed cannot, enter or leave it voluntarily." And again, at 276: "Since membership in their society is given, there is no question of the parties comparing the attractions of other societies." Thus, for the moment at least, the theory of justice as fairness does not address "opting in" or "opting out" of society, as subjects within the theory of political obligation.

91. JOHN RAWLS, THE LAW OF PEOPLES 8–9 (2001). Hereafter references to THE LAW OF PEOPLES will appear as LP. Rawls listed a number of primary causes for migration: "One is the persecution of religious and ethnic minorities, the denial of their human rights. Another is political oppression of various forms, as when the members of the peasant classes are conscripted and hired out by monarchs as mercenaries in their dynastic wars for power and territory. Often people are simply fleeing from starvation, as in the Irish famine of the 1840s. Yet famines are themselves in large part caused by political failures and the absence

of decent government. The last cause I mention is population pressure in the home territory, and among its complex of causes is the inequality and subjection of women. Once that inequality and subjection are overcome, and women are granted equal political participation with men and assured education, these problems can be resolved. Thus, religious freedom and liberty of conscience, political freedom and constitutional liberties, and equal justice for women are fundamental aspects of sound social policy for a realistic utopia. The problem of immigration is not, then, simply left aside, but is eliminated as a serious problem in a realistic utopia."

92. LP, at 8. The quote concludes a broader idea: "I argue that an important role of government, however arbitrary a society's boundaries may appear from a historical point of view, is to be the effective agent of a people as they take responsibility for their territory and the size of their population, as well as for maintaining the land's environmental integrity. Unless a definite agent is given responsibility for maintaining an asset and bears the responsibility and loss for not doing so, that asset tends to deteriorate. On my account the role of the institution of property is to prevent this deterioration from occurring. In the present case, the asset of the people's territory and its potential capacity to support them *in perpetuity*; and the agent is the people themselves politically organized. The perpetuity condition is crucial."

93. JOHN LOCKE, AN ESSAY CONCERNING UNDERSTANDING, KNOWLEDGE, OPINION, AND ASSENT §12 (Rand, ed., 1931).

NOTES TO CHAPTER 3

1. See Second Treatise, §95: The establishment of a commonwealth "injures not the freedom of the rest; they are left as they were in the liberty of the state of nature." Also, Second Treatise, §121: "Whenever the owner [of property], who has given nothing but such a tacit consent to the government, will, by donation, sale, or otherwise, quit the said possession, he is at liberty to go and incorporate himself into any other commonwealth, or to agree with others to begin a new one *in vacuis locis*, in any part of the world they can find free and unpossessed." Both statements imply a natural freedom to form and depart consensual governments.

2. Locke was often very pessimistic about human nature. This was how he once described his fellow Christians: "This is how it began. . . . A small weak band of Christians, destitute of everything, comes to a pagan country; the strangers beg the natives, in the name of common humanity, to succor them with the necessities of life. Their needs are satisfied, dwellings are granted them, and both races unite and form one people. The Christian religion takes root and spreads, but is not yet the stronger."

The natives soon become victims of predation. "At once compacts are broken and civil rights violated, in order that idolatry may be extirpated; and these innocent pagans, strict observers of what is right, and in no way offending against good morals and the civil law, are to be robbed of their lives and the goods and lands of their ancestors, unless they will forsake their ancient rites, and embrace new and strange ones. Then at last we see plainly what zeal for the church, combined with desire of domination, can lead to, and we are shown how easily religion and the salvation of souls become a pretext for rapine and ambition." JOHN LOCKE, A LETTER ON TOLERATION 113–115 (Gough, ed. and trans., 1968).

3. Second Treatise, §147.

4. Id., §145. Locke continued: "Hence, it is that the controversies that happen between any man of the society with those that are out of it are managed by the public, and an injury done to a member of their body engages the whole in the reparation of it."

5. "For a General Naturalization," in JOHN LOCKE, POLITICAL ESSAYS 324 (Mark Goldie, ed., 1997). The comments were made in the context of assessing the migration of French Huguenots to England, after the Edict of Nantes.

6. Second Treatise, §131.

7. See generally, LETTER, *supra* note 2.

8. Second Treatise, §22. "The liberty of man is to be under no other legislative power but that established by consent in the commonwealth, . . . The freedom of men under government is to have a standing rule to live by, common to every one of that society and made by the legislative power erected in it, a liberty to follow my own will in all things where the rule prescribes not, and not to be subject to the inconstant, uncertain, arbitrary will of another man; as freedom of nature is to be under no other restraint than the law of nature."

9. "As it is already common, and is rapidly tending to become the universal, condition of the more backward populations, to be either held in direct subjection by the more advanced, or to be under their complete political ascendancy. . . . There are in this age of the world few more important problems, than how to organize this rule, so as to make it a good instead of an evil to the subject people, providing them with the best attainable present government, and with the conditions most favorable to future permanent improvement." Considerations, at 454.

10. See also *A Few Words on Non-Intervention*, in COLLECTED WORKS, vol. 21, 118.

11. For the idea that "rights" are rather specific to particular cultures, namely English culture, and are thus not "universal," see Edmund Burke's classic essay on rights, reprinted in NON-SENSE UPON STILTS (Jeremy Waldron, ed., 1987).

12. Considerations, at 295.

13. Id., at 427.

14. LP, at 36. In *Perpetual Peace*, in KANT'S PHILOSOPHICAL WRITINGS 292–293 (Ernst Behler, ed., 1991), Kant writes the following passage, which is quoted directly in LP, at 36, fn. 40: "The idea of international law presupposes the separate existence of many independent but neighboring states. Although this condition is itself a state of war (unless a federative union prevents the outbreak of hostilities), this is rationally preferable to the amalgamation of states under one superior power, as this would end in one universal monarchy, and laws always lose their vigor what governments gain in extent; hence a soulless despotism falls into anarchy after stifling the seeds of the good."

Kant's passage continues: "Nevertheless, every state, or its ruler, desires to establish lasting peace in this way, aspiring if possible to rule the whole world. But nature wills otherwise. She employs two means to separate peoples and to prevent them from mixing: differences of language and religion. These differences involve a tendency to mutual hatred and pretexts for war, but the progress of civilization and men's gradual approach to greater harmony in their principles finally leads to peaceful agreement. This is not like the peace which despotism (in the burial ground of freedom) produces through a weakening of all powers; it is, on the contrary, produced and maintained by their equilibrium in liveliest competition."

Kant goes on to reason that money and commerce will be the driving forces behind larger federations of nation-states, joined to protect "mutual interest": "The spirit of commerce, which is incompatible with war, sooner or later gains the upper hand in every state. As the power of money is perhaps the most dependable of all powers (means) included under the state power, states see themselves forced, without any moral urge, to promote honorable peace and by mediation to prevent war wherever it threatens to break out."

15. LP, at 63.

16. See LP, at 62: "If a liberal constitutional democracy is, in fact, superior to other forms of society, as I believe it to be, a liberal people should have confidence in their convictions and suppose that a decent society, when offered due respect by liberal peoples, may be likely, over time, to recognize the advantages of liberal institutions and take steps toward becoming more liberal on its own."

17. LP, at 39: "It does not follow from the fact that boundaries are historically arbitrary that their role in the Law of Peoples cannot be justified. One the contrary, to fix on their arbitrariness is to fix on the wrong thing. In the absence of a world-state, there *must* be boundaries of some kind, which when viewed in isolation will seem arbitrary, and depend to some degree on historical circumstances."

Several contemporary theorists have agreed that even though boundaries are arbitrary, states may still have morally permissible reasons to enforce their borders. Consider the following passage from Jules Coleman and Sarah Harding,

Citizenship, Justice, and Political Borders, in JUSTICE IN IMMIGRATION (Bernard Schwartz, ed., 1995), 51–52: "Political borders are arbitrary from the moral point of view. One might argue that no one within a political territory thus has a right in justice to exclude others. The arbitrariness of political borders entails that there is no principled ground for any immigration policy other than open borders. Yet it hardly follows from that fact that those within a political border have no rightful claim to the territory and its resources than those outside the territory do. Some might take this to mean that countries have a right in morality to close their borders to immigrants. Both of these views, however, are unacceptable. Even if borders are arbitrary or conventionally set, it does not follow that they lack moral significance. Conventions, even arbitrary ones, can have morally significant consequences."

18. See generally, Theory, at 461–468.

19. Theory, at 475.

20. Rawls has been criticized, sometimes attacked, by a range of scholars charging that liberal accounts in general, and Rawls' theory in particular, are too "atomistic" and thus do not weigh fairly the moral and political value of immediate, apolitical attachments. See, for example, ALASDAIR MCINTYRE, AFTER VIRTUE: A STUDY IN MORAL THEORY (1980); CHARLES TAYLOR, SOURCES OF THE SELF: THE MAKING OF MODERN IDENTITY (1989); and MICHAEL SANDEL, LIBERALISM AND THE LIMITS OF JUSTICE (1998). For an overview of communitarian critiques of liberal theory, see LIBERALS AND COMMUNITARIANS (Stephen Mulhall and Adam Swift, eds., 1992).

21. See ROGERS SMITH, CIVIC IDEALS 10 (1997). A more detailed attack is on 481: "[Rawls] has always made the task of social unity artificially easy by adopting some inexcusably evasive premises. He explicitly assumes that he is theorizing only for a 'closed society' without relations to other ones, whose members 'enter into it only by birth and leave it only by death.' Such a society would have to deny its members all expatriation rights and reject all immigrants and refugees, however needy they may be. Those policies are inherently illiberal and undemocratic, and in most modern societies they could be enforced only by harsh coercive measures. These premises allow Rawls to theorize largely without regard to the tasks of nation-building, and therefore his views are useless for considering how liberal democratic polities can properly deal with them."

22. See, for example, Joseph Carens, *Aliens and Citizens: The Case for Open Borders*, 49 REV. OF POLITICS 251 (1987). Professor Carens' more recent work focuses on the political claims of immigrants and national minorities *already within* liberal nation-states. See JOSEPH CARENS, CULTURE, CITIZENSHIP, AND COMMUNITY: A CONTEXTUAL EXPLORATION OF JUSTICE AS EVEN-HANDEDNESS (2000). But the essence of his skepticism appears in other recent works, for example, PHILIP COLE, PHILOSOPHIES OF EXCLUSION: LIBERAL POLITICAL THEORY AND IMMIGRATION (2000). Cole claims that restrictive

immigration and naturalization rules are inconsistent with basic principles in liberal theory, especially those governing "internal" relations between persons within a liberal state.

23. See Will Kymlicka and W. J. Norman, *Return of the Citizen: A Survey of Recent Works on Citizenship Theory*, 104 ETHICS 352 (1994).

24. Whether the United States, as a nation, was ever fully a "liberal state"—in light of slavery, the subjugation of women, or the oppression of racial minorities—is of course a matter of considerable disagreement. One recent and persuasive account of the American ethos, SMITH, *supra* note 21, suggests that the United States has exhibited both liberal and illiberal characteristics, each fairly compelling and alternating, throughout the course of American history.

25. BRUCE ACKERMAN, SOCIAL JUSTICE AND THE LIBERAL STATE (1980).

26. See, for example, Joseph Carens, "Cosmopolitanism, Nationalism, and Immigration: False Dichotomies and Shifting Presuppositions," paper presented at the Conference on Cosmopolitanism and Nationalism, at Stanford University (Apr. 15–17, 1999). For a recent discussion of Carens' idea in the context of immigration law, please see Howard Change, *Immigration Restrictions as Employment Discrimination*, 78 CHICAGO-KENT L. REV. 291 (2003).

27. YAEL TAMIR, LIBERAL NATIONALISM 101, 110–111 (1993). As "partners in a shared way of life," belonging in a liberal society is indispensable: "Having developed this attitude, they cannot but care for other members, wish them well, delight in their success, and share in their misfortune. These feelings provide individuals with a reason to attend first to the needs and interests of their fellows. If the moral force of such feelings is denied, ruling out any special attention to fellow members, the social structure might collapse and we shall be left with isolated individuals and an abstract humanity."

28. Id., at 127. She quotes from MICHAEL WALZER, SPHERES OF JUSTICE 32 (1983).

29. WALZER, *supra* note 28.

30. See, SANDEL, *supra* note 20; TAYLOR, *supra* note 20; CHARLES TAYLOR, MULTICULTURALISM AND THE POLITICS OF RECOGNITION (Amy Gutmann, ed., 1994); THE ESSENTIAL COMMUNICATION READER (Amitai Etzioni, ed., 1998); and HENRY TAM, COMMUNITRIANISM: A NEW AGENDA FOR POLITICS AND CITIZENSHIP (1998).

31. JOSEPH RAZ, ETHICS IN THE PUBLIC DOMAIN 159 (1994).

32. See, for example, ARTHUR SCHLESINGER'S account in THE DISUNITING OF AMERICA (1992).

33. Neil MacCormick, "Nations and Nationalism." See also, Neil MacCormick, *Beyond the Sovereign State*, 56 MOD. L. REV. 1 (1993).

34. For more on these questions, see Henry Shue, *Mediating Duties*, 98 ETHICS 695 (1988); David Miller, *The Ethical Significance of Nationality*, 98

ETHICS 654 (1988); and even Joseph Raz, *National Self-Determination*, 87 J. PHIL. 448 (1990). For a thorough discussion of the issues involved, see SAMUEL SCHEFFLER, BOUNDARIES AND ALLEGIANCE (2001).

35. Daniel Philpott, *In Defense of Self-Determination*, 105 ETHICS 352, 385 (1995).

36. For useful discussions, see: CHARLES BEITZ, POLITICAL THEORY AND INTERNATIONAL RELATIONS (1979); JUSTICE IN IMMIGRATION, *supra* note 17; OPEN BORDERS? CLOSED SOCIETIES? (Michael Gibney, ed., 1988); IM-MIGRATION AND THE POLITICS OF CITIZENSHIP IN EUROPE AND NORTH AMERICA (Rogers Brubaker, ed., 1989); CHRISTIAN JOPPKE, IMMIGRATION AND THE NATION-STATE (1999); and FREE MOVEMENT: ETHICAL ISSUES IN THE TRANSNATIONAL MIGRATION OF PEOPLE AND MONEY (Brian Barry and Robert Goodin, eds., 1992). For discussions of the economic consequences of immigration, see: GEORGE BORJAS, FRIENDS OR STRANGERS: THE IMPACT OF IMMIGRANTS ON THE U.S. ECONOMY (1990); VERNON BRIGGS AND STEPHEN MOORE, STILL AN OPEN DOOR? U.S. IMMIGRATION POLICY AND THE AMERICAN ECONOMY (1994); STEPHEN MOORE, IMMIGRATION AND THE RISE AND DECLINE OF AMERICAN CITIES (1997); and JULIAN SIMON, THE ECONOMIC CONSEQUENCES OF IMMIGRATION (1999).

37. One such argument is by PETER SCHUCK AND ROGERS SMITH, CITI-ZENSHIP WITHOUT CONSENT (1985). Schuck and Smith have argued that American citizenship rules ought to embody consensualist values, such that birthright citizenship should not be presumptively granted. Persons born to American citizens should have a "provisional citizenship" until they are able to declare their intentions, while persons born to illegal immigrants would not have such provisional citizenship at all. Though this work has been praised in part, it has also received substantial criticism. See, for example, Joseph Carens, *Who Be-longs? Theoretical and Legal Questions about Birthright Citizenship in the United States*, 37 U. TOR. L. J. 413 (1987); David Schwartz, *The Amorality of Consent*, 74 CALIF. L. REV. 2143 (1986); and Gerald Neuman, *Back to Dred Scott?* 24 SAN DIEGO L. REV. 485 (1987).

38. Roger Nett, *The Civil Right We Are Not Ready For: The Right of Free Movement of People on the Face of the Earth*, 81 ETHICS 212, 218 (1971). See also, Timothy King, *Immigration from Developing Countries: Some Philosophi-cal Issues*, 93 ETHICS 525 (1983).

NOTES TO CHAPTER 4

1. See generally, GEORGE GORHAM, BIOGRAPHICAL NOTICE OF STEPHEN J. FIELD 3 (undated); and CARL BRENT SWISHER, STEPHEN J. FIELD, CRAFTSMAN OF THE LAW 5 (1930). For Field's early years in California, see

STEPHEN J. FIELD, CALIFORNIA ALCALDE 42 (1950). For his own account of his colorful history in California, see STEPHEN FIELD, PERSONAL REMINIS-CENCES OF EARLY DAYS IN CALIFORNIA (1893).

2. See SWISHER, *supra* note 1. Other leading scholarship on Field includes: PAUL KENS, JUSTICE STEPHEN FIELD (1997); Charles McCurdy, *Justice Field and the Jurisprudence of Government-Business Relations*, 61 J. AM. HIST. (1975), reprinted in AMERICAN LAW AND THE CONSTITUTIONAL ORDER, 246–266 (Lawrence Friedman and Harry Scheiber, eds., 1988); ROBERT MC-CLOSKEY, AMERICAN CONSERVATISM IN THE AGE OF ENTERPRISE (1951); and Howard Graham, *Justice Field and the Fourteenth Amendment*, 52 YALE L. J. 851 (1943). Field's contributions to the developing legal doctrine of "liberty of contract," typified by Lochner v. New York, 198 U.S. 45 (1905), is discussed later in this chapter.

3. ANDREW GYORY, CLOSING THE GATE: RACE, POLITICS, AND THE CHINESE EXCLUSION ACT 8 (1998).

4. RONALD TAKAKI, STRANGERS FROM A DIFFERENT SHORE: A HIS-TORY OF ASIAN AMERICANS 79 (1989)

5. CHARLES MCCLAIN, IN SEARCH OF EQUALITY: THE CHINESE STRUG-GLE AGAINST DISCRIMINATION IN NINETEENTH-CENTURY AMERICA 12 (1994). See also, Hudson Janisch, The Chinese, the Courts, and the Constitu-tion: A Study of the Legal Issues Raised by Chinese Immigration, 1850–1902 (1971) (unpublished JSD dissertation, University of Chicago Law School), one of the first serious studies of the specific impact of Chinese immigration on Ameri-can public law. The Foreign Miner's License Tax, Act of May 4, 1852, ch. 37, 1852 Cal. Stat. 84, 85. Takaki writes that by the time that the License Tax was voided by the Civil Rights Act of 1870, the state "had collected $5 million from the Chinese, a sum representing between 25 and 50 percent of all state revenue." TAKAKI, *supra* note 4, 82. For a history on the origins of anti-Chinese legislation in California, see LUCILE EAVES, A HISTORY OF CALIFORNIA LABOR LEGIS-LATION chs. 2–5 (1910).

6. Act of April 28, 1855, ch. 153, 1855 Cal. Stat. 194.

7. See the preamble to the Act of April 26, 1862, ch. 339, 1862 Cal. Stat. 462. Again, for a more thorough background into California labor legislation, see EAVES, *supra* note 5.

8. For a thorough discussion of class and race tensions in the 19th century, see ALEXANDER SAXTON, THE RISE AND FALL OF THE WHITE REPUBLIC: CLASS POLITICS AND MASS CULTURE IN NINETEENTH-CENTURY AMERICA (1990), ALEXANDER SAXTON, THE INDISPENSABLE ENEMY: LABOR AND THE ANTI-CHINESE MOVEMENT IN CALIFORNIA (1971); and RONALD TAKAKI, IRON CAGES: RACE AND CULTURE IN NINETEENTH-CENTURY AMERICA (1979). A recent study, GYORY, *supra* note 3, challenges the view that Chinese exclusion was driven primarily by organized labor. Gyory contends that national

politicians were behind the Act, and that most labor unions did not care much about the Chinese Question. His is an interesting, but still minority, opinion.

9. See Lin Sing v. Washburn, 20 Cal. 534 (1862), where Field dissented from the majority opinion striking down "The Act to Protect Free White Labor," which taxed the landing of passengers "ineligible for citizenship." The majority in *Lin Sing* followed precedents laid out by People v. Downer, 7 Cal. 169 (1857), and by the U.S. Supreme Court, in the Passenger Cases, 48 U.S. 282 (1849). Both precedents relied on the exclusive jurisdiction of the federal government in matters of immigration. In a series of cases regarding the Tax, for instance, Field exempted large numbers of Chinese miners working on private lands, as well as Chinese immigrants working in mining districts, but not as miners. In *Ex Parte Ah Pong*, 19 Cal. 106 (1861), the petitioner, Ah Pong, was a "washerman," not a miner, and so he was held not subject to the miners' tax. In Ah Hee v. Crippen, 19 Cal. 491 (1861), the petitioner was a miner working "upon the Mariposa estate, the property of Fremont and others, under a lease from the owners." Id., at 497. In his case, Field held that as a mere employee, working on nonpublic lands, Ah Hee should not be subject to the tax.

10. The first quote is from SUCHENG CHAN, ASIAN AMERICANS: AN INTERPRETIVE HISTORY 32 (1991), the second is from LUCY SALYER, LAWS HARSH AS TIGERS: CHINESE IMMIGRANTS AND THE SHAPING OF MODERN IMMIGRATION LAW 12 (1995). For accounts that rely on an economic explanation for anti-Chinese sentiment, see ALEXANDER SAXTON, *supra* note 8; P. CHIU, CHINESE LABOR IN CALIFORNIA, 1850–1880 (1963), and ELMER SANDEMEYER, THE ANTI-CHINESE MOVEMENT IN CALIFORNIA (1973). For a complex racial, cultural, and economic explanation, see RONALD TAKAKI, *supra* note 8. Finally, for a good account of the Chinese participation in the transcontinental railroad, see E. L. SABIN, BUILDING THE PACIFIC RAILWAY (1919); for a more general, recent discussion about the transcontinental railroad, see DAVID BAIN, EMPIRE EXPRESS: BUILDING THE FIRST TRANSCONTINENTAL RAILROAD (1999).

11. Of Chinese efforts against them, see MCCLAIN, *supra* note 5. Indeed, one of the central points of McClain's book is that the Chinese were hardly passive victims: "Far from being passive or docile in the face of official mistreatment, they reacted with indignation to it and more often than not sought redress in the courts. Indeed during the second half of the nineteenth century, the Chinese mounted court challenges to virtually every governmentally imposed disability under which they labored." Id., at 3. Professor McClain argues against some accounts of the Chinese that have portrayed them as passive sojourners; for example, see GUNTHER BARTH, BITTER STRENGTH: A HISTORY OF THE CHINESE IN THE UNITED STATES, 1850–1870 (1964).

12. Justice Field, Jury Instructions, 2 Sawyer 667, at 679–680 (Aug. 22, 1872).

13. 2 Sawyer at 680–681.

14. *See generally,* McCloskey, *supra* note 2, 111, where McCloskey writes: "[Field's] humanitarianism was not, indeed, of the type common to social reformers, who often identify themselves with the sufferers. It smacked rather of *noblesse oblige,* a sort of paternalistic attitude toward those who are put upon, a proprietary air toward constitutional rights. But this is not to disparage the sentiment."

15. Slaughter-House Cases, 83 U.S. 36, 105 (1872). Field's dissent came in response to the Court's decision to allow the State of Louisiana to grant an exclusive monopoly to a single private firm, the Crescent City Company, for the purpose of operating slaughter-houses in the state. Field insisted that the granting of a monopoly of this kind should be unconstitutional. Field's reluctance to uphold legislation he thought hostile to economic rights also appeared later, for instance, in his dissent in Munn v. Illinois, 94 U.S. 113 (1876).

In *Munn,* the Court upheld a provision in the Illinois State constitution that allowed the State Legislature to regulate heavily the prices charged by operators of grain elevators, which the state declared "public warehouses." This was Field in *Munn,* at 138, 140: "The declaration of the [Illinois] Constitution of 1870, that private buildings used for private purposes shall be deemed public institutions does not make them so. The receipt and storage of grain in a building for that purpose does not constitute the building a public warehouse. There is no magic in the language. . . . If this be sound law, if there be no protection, either in the principles upon which our government is founded, or in the prohibitions of the constitution against such invasion of private rights, all property and all business in the State are held at the mercy of a majority of its state legislature. The public has no greater interest in the use of buildings for the residences of families, nor, indeed, anything like so great an interest." (Unintentionally, Field had predicted rent control in Berkeley and Santa Monica.)

For Field, these types of state rules interfered with private property rights, thereby endangering individual liberties, particularly the liberty to pursue a lawful calling and the liberty of contract. The Louisiana rule should have been unconstitutional, according to Field's reasoning, because by granting a monopoly to one company it infringed on the liberty of other butchers to pursue a lawful trade; similarly, in *Munn,* Field suggested that the Illinois rule should have been unconstitutional because it amounted to a kind of regulatory taking, as well as an interference on the liberty of contract between farmers and operators of grain elevators. The state had no business choosing a winner in what should always be a competitive market, nor should it fix artificially the price of a commodity or service.

Field's early aversion to state interference in the market has led many scholars to conclude that he was an intellectual predecessor of the *Lochner* era, an era characterized by a general aversion to state regulation of private markets or of the terms of private labor contracts. Consider this passage, from PAUL KENS, *supra* note 2, 255–256: "In 1905 a 5 to 4 majority in *Lochner v. New York* relied on liberty of contract to invalidate a New York law limiting the hours of work in bakeries. Field had died by this time, but his influence was perhaps stronger than ever. . . . As if standing in for Field, [Justice Rufus] Peckham wrote a majority opinion that placed a heavy burden on the state to prove the legitimacy of its legislation. 'The mere assertion that the subject relates, though but in a remote degree, to the public health, does not necessarily render the enactment valid,' he wrote. 'The act must have a more direct relation, as a means to an end, and the end itself must be appropriate and legitimate.' Six years after Field's death, the transformation to his way of thinking on the matter of entrepreneurial liberty was complete." Peckham's remarks are from Lochner v. New York, 198 U.S. 45, 57–58 (1905).

16. 83 U.S. at 106.

17. Slaughter-House Cases, 111 U.S. 746, 756–757 (1884). In this version of the slaughterhouse cases, the primary issue was whether Louisiana's legislature could revoke the monopoly it had granted to the Crescent City Company. The Court's majority concluded that it could, but Field filed a separate opinion reiterating many of the ideas in his first dissent.

18. See, for instance, STEPHEN FIELD, ADDRESS AT THE CENTENNIAL CELEBRATION OF THE ORGANIZATION OF THE FEDERAL JUDICIARY (Feb. 4, 1890), reprinted in CHAUNCEY BLACK AND SAMUEL SMITH, SOME ACCOUNT OF THE WORK OF STEPHEN J. FIELD 485 (1895): "In 1776, [when Congress] declared the independence of the colonies, it proclaimed that the rights of man to life, to liberty and to the pursuit of happiness—having then arisen to a just appreciation of their true source—were held by him, not as a boon from king or parliament, or as the grant of any charter, but as the endowment of his Creator, and that to secure these rights—not to grant them—governments are instituted among men, deriving their just powers from the consent of the governed."

Similar phrases are found in STEPHEN FIELD, THE CHARACTER AND JUDICIAL LIFE OF CHIEF JUSTICE CHASE, REMARKS AT THE DINNER OF THE ASSOCIATED ALUMNI OF THE PACIFIC (Jul. 15, 1873), quoted in 2 SOME OPINIONS AND PAPERS OF STEPHEN J. FIELD 5 (1895). McCLOSKEY, *supra* note 2, 104, writes that for Field, the special character of American law appeared in a recognition of "rights which cannot be bartered away, or given away, or taken away"; "rights . . . echo with a sort of magic for him," and "Field . . . seized upon the term and made it the fulcrum of his legal and political theory."

19. *In re* Ah Fong, 3 Sawyer 144 (1874), and the appeal of this case to the Supreme Court, in Chy Lung v. Freeman, 92 U.S. 275 (1875).

20. 3 Sawyer, at 158.

21. Id., at 157.

22. *In re* Ah Yup, 5 Sawyer 155 (1878). See also, SALYER, *supra* note 10, 13. In 1870, the United States had amended naturalization rules, so that in addition to "any alien, being a free white person," the naturalization laws were "hereby extended to aliens of African nativity, and to persons of African descent." Ah Yup, 154–156. Prior to these amendments, the Naturalization Law of 1790, I U.S. Stat., ch. 3 (Mar. 26, 1790), allowed only for free "white persons" to become naturalized citizens. On this, see JAMES KETTNER, THE DEVELOPMENT OF AMERICAN CITIZENSHIP: 1608–1870 235–239 (1978). According to Sawyer's review of those amendments, he concluded that although Congress had extended naturalization to another "race," namely Americans of African descent, "Congress intended by this legislation to exclude Mongolians from the right of naturalization," and "a native of China, of the Mongolian race, is not a white person within the meaning of the act of Congress." Ah Yup, at 159.

23. The quote is from *Ex Parte* Newman, 9 Cal. 502, 528 (1858), a case concerning a state rule establishing the observation of the Sabbath.

24. See Ho Ah Kow v. Nunan, 5 Sawyer 552 (1879). Since the beginning of the Qing Dynasty, in the mid-17th century, Chinese men routinely wore their hair shaved in front, and in a long ponytail, or "queue," in back. The practice originated among the northern Manchus, who wore their hair in this manner to keep the hair out of their eyes during combat. After their conquest of the Han Chinese, the Manchus required all Han Chinese men to adopt the style as a sign of allegiance and obedience to the Manchus. The practice was bitterly resisted, and by the time the Manchus' Qing Dynasty collapsed, in 1911, Han Chinese men cut off their queues as a sign of rebellion and protest against the Manchu. See JONATHAN SPENCE, THE SEARCH FOR MODERN CHINA (1990).

25. See CHAN, *supra* note 10, 48. The change in procedure modified, of course, the original ruling in People v. Hall, 4 Cal. 399 (1854).

26. See MCCLAIN, *supra* note 5, 73–74.

27. 5 Sawyer at 564.

28. Id., at 554.

29. Id., at 559, 557.

30. Id., at 559.

31. Id., at 560.

32. Id., at 562. Emphasis and parentheses in the original.

33. Id., at 563, 562. Field's understanding of the Fourteenth Amendment—that it was a constitutional barrier against facially neutral state or local rules having a discriminatory purpose—would appear again, seven years later, in the landmark case, Yick Wo v. Hopkins, 118 U.S. 356, 373–374 (1886).

34. 5 Sawyer at 555.

35. Id., at 560.

36. Id., at 561.

37. Id., at 560.

38. McCLAIN, *supra* note 5, 74.

39. See SWISHER, *supra* note 1, 219 (1930). As the following passage from the same page shows, Swisher's biography of Field is riddled with language that is offensive to the Chinese, but it is nonetheless instructive of the aftermath of *Ho Ah Kow v. Nunan*: "Thereafter, when he stayed at the Palace Hotel in San Francisco, he was fairly swamped with attention from pig-tailed Mongolians, who with pathetic eagerness sought to perform services for him."

40. McCLAIN, *supra* note 5, 76.

41. See BLACK AND SMITH, *supra* note 18, 405.

42. See SWISHER, *supra* note 1, 220.

43. Id.

44. JOHN NORTON POMEROY, THE JUDICIAL CHARACTER OF JUDGE FIELD (May 6, 1881). He wrote: "It may be affirmed, I think, without any real doubt as to its correctness, that during the past year, by his deliberate and fearless discharge of duty, by following his own convictions to the law, and by rendering a decision in the now memorable Chinese Queue Case, which, however righteous and in accordance with the fundamental principles of constitutional law, awoke a storm of fierce opposition and hatred among all the lowest and most ignorant classes of the political party with which he was connected, Judge Field lost—nay, sacrificed—his chances, otherwise good, of a nomination by his party for the Presidency." Field and Pomeroy were close friends, and they apparently consulted on the queue ordinance case. In Field's defense, Pomeroy wrote a letter to the S. F. EVENING STAR on the same day Field read his opinion in open court; in that letter, Pomeroy defended Field and mentioned several arguments in favor of his decision, including the obligations of the Burlingame Treaty. Letter of John Norton Pomeroy to the S. F. EVENING STAR (Jul. 7, 1879), reprinted in 2 SOME OPINIONS AND PAPERS, *supra* note 18. There were other reasons why many Californians disliked Field intensely. See, for example, Charles McCurdy, *Stephen J. Field and the American Judicial Tradition*, in THE FIELDS AND THE LAW (1986), and SWISHER, *supra* note 1, chs. 3 and 9.

Specifically, Field did protect some Mexican land grants from white squatters, as in Ferris v. Coover, 10 Cal. 589 (1858), and Coryell v. Cain, 16 Cal. 567 (1860). On his protection of the railroads from state and federal taxation, see San Mateo v. Southern Pacific Rail-Road Company, 13 F. 145 (1882), the decision protecting railroads from state taxation, for which Field received the most criticism; and United States v. Stanford, 69 F. 25, and 161 U.S. 412 (1895). Sometimes, Field's protection to the railroads and their owners was very personal, as we see in SWISHER, *supra* note 1, 245: "When after Stanford's death the federal government tried to collect more than fifteen million dollars from his estate to apply on the debt owed by the California railroads to the government, Field, although he wrote none of the court opinions, gave every possible assistance to Mrs. Stanford in protecting her interest. The government failed to collect. 'Always your faithful friend,' Mrs. Stanford signed herself in a letter to him shortly after the case was won, 'and my prayers for years of usefulness here in this life.'"

45. Page Law, 18 Stat. 477 ch. 141, §§3 and 5 (Mar. 3, 1875).

46. Id., at 156. The position that Field took in *Ah Fong* became somewhat characteristic of his approach to government power more generally, in a broad range of cases. KENS, *supra* note 2, 211 (1997), explains: "[Field] believed that liberty would be best protected by confining government to a limited set of powers authorized by the Constitution. Federalism came into play in this respect. Field's theory of limited government confined the legislative activity of the states to their sphere of authority and federal activity to its sphere, not allowing one to entrench on the other. The state sphere of authority, known as the police powers of the states, was limited to protecting health, safety, morals, and peace and good order. The federal sphere of authority was confined to the powers enumerated in or implied by the Constitution." In this light, the state rule against "lewd and debauched women" entrenched on the federal sphere of authority, and so Field struck it down.

47. 5 Sawyer, at 563.

48. Interview with Justice Field, *A Possible Solution to the Chinese Problem*, S. F. ARGONAUT (Aug. 9, 1879), reprinted in 3 SOME PAPERS AND OPINIONS, *supra* note 18.

49. In a clear way, Field's approach in these immigration cases underscored his understanding of American federalism, with a strong and active federal government exercising its power where it was most appropriate, as in interstate commerce and foreign relations, and strong state governments exercising their appropriate "police powers," to tend toward the health, safety, and welfare of local political communities. It was a "dual federalism," ideally favoring neither states nor the federal government. Yet, among the judges of his time, Field seemed particularly likely to reassert federal authority in the wake of the Civil War. On this, generally, see William Wiecek, "The New Legal Order: Reconstruction and the Gilded Age," in AMERICAN LAW AND THE CONSTITUTIONAL ORDER, *supra* note 2, 235–245.

50. Interview with Justice Field, in SOME OPINIONS AND PAPERS, *supra* note 18.

51. Id. The full quote runs thus: "We may say to them, 'your people shall only come to the United States and shall only remain here for the purpose of general commerce; you shall be welcome to certain ports, and to none other; you shall engage only in foreign trade; you shall be excluded from all employments not connected with or incidental to foreign commerce; you shall be allowed the privilege of crossing our continent in pursuit of business; you shall be welcome to visit any part of our land; you may educate your youth in our colleges. But you shall not send to us an immigration to engage in the general industries of our

country; you shall not send a population to become permanent residents in the country; you shall not come into competition with our laborers; you shall not engage in mechanical and manufacturing employments; you shall not own or till our agricultural lands; nor shall you fill menial employments. . . .' Thus the question shall be solved, rationally, speedily, and peacefully."

52. Id.

53. CHAN, *supra* note 10; SPENCE, *supra* note 24; and more generally, FREDERIC WAKEMAN, THE FALL OF IMPERIAL CHINA (1975). The Burlingame Treaty itself can be taken as an instance of an "unequal treaty," one of many that the Chinese felt forced to sign at gunpoint. The Imperial Chinese would have thought that the "inalienable right of man to change his home and allegiance" was something very foreign and threatening, especially to Chinese sovereignty. The Chinese had never encouraged emigration—it was often punished by death—nor had they encouraged the ingress of "foreigners," the word itself being largely synonymous with "barbarians." That the treaty's signing was celebrated more in the United States than in a demoralized China speaks to the costs and benefits envisioned by the two parties. Moreover, the economic and political disruptions caused by foreign powers—including the United States—had been some of the primary reasons why so many poor Chinese immigrants had left their homelands, often in the face of starvation.

54. Interview with Justice Field, in SOME OPINIONS AND PAPERS, *supra* note 18, 3.

55. Open letter from Stephen Field to General Miller, *The Chinese Question*, S. F. MORNING CALL (Mar. 21, 1880), reprinted in 2 SOME OPINIONS AND PAPERS, *supra* note 18. Field and Miller were representative of the hostility toward the Chinese that had steadily been growing in the late 1870s. In fact, CARL BRENT SWISHER, MOTIVATION AND POLITICAL TECHNIQUE IN THE CALIFORNIA CONSTITUTION, 1878–1879 (1930), shows that they were just like many political and economic leaders in California, who, despite their numerous disagreements, were inclined to rail against the Chinese. By 1879, during the California constitutional conventions, the "Chinese Question" was a central concern. Harry Scheiber, *Race, Radicalism, and Reform: Historical Perspective on the 1879 California Constitution*, 17 HASTINGS CONST. L. Q. 35, 50 (1989), writes: "No single issue mobilized popular forces so effectively, or produced so powerful a response, as the racism and prejudice of the anti-Chinese movement."

56. SWISHER, *supra* note 1, 222.

57. See MCCLAIN, supra note 5, 147.

58. Id., at 148. Emphasis in the original.

59. Letter from Field to John Norton Pomeroy (Apr. 14, 1882), reprinted in HOWARD JAY GRAHAM, EVERYMAN'S CONSTITUTION 105 (1968).

60. Consider Ben Franklin's rhetorical question: "While we are Scouring our

Planet, by clearing America of Woods, and so making this Side of our globe reflect a brighter Light to the Eyes of Inhabitants of Mars or Venus, why should we in the Sight of Superior Beings, darken its People? Why increase the Sons of Africa, by Planting them in America, where we have so fair an opportunity, by excluding all Blacks and Tawneys, of increasing the lovely White?" Benjamin Franklin, *Observations Concerning the Increase of Mankind*, in 4 THE PAPERS OF BENJAMIN FRANKLIN 234 (Leonard Labaree ed., 1959). The remarks came to my attention through TAKAKI, *supra* note 8, 14.

61. *In re* Ah Sing, 13 F. 286 (1882). More specifically, Field wrote: "An American vessel is deemed a part of the territory of the state within which its home port is situated, and as part of the territory of the United States." Id., at 289.

62. *In re* Ah Tie, 13 F. 291 (1882).

63. *In re* Low Yam Chow, 13 F. 605 (1882).

64. Id., at 611.

65. Id.

66. Id., at 608.

67. Id., at 611. In a concurring opinion, District Judge Hoffman warned customs officials not to upset the compromise embodied in the Exclusion Act: "Nothing would more gratify the enemies of the bill than that in its practical operation it should be found to be unreasonable, unjust and oppressive. [If so], its repeal cannot long be averted." Id., at 616–617.

68. *In re* Ah Lung, 18 F. 28 (1883).

69. Id., at 32.

70. Id., at 30–31.

71. Id., at 32. (Emphasis in the original.)

72. SALYER, *supra* note 10, 19. (Emphasis in the original.) See 23 Stat. 115 (Jul. 5, 1884).

73. *In re* Ah Moy, 21 F. 785 (1884), and *In re* Kew Ock, 21 F. 789 (1884).

74. *In re* Tung Yeong, 19 F. 184 (1884), and *In re* Leong Yick Dew, 19 F. 493, on 493 (1884).

75. *In re* Cheen Heong, 21 F. 791, 793 (1884). Field's assertion that the Chinese could not be trusted to testify truthfully echoed Chief Justice Hugh Murray's reasoning in People v. Hall, 4 Cal. 399 (1854). In that case, the California Supreme Court overturned George Hall's conviction for murder on the grounds that Chinese witnesses had improperly testified during his trial. This is what Murray wrote to justify the exclusion of the Chinese from the administration of justice: "The anomalous spectacle of a distinct people, living in our community, recognizing no laws of this State, except through necessity, bringing with them their prejudices and national feuds, in which they indulge in open violation of law; whose mendacity is proverbial; a race of people whom nature has marked as inferior, and who are incapable of progress or intellectual development

beyond a certain point, as their history has shown; differing in language, opinions, color, and physical conformation; between whom and ourselves nature has placed an impassable difference, is now presented, and for them is claimed, not only the right to swear away the life of a citizen, but the further privilege of participating with us in administering the affairs of our Government." 4 Cal., 404–405.

76. *In re* Ah Moy, 21 F. 808 (1884).

77. The quote is actually from Judge Lorenzo Sawyer's dissent. "I think it would be a great hardship, not to say a gross violation of her personal rights, to refuse [bail] upon security satisfactory to the court. I think she should be admitted to bail." Id., at 810. On the exclusionist tendency during these years, generally, see TAKAKI, *supra* note 1, 231–239. On immigration procedure and the tendency to incarcerate deportable aliens, since the Chinese exclusion period, see Hiroshi Motomura, *The Curious Evolution of Immigration Law: Procedural Surrogates for Substantive Constitutional Rights*, 92 COLUM. L. REV. 1625 (1992).

78. *In re* Look Tin Sing, 21 F. 905 (1884).

79. Id., at 906.

80. Id., at 910. This reading of the citizenship clause of the Fourteenth Amendment was clearly controversial, and it reflected a very controversial history. The framers of the Reconstruction amendments thought about the Chinese immigrants in their deliberations, and many felt that the children of those immigrants should not be granted citizenship as a birthright. For a thorough discussion of this topic, see John Hayakawa Torok, *Reconstruction and Racial Nativism: Chinese Immigrants and the Debates on the 13th, 14th and 15th Amendments and Civil Rights Laws*, 3 ASIAN L. J. 55 (1996). Field maintained: "The clause as to citizenship was inserted in the [14th] amendment not merely as an authoritative declaration of the generally recognized law of the country, so far as the white race is concerned, but also to overrule the doctrine of the *Dred Scott Case*. . . . When it was adopted, the naturalization laws of the United States excluded colored persons from becoming citizens . . . [but] the inability of persons to become citizens under those laws in no respect impairs the effect of their birth, or of mere birth of their children, upon the status of *either* as citizens under the amendment in question." 21 F., at 909. Emphasis in the original.

81. 21 F., at 910–911.

82. See United States v. Wong Kim Ark, 169 U.S. 649 (1898). Gray's majority opinion in that decision follows Field's reasoning very closely, particularly his review of English and American common-law rules on citizenship, and his interpretation of the 14th Amendment.

83. 21 F., at 910.

84. *Chew Heong v. United States*, 112 U.S. 536, 537 (1884).

85. Id., at 555, 559–560. Harlan continued: "It would be a perversion of the

language used to hold that such regulations apply to Chinese laborers who had left the country with the privilege, secured by treaty, of returning, but who, by reason of their absence when those legislative enactments took effect, could not obtain the required certificates."

86. Id., at 562.

87. Id.

88. Id., at 574–575.

89. Id., at 577. On 562, in favor of carrying out the spirit and letter of the Exclusion Act, irrespective of the language of the earlier treaty, Field insisted that the treaty did not limit the Act, for both were on equal constitutional footing.

90. Id., at 565.

91. Id.

92. Id.

93. Id., at 568.

94. Id., at 568. Consider SWISHER, *supra* note 1, 209–210: "[Chinese] laborers competed actively and successfully with white laborers, and did, for instance, a substantial part of the work in the construction of the Central Pacific Railroad. Many of them hired out to work on farms. They served as cooks and helpers in many households. They took over a large part of the laundry business in the cities, and made themselves generally useful wherever unskilled labor was needed. They lived on next to nothing, and worked for wages which white men would not accept. Add to these facts their peculiar mannerisms of speech, of dress, and of general living, and it is not surprising that the Chinese were highly unpopular with a large percentage of the Californians, particularly of the workers, and that they became increasingly unpopular with the increase in the number of yellow immigrants arriving in the country." Swisher's words and diction, as well as his own unexplored prejudices toward the Chinese, follow Field's very closely—the biographer seems to have taken on something of his subject's persona.

95. Even though Field was known to have violently disliked men like Dennis Kearney, the leader of the Workingmen's Party in California, a political organization built around Chinese exclusion, he sadly adopted his rhetoric here. The slogan, and the argument that the Chinese "underlived" whites, belonged to Kearney. On the relationship, or lack thereof, between Kearney and Field, see SWISHER, *supra* note 1, 250, 403; on the Workingmen's Party, and their strategy to unify white workers through their violent opposition to Chinese immigration, see SALYER, *supra* note 10, 12. On these matters, TAKAKI, *supra* note 8, 29, offers these thoughts: "Capital used Chinese laborers as a transnational reserve army to weight down white workers during periods of economic expansion and to hold white labor in check during periods of over-production. Labor was a major cost of production, and employers saw how the importation of Chinese workers could boost the supply of labor and drive down the wages of both

Chinese and white workers. The resulting racial antagonism generated between the two groups helped to ensure a divided working class and a dominant employer class." See also, JOHN HIGHAM, STRANGERS IN THE LAND: PATTERNS OF AMERICAN NATIVISM, 1860–1925 (1978), and SANDMEYER, *supra* note 10.

96. *Chew Heong*, 112 U.S., at 578. Justice Bradley put it more directly: "Chinese of the lower classes have little regard for the solemnity of an oath." Id., at 579. Bradley, dissenting.

97. Id., at 578.

98. Id., at 568.

99. Id., at 567.

100. Id., at 569. McCurdy compares Field's racist sentiments here to those of Theodore Sedgwick, who, McCurdy contends, heavily influenced Field's thinking on these matters. In THEODORE SEDGWICK, PUBLIC AND PRIVATE ECONOMY (1836), reprinted in McCurdy, *supra* note 44, 17, Sedgwick wrote: "It is enough for us to know that the Supreme Being has seen fit to separate his people on this earth into various families, and that the white man stands at the head of these families. As the white people, then, are at the head of the human families, they are bound to advance, to go forward in the race of civilization, and never backward by amalgamation, intermarriage, or any kind of corruption of pure blood. The interests of humanity [and] of free government . . . depend upon the white man's retaining his superiority."

NOTES TO CHAPTER 5

1. For specific histories of Chinese beyond the West Coast, see Edward Rhoads, *The Chinese in Texas*, 81 SOUTHWESTERN HIST. Q. 1 (1977); ROBERT QUAN, LOTUS AMONG THE MAGNOLIAS: THE MISSISSIPPI CHINESE (1982); JAMES LOEWEN, THE MISSISSIPPI CHINESE: BETWEEN BLACK AND WHITE (1988); CHINESE IMMIGRANTS AND AMERICAN LAW (Charles McClain, ed., 1994); ARTHUR BONNER, ALAS! WHAT BROUGHT THEE HITHER? THE CHINESE IN NEW YORK 1800–1950 (1997); and Edward Rhoads, *Asian Pioneers in the Eastern United States: Chinese Cutlery Workers in Beaver Falls, Pennsylvania, in the 1870s*, 2 J. ASIAN AMER. STU. 119 (1999).

2. The most famous phrase from that most famous case ran thus: "Though the law be fair on its face and impartial in appearance, yet, if it is applied and administered by public authority with an evil eye and an unequal hand, so as practically to make unjust and illegal discriminations between persons in similar circumstances, material to their rights, the denial of equal justice is still within the prohibition of the Constitution." 118 U.S., at 373–374.

3. 13 F. 229, at 233 (1882).

4. Id. On laundries and economic rights, see Thomas Joo, *New "Conspiracy*

Theory" of the Fourteenth Amendment: Nineteenth-Century Chinese Civil Rights Cases and the Development of Substantive Due Process Jurisprudence, 29 U.S.F. L. REV. 353 (1995). For many legal scholars, Field's legal theory on economic rights form the groundwork for cases like Lochner v. New York, 198 U.S. 45 (1905), as discussed in the last chapter. See also Charles McCurdy, *Justice Field and the Jurisprudence of Government-Business Relations*, 61 J. AM. HIST. (1975), reprinted in AMERICAN LAW AND THE CONSTITUTIONAL ORDER, 246–266 (Lawrence Friedman and Harry Scheiber, eds., 1988); and Howard Graham, *Justice Field and the Fourteenth Amendment*, 52 YALE L. J. 851 (1943). Field himself expresses his views well in the two *Slaughter-House Cases*, 83 U.S. 36, at 89, 106 (1873), and 111 U.S. 746, 754–760 (1884), and in Munn v. Illinois, 94 U.S. 113, 138–154 (1876), as discussed in the last chapter, note 15. Later in his essay, on 265, McCurdy, suggested that Field's economic jurisprudence was mistaken by the Court in the 1920s: "The Court had not only transformed Field's police-power dicta into an iron law of 'liberty to contract,' but also had permitted the states to devolve eminent domain powers." Graham, on 856–857, suggested that in cases involving "economic liberty," Field was especially concerned about "communistic," or "Marxist" legislation. He says this, on 857: "Like many Americans living in the chaos of the Reconstruction period, fearful that their new industrial order might be jeopardized almost at the moment of its birth, Justice Field was appalled at the recrudescence of revolution in Europe. Under the cumulative impact of successive shocks, and because his personal experiences abroad and in California rendered him particularly sensitive to these influences, he became an apostle of reaction, determined, in his own later phrase, 'to strengthen, if I could, all conservative men.' The evidence is clearly such as to mark the Paris Commune as an important pivot in American constitutional history, a chronological and doctrinal key both to Justice Field's career and to the historical evolution of the Fourteenth Amendment."

5. *Soon Hing v. Crowley*, 113 U.S., at 710. This case has a companion case, decided by Field on the same day. In *Barbier v. Connolly*, 113 U.S. 27 (1885), Field also denied that there was a Fourteenth Amendment equal protection violation against the same laundry ordinances in San Francisco. In *Barbier*, the primary plaintiffs were French, and they alleged that the City was targeting laundries in violation of Field's earlier decision in *Quong Woo*. For greater background and detail, see CHARLES MCCLAIN, IN SEARCH OF EQUALITY: THE CHINESE STRUGGLE AGAINST DISCRIMINATION IN NINETEENTH-CENTURY AMERICA 126 (1994).

6. See, again, MCCLAIN, *supra* note 5, ch. 4.

7. See SUCHENG CHAN, ASIAN AMERICANS: AN INTERPRETIVE HISTORY (1991); CHINESE IMMIGRANTS AND THE LAW, *supra* note 1; MCCLAIN, *supra* note 5; LUCY SALYER, LAWS HARSH AS TIGERS: CHINESE IMMIGRANTS AND THE SHAPING OF MODERN IMMIGRATION LAW (1995).

8. CHAN, *supra* note 7, 48–49. On the issue of violence against Chinese immigrants during this era, see generally, ANTI-CHINESE VIOLENCE IN NORTH AMERICA (Roger Daniels, ed., 1978), and McCLAIN, *supra* note 5, ch. 7.

9. McCLAIN, *supra* note 5, 173–176, at 173.

10. Id.

11. CHAN, *supra* note 7, 51.

12. The best account of Baldwin v. Franks, 120 U.S. 678 (1887), is in Mc-CLAIN, *supra* note 5, ch. 7. Technically odd, the case tested the holding of the Court in the notorious case of United States v. Harris, 106 U.S. 629 (1882). In that earlier case, the Court overturned the federal convictions of several white men in Tennessee who had beaten four black prisoners and murdered one of them while they were in the custody of a state deputy sheriff. Following United States v. Cruikshank, 92 U.S. 542 (1875), the Court held that when *private* citizens conspire to "deprive" one another of Fourteenth Amendment protections, it is not within the federal power to punish the wrongdoers, because the Fourteenth Amendment specifically prohibits a *state* from depriving those rights, but says nothing of what individual private citizens do to one another. Thus, the portions of the Civil Rights Act of 1871 that concern criminal conspiracies to deprive equal protection or due process were not constitutional because they pertained to private conduct. This logic—that Fourteenth Amendment violations could be reviewed in federal courts only when "state action" was involved—gained its clearest expression in the Civil Rights Cases, 109 U.S. 3 (1883). Of the corruption of local officials, see McCLAIN, *supra* note 5, at 175: "Given the temper of the times in the West, it seemed to the Chinese entirely unrealistic to expect local authorities to use municipal law to blunt what were in effect the manifestations of a quasi-political movement enjoying wide societal support—especially when these local authorities were themselves more often than not in the movement's vanguard."

13. 120 U.S., at 691.

14. Id., at 702.

15. Id., at 707.

16. Scott Act, 25 Stat. 504 (Oct. 1, 1888).

17. CHAN, *supra* note 7, 55.

18. Chae Chan Ping v. United States, 130 U.S. 581, 603, 606 (1889).

19. Id., at 594, 595.

20. Id., at 595.

21. Id., at 598.

22. Id., at 603.

23. Id., at 595.

24. Id.

25. Id., at 595.

26. Id., at 596.

27. Id., at 602–603. He continued: "We do not mean to intimate that the moral aspects of legislative acts may not be proper subjects of consideration. Undoubtedly they may be, at proper times and places, before the public, in the halls of Congress, and in all the modes by which the public mind can be influenced. Public opinion thus enlightened, brought to bear upon legislation, will do more than all other causes to prevent abuses; but the province of the courts is to pass upon the validity of laws, not to make them, and when their validity is established, to declare their meaning and apply their provisions. All else lies beyond their domain."

28. Id.

29. Id., at 605. Field, quoting Justice John Marshall in *Cohens v. Virginia*, 19 U.S. 264, 413–414 (1821). The quote continues: "In war, we are one people. In making peace we are one people. In all commercial regulations, we are one and the same people. In many other respects, the American people are one; and the government which is alone capable of controlling and managing their interests in all these respects, is the government of the Union. It is their government, and in that character they have no other. America has chosen to be in many respects, and to many purposes, a nation; and for all these purposes her government is complete; to all these objects, it is competent. The people have declared, that in the exercise of all powers given for these objects, it is supreme. It can then in affecting these objects legitimately control all individuals or governments within the American territory. The constitution and laws of a State, so far as they are repugnant to the Constitution and laws of the United States, are absolutely void."

30. 130 U.S., at 606.

31. Id., at 603. This claim of federal power *was*, however, controversial, in light of the history of state rules regarding immigration, prior to federal legislation. See GERALD NEUMAN, STRANGERS TO THE CONSTITUTION: IMMIGRANTS, BORDERS, AND FUNDAMENTAL LAW ch. 2 (1996). That the federal government could claim powers not expressly enumerated in the Constitution was clearly controversial and reflected a new political reality. See Louis Henkin, *The Constitution and United States Sovereignty*, 100 HARV. L. REV. 853, 855 (1987): "That the federal government had unenumerated powers probably would not have been claimed, and surely would not have been accepted, before Union victory in the Civil War, vanquished states' rights and established federal supremacy by constitutional amendments imposed as the peace treaty of the war."

32. 130 U.S., at 606.

33. Id.

34. Id., at 609.

35. Scalia, dissenting, in Zadvydas v. Davis, and Immigration and Naturalization Service v. Kim Ho Ma, 533 U.S. 678 (2001).

36. Justice Brewer, quoted in Owen Fiss, *David J. Brewer: The Judge as Missionary*, in THE FIELDS AND THE LAW 53 (1986).

37. Brewer, however, was not particularly sympathetic to other racial groups in America—like his uncle, Justice Field, who had by now written the dissent in *Strauder v. Virginia* and had sided with the majority in the *Civil Rights Cases*, Brewer often decided against African American claims for relief from the Court. Yet "Brewer consistently spoke out in protest against the treatment of the Chinese and did so in the most forceful terms." Field sometimes took exception to Brewer's dissents, but within a few years, as we shall see, Field and Brewer drew closer together during the final years of Field's tenure. By the time Brewer joined the bench, in 1889, Field was already seventy-three years old. Of Field's attitude toward African Americans and the rising era of Jim Crow, see Strauder v. West Virginia, 100 U.S. 303 (1879); *Ex Parte* Virginia, 100 U.S. 339 (1879), and the Civil Rights Cases, 109 U.S. 3 (1883). In the Virginia cases, Field dissented in a decision striking down the exclusion of African Americans from juries. In the *Civil Rights Cases*, Field did not write, but merely joined, the majority opinion, which struck down the Civil Rights Act of 1875 that provided for civil and criminal penalties against any private person discriminating against African Americans seeking to use private facilities equally with others. On Brewer, see Fiss, *supra* note 36, 55. Fiss shows, again, how Brewer wasn't particularly protective of African Americans. For instance, see Louisville, New Orleans and Texas Railway Company v. Mississippi, 133 U.S. 587 (1890), which in many ways is a predecessor of Plessy v. Ferguson, 163 U.S. 537 (1896). In the Mississippi case, Brewer held that a state law requiring separate accommodations for black and white passengers did not violate the commerce clause, because the state rule only applied to intrastate commerce. Harlan dissented, as he did in *Plessy*. On Brewer generally, see MICHAEL BRODHEAD, DAVID J. BREWER, THE LIFE OF A SUPREME COURT JUSTICE, 1837–1910 ch. 8 (1994).

38. Quock Ting v. United States, 140 U.S. 417, 418 (1891).

39. Id., at 419–420. Field continued: "A boy of any intelligence, arriving at that age, would remember, even after the lapse of six years, some words of the language of the country, some names of the streets or places or some circumstances that would satisfy one that he had been in the city before. But there was nothing whatever of this kind shown. He gave the name of no person he had seen; he described no locality or incident relating to his life in the city, nor did he repeat a single word of the language, which he must have heard during the greater part of several years, if he was there. The testimony of the father was also devoid of any incident or circumstance corroborative of his statement."

40. RONALD TAKAKI, STRANGERS FROM A DIFFERENT SHORE 117 (1989).

41. 140 U.S., at 423.

42. Id., at 424.

43. BILL ONG HING, MAKING AND REMAKING OF ASIAN AMERICA THROUGH IMMIGRATION POLICY, 1850–1990 73–74 (1993).

44. Id., at 74; and TAKAKI, *supra* note 40, 234. For an extensive discussion of how immigration authorities attempted to sort through Chinese entrants, and of how the entrants sought to evade the immigration law, see Kitty Calavita, *The Paradoxes of Race, Class, Identity, and "Passing": Enforcing the Chinese Exclusion Acts, 1882–1910*, 25 LAW & SOC. INQUIRY 1 (2000).

45. 140 U.S., at 428.

46. Geary Act, 27 Stat. 25 (May 5, 1892).

47. Id., §4.

48. HING, *supra* note 43, 25: "Claiming that Chinese names and faces were all alike, the nativists argued that a registration requirement was necessary to distinguish those who were legally in the United States prior to exclusion from those who might have been smuggled in afterward."

49. Fong Yue Ting v. United States, 149 U.S. 698, 704–705 (1893). On the organized civil disobedience of the Chinese in response to the Geary Act, see McCLAIN, *supra* note 5, 203–206. McClain drew this quote, on 206, from the Equal Rights League, a Chinese American organization: "We feel keenly the disgrace unjustly and maliciously heaped upon us by cruel Congress. That for the purpose of prohibiting Chinese immigration more than one hundred thousand honest and respectable Chinese residents should be made to wear the badge of disgrace as ticket-of-leave men in your penitentiaries; that they should be tagged and branded as a whole lot of cattle for the slaughter; that they should be seen upon your streets with tearful eyes and heavy hearts, objects of scorn and public ridicule."

50. Id., at 705, 706, 713, 714, 720, 722, 724, 730, 731.

51. Id., at 714. The naturalization law to which Justice Gray refers is the Naturalization Act of 1790, which stipulates that only "white persons" could become naturalized citizens. See JAMES KETTNER, THE DEVELOPMENT OF AMERICAN CITIZENSHIP: 1608–1870 (1978).

52. 149 U.S., at 707. He went on: "The power to exclude aliens and the power to expel them rest upon one foundation, are derived from one source, are supported by the same reasons, and are in truth but parts of one and the same power." And also, "The power of Congress, therefore, to expel, like the power to exclude aliens, or any specified class of aliens, from the country, may be exercised entirely through executive officers; or Congress may call in the aid of the judiciary to ascertain any contested facts on which an alien's right to be in the country has been made by Congress to depend." Id., at 714.

53. Id., at 707, 708, and 709.

54. Id., at 724.

55. Id., at 730.

56. Id.

57. Id., at 714.

58. Id., at 731.

59. Id., at 746.
60. Id.
61. Id. The law to which Justice Field refers concerns sedition, 1 Stat. 570.
62. Id., at 748.
63. Id., at 749.
64. Id., at 759.
65. Id., at 751.
66. Id.
67. Id., at 750.
68. Id., at 754.
69. Id., at 749.

70. On the practice of "mixed juries," which Field invoked, See MARIANNE CONSTABLE, THE LAW OF THE OTHER: THE MIXED JURIES AND CHANGING INTERPRETATIONS OF CITIZENSHIP, LAW, AND KNOWLEDGE (1994). Constable shows how the practice of "mixed juries"—juries composed half of citizens, half of aliens or denizens, depending on the parties to the suit—were used in England up until the time of the Norman Conquest, after which the conquerors eliminated the practice.

71. 149 U.S., at 754–755.
72. Id., at 755.
73. Id., at 760.

74. Id., at 750. He continued: "The unnaturalized resident feels it to-day, but if Congress can disregard the guaranties with respect to any one domiciled in this country with its consent, it may disregard the guaranties with respect to naturalized citizens. What assurance have we that it may not declare that naturalized citizens of a particular country cannot remain in the United States after a certain day, unless they have in their possession a certificate that they are of good moral character and attached to the principles of our Constitution, which certificate they must obtain from a collector of internal revenue upon the testimony of at least one competent witness of a class or nationality to be designated by the government? What answer could the naturalized citizen in that case make to his arrest for deportation, which cannot be urged in behalf of the Chinese laborer of today?" Id., at 761.

75. Id., at 737–738.
76. Id., at 744.
77. See CHAN, *supra* note 7, 51.
78. 149 U.S., at 756.
79. Alan Westin, *Stephen J. Field and the Headnote to* O'Neil v. Vermont: *A Snapshot of the Fuller Court at Work*, 67 YALE L. J. 363, 381 (1958).
80. Id., at 382. Specifically, Field said: "As a general rule, it would be dangerous to increase the bench for the purpose of correcting a bad decision, but where that decision goes to the very essentials of Constitutional Government, the ques-

tion of an increase of the bench may properly be considered and acted upon. Surely the American people are not to submit to such a doctrine as has been announced in this case—which is nothing else than the Safeguards of the Constitution for life, liberty and property can be suspended by Congress, with reference to any class, at its pleasure." (Westin quotes from a letter from Field to Dickensen, in *Dickensen Papers*, Manuscript Division, Library of Congress, Washington, D.C., June 17, 1893.)

Whatever the efficacy of court-packing, Field's faith in Harlan may have been misplaced. Justice Harlan's experience with Chinese immigrants is detailed in Gabriel Chin, *The Plessy Myth: Justice Harlan and the Chinese Cases*, 82 IOWA L. REV. 151 (1996). Chin points out that Harlan's opinion in *Chew Heong* may have been an exception to his general practice of using degrading, racist language toward the Chinese, and of ruling against them in court. "Harlan's voting record as a whole . . . shows that his animosity towards the Chinese was fixed and strong." Id., at 158. At any rate, Field was very disturbed with the original decision: "That decision has affected me very unpleasantly. I am not willing that any one of [the Constitutional Amendments] should be given up; nor am I willing to have it held that Congress has the power to suspend their guaranty and security with reference to any person who is a subject at peace with us and who is a resident in our country by our consent."

81. CARL BRENT SWISHER, STEPHEN J. FIELD, CRAFTSMAN OF THE LAW 442–444 (1930).

82. Wong Wing v. United States, 163 U.S. 228 (1896).

83. Id., at 234–235. The most important of the "previous decisions" cited by Shiras was probably *Lem Moon Sing v. United States*, 158 U.S. 538, which held that "the decisions of the appropriate immigration or custom officers should be *final*, unless reversed on appeal to the Secretary of the Treasury," and that thus, exclusion could be "enforced exclusively through executive officers, without judicial intervention." Justice Harlan, in his majority opinion for Lem Moon Sing, relied on another case, Nishimura Ekiu v. United States, 142 U.S. 651 (1892). The doctrine appears again in Yamataya v. Fisher, 189 U.S. 86 (1903), United States v. Sing Tuck, 194 U.S. 161 (1904), and United States v. Ju Toy, 198 U.S. 253 (1905). "Judicial interference" was only warranted in cases where executive officers showed clear prejudice to the petitioner, as was alleged in Chin Yow v. United States, 208 U.S. 8 (1908); Tang Tun v. Edsell, 223 U.S. 673 (1912); and Kwock Jan Fat v. White, 253 U.S. 454 (1920).

84. SALYER, *supra* note 7, 116. The Ninth Circuit, in particular, was noted for the number and frequency of habeas corpus petitions granted in immigration matters. See generally, Christian Fritz, *A Nineteenth Century "Habeas Corpus Mill": The Chinese before the Federal Courts of California*, 32 AM. J. LEGAL HIST. 347, 371–372 (1988). Even the Ninth Circuit, however, would turn against Chinese litigants soon, as it was staffed with a new round of judges,

some of whom had pushed for restrictive legislation themselves while serving in Congress. For more background on that shift, see DAVID FREDERICK, RUGGED JUSTICE (1994), esp. ch. 3, 62–77.

85. See Kew Ock, 21 F., at 790. Field had said there, to another petitioner who had been without another kind of certificate, that "the remedy, if he is to have any, must come from the officers in Washington who have control over the collector. The court has no jurisdiction to supervise his actions towards the petitioner, and direct the special performance of any neglected duty to him."

86. *Wong Wing*, 163 U.S., at 235.

87. Id., at 237.

88. Id., at 238. Shiras said, specifically, "All persons within the territory of the United States are entitled to the protections guaranteed by [the Fifth and Sixth] amendments, and that even aliens shall not be held to answer for a capital crime or other infamous crime, unless on a presentment or indictment of a grand jury, nor be deprived of life, liberty or property without due process of law."

89. Id., at 239.

90. Id., at 242–243.

91. Id., at 241.

92. Id. He continued: "Imprisonment at hard labor for a definite period is not only punishment, but it is punishment of an infamous character. . . . Imprisonment at hard labor in a state prison is also *servitude*, to which no person under the constitution can be subjected except as punishment for crime, whereof he shall have been duly convicted." Id., at 242. Emphasis in the original.

93. Id., at 243.

94. SWISHER, *supra* note 81, 448.

95. See McCurdy, *supra* note 4; ROBERT McCLOSKEY, AMERICAN CONSERVATISM IN THE AGE OF ENTERPRISE (1951); Graham, *supra* note 4; and SWISHER, *supra* note 81.

96. For helpful historical insights into its original political appeal and then its demise, see Michael Les Benedict, *Laissez Faire and Liberty: A Revaluation of the Meaning and Origins of Laissez Faire Constitutionalism*, 3 LAW & HIST. REV. 293 (1985); HOWARD GILLMAN, THE CONSTITUTION BESIEGED: THE RISE AND DEMISE OF LOCHNER ERA POLICE POWERS JURISPRUDENCE (1993); and G. EDWARD WHITE, THE CONSTITUTION AND THE NEW DEAL (2002).

97. See, for example, Lapina v. Williams, 232 U.S. 78 (1914); Missouri v. Holland, 252 U.S. 416 (1920); United States v. Curtiss-Wright Export, 299 U.S. 304 (1936); Bridges v. Wixon, 326 U.S. 135 (1945); Dennis v. United States, 341 U.S. 494 (1951); Shaughnessy v. United States, 345 U.S. 206 (1953); Boutilier v. Immigration and Naturalization Service, 387 U.S. 118 (1967); Graham v. Richardson, 403 U.S. 365 (1971); Kleindienst v. Mandel, 408 U.S. 753 (1972);

Fiallo v. Bell, 430 U.S. 787 (1977); Jean v. Nelson, 727 F.2d 957 (1984); Jean v. Nelson, 472 U.S. 846 (1985); Bruno v. Albright, 339 U.S. App. D.C. 78 (1999); and Zadvydas v. Davis, 533 U.S. 678 (2001).

98. Jean v. Nelson, 472 U.S. 846 (1985), Marshall dissenting. In another dissenting opinion, in Kleindienst v. Mandel, 408 U.S. 753 (1972), Marshall had criticized the Chinese Exclusion Cases and the plenary powers doctrine. The case concerned the exclusion of a European intellectual for his political ideas, an exclusion that the Court's majority had upheld. The majority had relied on the exclusion cases, to which Marshall replied: "These are not the strongest precedents in the United States Reports, and the majority's baroque approach reveals its reluctance to rely upon them completely . . . all governmental power—even the war power, the power to maintain national security, or the power to conduct foreign affairs—is limited by the Bill of Rights. When individual freedoms of Americans are at stake, we do not blindly defer to broad claims of the Legislative Branch or Executive Branch, but rather we consider those claims in light of the individual freedoms." One might suppose that Field would have approved of this statement.

99. See, for example, United States v. Gue Lim, 176 U.S. 459 (1900); Traux v. Raich, 239 U.S. 33 (1915); and Flemming v. Nestor, 363 U.S. 603 (1960).

100. See the majority opinion by Justice Rhenquist, and the dissenting opinion by Justice Souter, each in Demore v. Kim, 2003 U.S. LEXIS 3428 (2003). The lower federal Circuit Courts have also divided on the meaning and significance of *Wong Wing*, especially in light of new immigration rules passed in 1996. In part, these rules provide for indefinite detention of aliens, at least in theory. Please see, for example: Zadvyas v. Underdown, 185 F. 3d 279 (1999); and Ma v. Reno, 208 F. 3d 815 (2000). Issues in both of these cases were raised again before the Supreme Court in Zadvydas v. Davis, 533 U.S. 678 (2001), then settled in favor of the immigrant plaintiffs by a majority relying in part on Field's reasoning in *Wong Wing*. In part of the majority opinion, Justice Breyer agreed that the detention of aliens—especially over indefinite periods—should be subject to judicial review.

101. Hiroshi Motomura, *The Curious Evolution of Immigration Law: Procedural Surrogates for Substantive Constitutional Rights*, 92 COLUM. L. REV. 1625 (1992). For more background into this curious evolution, see also, Peter Schuck, *The Transformation of Immigration Law*, 84 COLUM. L. REV. 1 (1984).

NOTES TO CHAPTER 6

1. The figures for European immigration are from the IMMIGRATION AND NATURALIZATION SERVICE, STATISTICAL YEARBOOK Table 2 (1989); the

figures for the Chinese American population are from RONALD TAKAKI, STRANGERS FROM A DIFFERENT SHORE 111–112 (1989).

2. TAKAKI, *supra* note 1, 231.

3. United States v. Sing Tuck, 194 U.S. 161 (1904).

4. The first of these cases was, from Justice Field's time, Lem Moon Sing v. United States, 158 U.S. 538 (1895). That case was followed by Fuk Yong Yo v. United States, 185 U.S. 296 (1902); Chin Bak Kan v. United States, 186 U.S. 193 (1902); and Yamataya v. Fisher, 189 U.S. 86 (1903).

5. See 194 U.S., at 167–170.

6. For a thorough discussion of the divisions among federal courts over Chinese habeas corpus petitions, see generally, LUCY SALYER, LAWS HARSH AS TIGERS pt. II (1995).

7. 194 U.S. at 168.

8. Id., Brewer's quote is at 177, Holmes at 170.

9. See SALYER, *supra* note 6.

10. See United States v. Ju Toy, 198 U.S. at 253, 255 (1905).

11. See, for example, *In re* Jung Ah Lung, 25 Fed. Rep. 141 (1885), Gee Fook Sing v. United States, 49 Fed. Rep. 146 (1892), and *In re* Jew Wong Loy, 91 Fed. Rep. 240 (1898).

12. 198 U.S., at 263.

13. See, for example, Chin Yow v. United States, 280 US 8, 12 (1907), where "the petitioner was prevented by the officials of the Commissioner from obtaining testimony, including that of named witnesses." In Kwock Jan Fat v. White, 253 U.S. 454 (1919), immigration officials prohibited the testimony of three "important white witnesses" who could establish the petitioner's claim of birthright citizenship. Justice Clarke concluded, "It is better that many Chinese immigrants should be improperly admitted than that one natural born citizen of the United States should be permanently excluded from his country." Id., at 464. The sentiment was repeated again in Ng Fung Ho v. White, 259 U.S. 276, 284–285 (1922), by Justice Brandeis: "To deport one who so claims to be a citizen obviously deprives him of liberty. . . . It may result also in loss of both property and life, of all that makes life worth living. . . . Against the danger of such deprivation without the sanction afforded by judicial proceedings, the Fifth Amendment affords protection in its guarantee of due process of law."

14. In 1925, for example, in Kaplan v. Tod, 267 U.S. 228 (1925), the same fiction appeared again. The facts were heartbreaking: "The appellant was born in Russia. On July 20, 1914, being then about thirteen years old, she was brought to this country, where her father already was, by her mother. Upon examination she was certified to be feeble-minded, and was ordered to be excluded, but before the order was carried into effect the European war had begun. Deportation necessarily was suspended, and she was kept at Ellis Island until June, 1915." Id., at 230. Afterward, she stayed with the Hebrew Sheltering and

Immigrant Aid Society, in New York City, until 1920, when her father became a naturalized citizen. Amazingly, in 1923, the Immigration Service filed an order to have the petitioner deported, based on the original order of 1914. And despite nine years in the country, and despite the naturalization of her father, and despite his repeated pleas to have his daughter live with him and his wife in New York, Holmes ruled that because she had never lawfully "entered" the United States, she remained subject to the exclusion order. Holmes said: "The appellant could not lawfully have landed in the United States in view of the express prohibition of the [immigration law], and until she landed 'could not have dwelled in the United States.' Moreover, while she was at Ellis Island she was regarded as stopped at the boundary line and kept there unless and until her right to enter should be declared. When her prison bounds were enlarged by committing her to the custody of the Hebrew Society, the nature of her stay within the territory was not changed. She was still in theory of law at the boundary line and had gained no foothold in the United States. She never has been dwelling in the United States. . . . Still more clearly she never has begun to reside permanently in the United States." Id.

Citing *Ju Toy*, Holmes upheld the order for this "feeble-minded" girl, nine years in the United States, to leave the country, her mother, and her father, all because, in the legal fiction of immigration law that he had created, she was never really in the country at all. "Theoretically she is in custody at the limit of the jurisdiction awaiting the order of the authorities." Id., at 231.

The fiction appeared several decades later in a set of important cases involving exclusion proceedings in the 1950s, one of which involved a Chinese alien. In that case, Leng May Ma v. Barber, 357 U.S. 185 (1958), Justice Clark said: "For over a half century this Court has held that the detention of an alien in custody pending determination of his admissibility does not legally constitute an entry though the alien is physically within the United States." Also, "The parole of aliens seeking admission is simply a device through which needless confinement is avoided while administrative proceedings are conducted. It was never intended to affect an alien's status, and to hold that petitioner's parole placed her legally 'within the United States' is inconsistent with the congressional mandate, the administrative concept of parole, and the decisions of this Court." Justice Clark didn't think this a bad thing: "Certainly this policy reflects the humane qualities of an enlightened civilization." Id., at 188 and 190.

15. See LISA LOWE, IMMIGRANT ACTS: ON ASIAN AMERICAN CULTURAL POLITICS 6 (1998).

16. JONATHAN SPENCE, THE SEARCH FOR MODERN CHINA 161 (1990).

17. TAKAKI, *supra* note 1, 235–236 (1989). For recent scholarship on Chinese immigrants creating family relationships, forging documents, and misrepresenting their true place of birth, all to evade immigration rules, see Mae Ngai, *Legacies of Exclusion: Illegal Chinese Immigration during the Cold War Years,*

18 J. AMER. ETHN. HIST. 3 (1998); XIAOJIAN ZHAO, REMAKING CHINESE AMERICA: IMMIGRATION, FAMILY, AND COMMUNITY, 1940–1965 (2002); and Madeline Hsu, *Gold Mountain Dreams and Paper Son Schemes*, CHINESE AMERICA: HISTORY AND PERSPECTIVES (1997). For examples of some of the more creative ways that the Chinese used to enter the country illegally, including the use of empty peanut shells, see ERICA LEE, AT AMERICA'S GATES: CHINESE IMMIGRATION DURING THE EXCLUSION ERA 1882–1943 (2003).

18. United States v. Wong Kim Ark, 169 U.S. 649 (1898).

19. United States v. Wong You, 223 U.S. 67, 69 (1912).

20. See, for example, Tang Tun v. Edsell, 223 U.S. 673 (1912), with Justice Hughes writing for a majority; United States v. Woo Jan, 245 U.S. 552 (1917), with Justice McKenna writing for a majority; Yee Won v. White, 256 U.S. 399 (1921), with Justice McReynolds writing for a majority; and Quon Quon Poy v. Johnson, 273 U.S. 352 (1927), with Justice Sanford writing for the majority. See also, Tod v. Waldman, 266 U.S. 113 (1924), where Chief Justice Taft cited Holmes' decisions to uphold an exclusion order against a Jewish petitioner. The petitioner was judged likely to become a public charge on the grounds that he was illiterate.

For the efforts of the lower federal courts in sorting through Chinese petitions, see SALYER, *supra* note 6, ch. 7 (1995).

21. The quotations are from Kwock Jan Fat v. White, 253 U.S. 454, 464 (1919). See also, Ng Fung Ho v. White, 259 U.S. 276 (1922), where executive officers similarly excluded compelling evidence and testimony of American citizenship.

22. See Roger Daniels, *No Lamps Were Lit for Them: Angel Island and the Historiography of Asian American Immigration*, 17 J. AMER. ETHN. HIST. 3 (1997).

23. Id.

24. TAKAKI, *supra* note 1, 238.

25. See Judy Yung, *A Bowlful of Tears: Chinese Women Immigrants on Angel Island*, 2 FRONTIERS (1977); Connie Yu, *Rediscovered Voices: Chinese Immigrants and Angel Island*, 4 AMERASIA (1977); and ISLAND: POETRY AND HISTORY OF CHINESE IMMIGRANTS ON ANGEL ISLAND, 1910–1940 (Him Mark Lai, Genny Lim, and Judy Yung, eds., 1980).

26. See generally, TAKAKI, *supra* note 1, 202–204; PAUL SPICKARD, JAPANESE AMERICANS: THE FORMATION AND TRANSFORMATION OF AN ETHNIC GROUP chs. 3 and 4 (1996); SUCHENG CHAN, ASIAN AMERICANS: AN INTERPRETIVE HISTORY ch. 3 (1991); for additional background and history, see FRANK CHUMAN, THE BAMBOO PEOPLE: THE LAW AND JAPANESE-AMERICANS ch. 2 (1976); TERUKO KACHI, THE TREATY OF 1911 AND THE IMMIGRATION AND ALIEN LAND LAW ISSUE BETWEEN THE UNITED STATES AND JAPAN, 1911–1913 (1978).

27. CHARLES MCCLAIN, IN SEARCH OF EQUALITY: THE CHINESE STRUGGLE AGAINST DISCRIMINATION IN NINETEENTH-CENTURY AMERICA 142 (1994).

28. For background on the Meiji Restoration, see JAMES HOARE, JAPAN'S TREATY PORTS AND FOREIGN SETTLEMENTS: THE UNINVITED GUESTS, 1858–1899 (1994); W. G. BEASLEY, THE MEIJI RESTORATION (1972); CONRAD TOTMAN, EARLY MODERN JAPAN (1995); and W. G. BEASLEY, THE JAPANESE EXPERIENCE: A SHORT HISTORY OF JAPAN (1999).

29. See generally, EVELYN NAKANO GLENN, ISSEI, NISEI, WAR BRIDE: THREE GENERATIONS OF JAPANESE AMERICAN WOMEN IN DOMESTIC SERVICE (1986); and YUJI ICHIOKA, THE ISSEI: THE WORLD OF THE FIRST GENERATION JAPANESE IMMIGRANTS, 1885–1924 (1988).

30. See generally, TAKAKI, *supra* note 1, 188–197; SPICKARD, *supra* note 26, ch. 4. From SPICKARD, 38: "Already in 1910, Japanese men had become the largest single group of laborers in the California fields. In the following decade, they became the owners (or at least the operators) of a significant number of farms as well. Between 1910 and 1920, the number of Japanese-run farms in Los Angeles County tripled; their acreage multiplied by a factor of seven; and their holdings grew to five percent of the county's total farmland. So Issei were both bosses and workers in the West Coast's factories in the fields. One 1929 survey counted more than 64,000 Japanese Americans working in California agriculture: 13,000 field hands and 51,000 independent farmers exercising various degrees of ownership."

31. For detailed discussions of the Alien Land Laws, see Robert Higgs, *Landless by Law: Japanese Immigrants in California Agriculture to 1941*, 38 J. ECON. HIST. 205 (1978), and Dudley McGovney, *The Anti-Japanese Land Laws of California and Ten Other States*, 35 CAL. L. REV. 7 (1947).

32. Higgs, *supra* note 31, 215.

33. SPICKARD, *supra* note 26, 57–58.

34. Id., at 60.

35. See TAKAKI, *supra* note 1, 205.

36. See McGovney, *supra* note 31.

37. TAKAKI, *supra* note 1, 206–207; and McGovney, *supra* note 31, 7–8.

38. SPICKARD, *supra* note 26, 60.

39. See TAKAKI, *supra* note 1, 315, 342–343, and Juanita Lott, *Demographic Changes Transforming the Filipino American Community*, in FILIPINO AMERICANS: TRANSFORMATION AND IDENTITY 12–13 (Maria Root, ed., 1997).

40. BRUNO LASKER, FILIPINO IMMIGRATION 92–93 (1930, 1969).

41. Donald Elliot Anthony, *Filipino Labor in Central California*, 16 SOCIOL. & SOC. RES. 149, 149 and 156 (1931). For similar sentiments see also, John Burma, *The Background and Current Situation of Filipino-Americans*, 30 SOC.

FORCES 42, 47 (1951). Burma wrote: "The crux of the most active and bitter discrimination and dislike seems to be the Filipino's refusal to accept his 'place' as an inferior. He typically considers himself white, with all the prerequisites thereto appertaining in our culture. He has been taught on the Islands that all men are created equal, and his pride and sensitivity will not permit him to passively assume the role of an inferior as did the Chinese coolie a generation or two before him."

42. Consider this explanation, from Rhacel Parrenas, *"White Trash" Meets the "Little Brown Monkeys": The Taxi Dance Hall As a Site of Interracial and Gender Alliances between White Working Class Women and Filipino Immigrant Men in the 1920s and 1930s*, 24 AMERASIA 115, 123 (1998): "In American society, race privilege is highly signified by male access to the bodies of women historically, making women's bodies a battleground among men. . . . Focusing on women's bodies as properties of men and symbols of their racial positioning in society emphasizes how systems of race, gender, and class in the United States have historically intersected in their construction."

43. See, for example, LASKER, *supra* note 40; Anthony, *supra* note 41; Burma, *supra* note 41; Emory Bogardus, *What Race Are Filipinos?* 16 SOCIOL. & SOC. RES. 274 (1932); Benicio Catapusan, *Filipino Intermarriage Problems in the United States*, 22 SOCIOL. & SOC. RES. 265 (1938); Severino Corpus, *Second Generation Filipinos in Los Angeles*, 22 SOCIOL. & SOC. RES. 446 (1938); Constance Panunzio, *Intermarriage in Los Angeles, 1924–1933*, 47 AMER. J. SOCIOL. 690 (1942). For specific statistics that "measure" the extent of Filipino-white marriages, see Catapusan; Corpus; Panunzio; and M. Annella, *Some Aspects of Interracial Marriage in Washington, D.C.*, 25 J. NEGRO ED. 380 (1956). For a discussion of miscegenation rules and their impact on Filipino-white couples, see Nellie Foster, *Legal Status of Filipino Intermarriages in California*, 16 SOCIOL. & SOC. RES. 441 (1932). And finally, for a contemporary discussion of the cultural and political significance of Filipino-white unions, see Parrenas, *supra* note 42.

44. Bogardus, *supra* note 43, 11–12.

45. LASKER, *supra* note 40, 93.

46. Catapusan, *supra* note 43, 267. Burma, *supra* note 41, 46–47, cites and relies on Catapusan for the same point. Indeed, Burma's phrasing is almost exactly the same at Catapusan's.

47. Panunzio, *supra* note 43, 696. He continues: "These consisted mainly of poor rural girls from the Middle West, part of the army of drifting young people characteristic of that time who had been attracted to Los Angeles by the glamour of Hollywood and who had become 'stars,' not in the cinema studios, but in the taxi-dance halls of the community. These young women, separated from their families and therefore beyond the enforcement reach of the mores, were attracted to the Filipino boys, perhaps because they were lonely and in need of

companionship and because the Filipinos, themselves mere boys away from home and craving for fellowship, gave them a ready, simple, direct response. More tangible still, these girls, in that period of widespread unemployment, were much in need of financial support and gladly accepted it from the Filipinos, who in fact gave it to them willingly, often joyously, sometimes with a lavish hand. Cases have been known of Filipino boys spending as much as three-fourths of their earnings on their taxi-dance-hall companions for clothing, food, shelter, and other needs."

48. Barrows was the former director of the American-sponsored educational system in the Philippines; he is quoted in LASKER, *supra* note 40, 98. Barrows continued: "The evidence is very clear that, having no wholesome society of his own, [the Filipino] is drawn into the lowest and least fortunate associations. . . . Everything in our rapid, pleasure-seeking life and the more or less shameless exhibitionism that accompanies it contributes to overwhelm these young men who, in most cases, are only a few years removed from the even, placid life of a primitive native barrio."

49. LASKER, *supra* note 40, 99.

50. Bogardus, *supra* note 43, 25; Burma, *supra* note 41, 46.

51. Norman Hayner, *Social Factors in Oriental Crime*, 43 AMER. J. SOCIOL. 908, 917 (1938).

52. Panunzio, *supra* note 43, 695.

53. Burma, *supra* note 41, 46, 47.

54. Catapusan, *supra* note 43. Catapusan listed a number of difficulties faced by the couple: the threat of either or both losing employment; estrangement from family and friends; estrangement from their own children; conflicts in the home over household responsibilities and duties; and "the parents' wide difference in temperament," presumably based on their racial background.

55. Benicio Catapusan, THE FILIPINO OCCUPATIONAL ACTIVITIES IN LOS ANGELES 84 (MA Thesis, University of Southern California, 1934).

56. Consider this passage from BULOSAN, AMERICA IS IN THE HEART 144–145 (1943):
One day a Filipino came to Holtville with his American wife and their child. It was blazing noon and the child was hungry. The strangers went to a little restaurant and sat down at a table. When they were refused service, they stayed on, hoping for some consideration. But it was no use. Bewildered, they walked outside; suddenly the child began to cry with hunger. The Filipino went back to the restaurant and asked if he could buy a bottle of milk for his child.
"It is only for my baby," he said humbly.
The proprietor came out from behind the counter. "For *your* baby?" he shouted.
"Yes, sir," said the Filipino.
The proprietor pushed him violently outside. "If you say *that* again in my

place, I'll bash in your head!" he shouted aloud so that he would attract attention. "You goddamn brown monkeys have your nerve, marrying our women. Now get out of this town!"

"I love my wife and my child," said the Filipino desperately.

"*Goddamn* you!" The white man struck the Filipino viciously between the eyes with his fist.

Years of degradation came into the Filipino's face. All the fears of his life were here—in the white hand against his face. Was there no place where he could escape? Crouching like a leopard, he hurled his whole weight upon the white man, knocking him down instantly. He seized a stone the size of his fist and began smashing it into the man's face. Then the white men in the restaurant seized the small Filipino, beating him unconscious with pieces of wood and with their fists.

He lay inert on the road. When two deputy sheriffs came to take him away, he looked tearfully back at his wife and child.

57. Foster, *supra* note 43.

58. The first two cases are People v. Yatko, No. 24795, Superior Court of Los Angeles County (1925); and Robinson v. Lampton, County Clerk of Los Angeles County, No. 2496504 (1930). The two latter cases are Laddaran v. Laddaran, No. 095459, Petition for Annulment of Marriage, Superior Court of Los Angeles County (1931); and Murillo v. Murillo, No. D97715, Petition for Annulment of Marriage, Superior Court of Los Angeles County (1931). A full discussion of these cases is in Foster, *supra* note 43.

59. Foster, *supra* note 43, 449.

60. Id., at 449–450. The circular continues: "Are you willing to defend your right UNDER GOD-GIVEN PRINCIPLE OF MARRIAGE AND HAPPINESS? Or shall we allow ourselves to be restrained by laws motivated by unjust discrimination, in defiance of the laws of God and reason? . . . Now, FILIPINOS, DO YOU WANT TO BE CALLED MONGOLIANS? IF YOUR ANSWER IS 'NO' SUPPORT THE FIGHT OF GAVINO C. VISCO BY SUBSCRIBING TO HIS LEGAL FUND LIBERALLY . . . REMEMBER THIS DOES NOT ONLY AFFECT GAVINO C. VISCO, BUT AFFECTS EVERY FILIPINO IN THE STATE OF CALIFORNIA." For a contemporary discussion of this type of race-based strategy, see Victor Romero, *'Aren't You Latino?': Building Bridges upon Common Misperceptions*, 33 U.C. DAVIS L. REV. 837 (2000).

61. Roldan v. Los Angeles County, 129 Cal. App. 267, 268 (1933).

62. Id., at 273.

63. People v. Godines, 17 Cal. App. 2d 721, 722–723 (1936).

64. Id., at 726.

65. Id., at 722–724. The controlling passage, on 727, reads: "While we recognize the fundamental difference between a decree of divorce, whereby a marriage is dissolved, and a judgment of annulment, whereby it is adjudged that a

marriage was never valid, we are of the opinion that within the meaning of the language we have quoted from section 1881 of the Code of Civil Procedure, there is a period during the marriage even in the case of an annulled marriage and that after the annulment, a communication theretofore made by the wife to the husband may not be received in evidence over her objection. No authority to the contrary is cited to us and none has been discovered by us." §1881 reads: "A husband cannot be examined for or against his wife without her consent; nor a wife for or against her husband, without his consent; nor can either . . . be, without the consent of the other, examined as to any communication made by one to the other." Emphasis in the original.

66. Id., at 723.

67. Panunzio, *supra* note 43, 697.

68. See VOICES, A FILIPINO AMERICAN ORAL HISTORY (Joan Cordova and Alexis Canillo, eds., 1984) [no page numbers in the original].

69. See Catapusan, *supra* note 43, 265, for figures about Filipino marriage. Parrenas, *supra* note 42, 119–120, offers this discussion of the reasons behind the gender imbalance among Filipino immigrants: "Filipina women constituted less than ten percent of the Filipino American population in 1930. The absence of Filipina women in the community is of no surprise considering that single women were less likely to migrate on their own during that time and that the wages of Filipino men could ill afford to meet the standard of living for raising families in the United States. Moreover, the passage of the Tydings-McDuffie Act in 1934, which curtailed Filipino migration to fifty persons per year and declared Filipinos 'aliens' ineligible for citizenship, all together prevented women and families from migrating to the United States from the Philippines. As a result, Filipino Americans remained restricted to primarily bachelor communities."

70. Panunzio, *supra* note 43, 695: "[In 1930], [Filipino] marriages with non-whites included 37 unions with Negresses, nearly all of whom were born in the United States, 26 with Mexican women, 8 with American Indians, 2 with Japanese, and 1 with a Chinese."

71. Annella, *supra* note 43, 380–382. Annella's study focused more heavily on white-black interracial marriages, and she did not provide crucial details about the numbers of Filipinos marrying other Asians or Mexicans. Thus, there is no way to compare the rate of outmarriage among Filipinos across different racial groups, except between Filipino-white and Filipino-black marriages.

72. See generally, Peggy Pascoe, *Miscegenation Law, Court Cases, and Ideologies of 'Race' in Twentieth-Century America*, INTERRACIALISM: BLACK-WHITE INTERMARRIAGE IN AMERICAN HISTORY, LITERATURE, AND LAW 183–184 (Werner Sollors ed., 2000).

73. See, Severino Corpus, *Second Generation Filipinos in Los Angeles*, SOCIOL. & SOC. RES. 446 (1938), and TAKAKI, *supra* note 1, 342–343.

74. As there are relatively few historical records on this subject, it is difficult to know the extent to which this rule was enforced against white women marrying Filipino men, although there are popular reports of Japanese American women stripped of their American citizenship for marrying Japanese immigrant men, and a white woman stripped of her citizenship for marrying a Korean man, both related in Ann Marie Nicolosi, *"We Do Not Want Our Girls to Marry Foreigners": Gender, Race, and American Citizenship*, 13 NAT. WOMEN'S STUD. ASSO. J. 1 (2001). On the Expatriation Act and the Cable Act, including extensive discussion of the congressional debates around derivative citizenship for women, see: CANDICE BREDBENNER, A NATIONALITY OF HER OWN: WOMEN, MARRIAGE, AND THE LAW OF CITIZENSHIP (1998) and LINDA KERBER, NO CONSTITUTIONAL RIGHT TO BE LADIES: WOMEN AND THE OBLIGATIONS OF CITIZENSHIP (1998). Two recent works that discuss the history of miscegenation rules during this and other periods are: RACHEL MORAN, INTERRACIAL INTIMACY: THE REGULATION OF RACE AND ROMANCE (2001) and RANDALL KENNEDY, INTERRACIAL INTIMACIES: SEX, MARRIAGE, IDENTITY, AND ADOPTION (2003). Both books discuss interracial marriages between whites and Asians, but neither does so extensively.

NOTES TO CHAPTER 7

1. Sutherland and Pierce, along with Van Devanter and McReynolds, were known as the "Four Horsemen," as in Four Horsemen of the Apocalypse. Generally, they were very conservative and not regarded as sympathetic to underprivileged litigants. See Barry Cushman, *The Secret Lives of the Four Horsemen*, 83 VA. L. REV. 559 (1997). Cushman is actually inclined to think that "here and there one finds shreds of biographical evidence suggesting that something like the milk of human kindness may have flowed in parsimonious quantities through their veins." Id., at 560. For general biographical information on Sutherland and Butler specifically, including cursory discussions of the naturalization cases and the Alien Land cases, see David Burner, *Pierce Butler*, in 3 THE LIVES OF THE JUSTICES OF THE UNITED STATES SUPREME COURT, 1789–1969: THEIR LIVES AND MAJOR OPINIONS 2183 (Leon Friedman and Fred Israel, eds., 1969); JOEL PASCHAL, MR. JUSTICE SUTHERLAND: A MAN AGAINST THE STATE (1951); and Harold Stephens, *Mr. Justice Sutherland*, 31 A.B.A. J. 446 (1945).

2. Ozawa v. United States, 260 U.S. 178 (1922), and United States v. Thind, 261 U.S. 204 (1923). For a discussion of the background and legal strategy behind Ozawa, see Yuji Ichioka, *The Early Japanese Immigrant Quest for Citizenship*, 4 AMERASIA 12 (1977). For an excellent discussion of both cases, see IAN

HANEY LOPEZ, WHITE BY LAW: THE LEGAL CONSTRUCTION OF RACE (1996).

3. LOPEZ, *supra* note 2.

4. Ichioka, *supra* note 2, 11.

5. Id.

6. Withington, quoted from "Brief for Ozawa," reprinted in: The Consulate General of Japan, DOCUMENTAL HISTORY OF LAW CASES AFFECTING JAPANESE IN THE UNITED STATES, 1916–1924 vol. 1 (1978), 18. For the proposition that Japanese were not black, Withington cited the constitution for the State of Oklahoma, which distinguished persons of African descent from all other "races": "Whatever in this constitution and laws of this state the words 'colored' or 'colored person,' 'negro,' or 'negro race' are used, the same shall be construed to mean to apply to all persons of African descent. The term 'white race' shall include all other persons." Id., at 36. The quote on miscegenation appears on 49.

7. 260 U.S., at 184.

8. See, for example, Withington's "Brief," at 25–26, 38–39, 41–42, 44–45, and Wickersham's "Arguments," in DOCUMENTAL HISTORY, *supra* note 6.

9. His thoughts on Japanese women, families, and crime appear in Withington's "Brief" on 38, 49–50. The phrasing of Japanese as "Yankees of the Orient" appears on 44.

10. 260 U.S., at 184.

11. Id.

12. I am indebted to my former colleague Shirley Thompson for showing me the parallels. See Shirley Thompson, *'Ah Toucoutou, ye conin vous': History and Memory in Creole New Orleans*, 53 AMER. QUART. 232 (2001), and also Teresa Zackodnik, *Fixing the Color Line: The Mulatto, Southern Courts, and Racial Identity*, 53 AMER. QUART. 420 (2001).

13. 260 U.S., at 197–198.

14. 261 U.S., at 205–207.

15. Id., at 212.

16. Id., at 214–215.

17. See generally, RONALD TAKAKI, STRANGERS FROM A DIFFERENT SHORE 297–300 (1989); and SUCHENG CHAN, ASIAN AMERICANS 54–56 (1991).

18. Consider the following passage, written by a prominent diplomat in the Department of State: "My investigations have convinced me personally that the only thoroughly satisfactory method of providing against discriminatory treatment of Japanese aliens would be by Congressional action granting people of the Yellow race the privilege of naturalization. I wish that the Congress might feel justified in taking such action. Its effect . . . would be limited to one generation,

and yet in so doing, we would totally change the existing spirit of irritation and resentment which now characterizes our contact with the Orient. We would remove from the peoples of China and Japan the stigma that is placed upon them in thus removing the *racial* discrimination, and we could more vigorously enforce restrictions on immigration as an *economic* protection to our own people. As early as 1906, President Roosevelt, seeing as he did so clearly throughout his entire public life the international value of the closest friendship and understanding with Japan, in his annual message to Congress said: 'I recommend to the Congress that an act be passed specifically providing for the naturalization of the Japanese who come here intending to become American citizens.'" Roland Morris, U.S. Department of State, *Japanese Immigration and Alleged Discriminatory Legislation against Japanese Residents in the United States* (1921, 1978).

Restrictions against Asian migration were not always seen as incompatible with extending the right of naturalization to Asian immigrants already in the United States. Consider another passage, written by an American missionary in 1918: "While, on the one hand, [our policy] should provide real protection for the Pacific coast States from the dangers of excessive Asiatic immigration; it should also, on the other hand, give to Asiatics the same courtesy of treatment and the same equality of rights as America readily accords to all other people, whether they come from Europe, Africa, or South America." SIDNEY GULICK, AMERICAN DEMOCRACY AND ASIATIC CITIZENSHIP ix (1918, 1978).

19. United States v. Balsara, 180 F. 694 (2d. Cir. 1910); *In re* Mozumdar, 207 F. 115 (E.D. Wash. 1913); and *In re* Singh, 257 F. 209 (S.D. Cal. 1919). In two other cases regarding naturalization, one by a Japanese immigrant petitioner, *In re* Saito, 62 F. 126 (C.C.D. Mass. 1894), and another by an Asian Indian petitioner, *In re* Singh, 246 F. 496 (E.D. Pa. 1917), the federal courts denied each application on racial grounds similar to the ones outlined by Sutherland.

20. Terrace v. Thompson, 263 U.S. 197 (1923); Porterfield v. Webb, 263 U.S. 225 (1923); Webb v. O'Brien, 263 U.S. 313 (1923); and Frick v. Webb, 263 U.S. 326 (1923).

21. See generally, Geer v. Connecticut, 161 U.S. 519 (1896); Patsone v. Pennsylvania, 232 U.S. 138, 143 (1914); Traux v. Raich, 239 U.S. 33 (1915); and Heim v. McCall, 239 U.S. 175, 177 (1915).

22. 263 U.S., at 221.

23. 263 U.S., at 324.

24. Consider the following passage, written in 1921: "Control of those rich lands [in California] means in time control of the products, and control of the markets. Control of the products of the soil by a unified interest such as the Japanese will lead to economic control of the country. That will be followed in time by political control through force of numbers induced by the heavy birth rate. That condition is not at hand in Hawaii [. . .] The birth rate will insure increase, rather than decrease, of the Japanese population in this state [. . .]

Rather than invite such disaster, better let some land lie idle, and a few large landholders make less profit, and even see production decrease somewhat, as opponents claim will result if this measure carries." V. S. McClatchy, quoted in Morris, *supra* note 18, 261.

25. 263 U.S. at 334. These decisions overturned important state court precedents challenging the Alien Land Laws. See for example, *In re* Yano, 188 Cal. 645 (1922), the logic of which reappears in Oyama v. California, 332 U.S. 633 (1948).

26. See LISA LOWE, IMMIGRANT ACTS (1996).

27. That white racial identity is a form of property is explained in Cheryl Harris, *Whiteness as Property*, 106 HARV. L. REV. 1707 (1993).

28. See generally, TAKAKI, *supra* note 17, 212–229; and Karen Leonard, *The Pahkar Singh Murders: A Punjabi Response to California's Alien Land Laws,"* 11 AMERASIA 75 (1984).

29. Again, see McClatchy, *supra* note 24: "Rather than invite such disaster, better let some land lie idle, and a few large landholders make less profit, and even see production decrease somewhat, as opponents claim will result if this measure carries."

30. See Cockrill v. California, 268 U.S. 258 (1925), on the Alien Land Law; Gong Lum v. Rice, 275 U.S. 78 (1927), with Justice Taft writing to uphold segregated schools in Mississippi for children of Chinese ancestry; and Roldan v. County of Los Angeles, 129 Cal. App. 267 (1933), and People v. Godines, 17 Cal. App. 2d 721 (1936), both concerning antimiscegenation statutes in California.

31. 261 U.S., at 215.

32. JOHN HIGHAM, STRANGERS IN THE LAND: PATTERNS OF AMERICAN NATIVISM, 1860–1925 300 (1963).

33. Id., at 319: "Johnson's purpose was fixed. He wanted to put European immigration on two per cent quotas computed from the 1890 census, thereby cutting the Italian quota from 42,000 to about 4,000, the Polish from 31,000 to 6,000, the Greek from 3,000 to 100. Also, if possible, he wanted to exclude completely the Japanese, sweeping aside the Gentlemen's Agreement of 1907. Some members of the House Committee doubted the wisdom of flouting a treaty obligation, but the passions of the southern and western committeemen carried the day. Since other Orientals were already barred, they argued, it was no discrimination to treat the Japanese like the rest of their race."

34. Id., at 321. For a recent and thorough review of the legislation leading up to and including the Immigration Act of 1924, see Mai Lgai, *The Architecture of Race in American Immigration Law: A Reexamination of the Immigration Act of 1924*, 86 J. AMER. HIST. 67 (1999).

35. See STEPHEN LEGOMSKY, IMMIGRATION LAW AND POLICY 119 (1992).

36. Some excellent accounts include: Jacobus TenBroek, Edward Bernhart, and Floyd Matson, Prejudice, War, and the Constitution: Causes and Consequences of the Evacuation of Japanese Americans in World War II (1970); Roger Daniels, Concentrations Camps USA: Japanese Americans and World War II (1971); and Peter Irons, Justice at War: The Story of the Japanese American Internment Cases (1983).

37. Paul Spickard, Japanese Americans 102 (1996).

38. Id., at 102.

39. Id., at 102. At least one similarity to Plessy's case is notable. According to Spickard, Yasui wanted to be arrested and cited: "I had an awful time getting arrested. I was getting tired walking around town, and I approached a policeman at eleven o'clock at night. I pulled out this order that said all persons of Japanese ancestry must be in their place of abode, and I pulled out my birth certificate and said, 'Look, I'm a person of Japanese ancestry, arrest me.' And the police said, 'Run along home, you'll get in trouble.' I actually had to go down to the Second Avenue police station and talk to the sergeant and tell him what I wanted to do. He said, 'Sure, we'll oblige you.' So they threw me in the drunk tank until Monday morning, which was a miserable experience."

40. Id., at 103.

41. Justice Black's opinion in Korematsu v. United States, 323 U.S. 214 (1944), included the concept of "strict scrutiny" in race cases. On 223, he wrote: "It should be noted, to begin with, that all legal restrictions which curtail the civil rights of a single racial group are immediately suspect. That is not to say that all such restrictions are unconstitutional. It is to say that courts must subject them to the most rigid scrutiny. Pressing public necessity may sometimes justify the existence of such restrictions; racial antagonism never can. . . . Our task would be simple, our duty clear, were this a case involving the imprisonment of a loyal citizen in a concentration camp because of racial prejudice."

42. Ex parte Mitsuye Endo, 323 U.S. 283 (1944).

43. Id., at 302.

44. Takaki, supra note 17, 397.

45. Id., at 399.

46. Eric Muller, Free to Die for Their Country: The Story of the Japanese American Draft Resisters in World War II (2001).

47. Takaki, *supra* note 17, 401–402.

48. The key cases concerning Japanese immigrant veterans are: *In re* Saito, 62 F. 126 (C.C.D. Mass., 1894); *In re* Buntaro Kumagai, 163 F. R. 922 (D.C.W.D. Wash. N.D., 1908); Bessho v. United States, 178 F. 245 (C.C.A. 4, 1910); Sato v. Hall, 191 Cal. 510 (1923); and Toyota v. United States, 268 U.S. 402 (1925). In *Toyota*, "Hidemitsu Toyota, a person of the Japanese race, born in Japan, entered the United States in 1913. He served substantially all the time

between November of that year and May, 1923, in the United States Coast
Guard Service. This was a part of the naval force of the United States nearly all
of the time the United States was engaged in the recent war. He received eight or
more honorable discharges, and some of them were for service during the war."
Id., at 406. Still, a majority of the court, speaking again through Butler, upheld
his denial of naturalization citing congressional statutes allowing only free white
persons and persons of African nativity the right to become citizens. A Korean
serviceman was denied naturalization in Charr, 273 F. 207 (1921).

Filipino veterans were denied the same in two cases: *In re* Alverto, 198 Fed.
688 (1912), and *In re* Rallos, 241 Fed. 686 (1917). In May 1918, Congress
made a special exception to provide for the naturalization of Filipinos who had
served "in the United States Navy or Marine Corps or the Naval Auxiliary Service." See Toyota, 268 U.S. 407.

49. TAKAKI, *supra* note 17, 413.

50. For recent discussions on the Internal Security Act, see Mari Matsuda,
McCarthyism, the Internment and the Contradictions of Power, 19 B.C. THIRD
WORLD L. J. 9 (1998); Natsu Taylor Saito, *Model Minority, Yellow Peril: Functions of "Foreignness" in the Construction of Asian American Legal Identity*, 4
ASIAN L. J. 71 (1997); and William M. Wiecek, *The Legal Foundations of Domestic Anticommunism: The Background of Dennis v. United States*, 2001 SUP.
CT. REV. 375. For a useful overview of this period in Chinese American history,
see IRIS CHANG, THE CHINESE IN AMERICA: A NARRATIVE HISTORY ch. 14
(2003).

51. VICTOR NEE AND BRETT DE BARY NEE, LONGTIME CALIFORN': A
DOCUMENTARY STUDY OF AN AMERICAN CHINATOWN (1973), 211–212.

52. Consider the following recollection, by a chemist, Franklin Woo, quoted
in NEE AND NEE, at 216: "We knew the FBI was keeping a close eye on us, and
we even suspected that there was an informer among us. I guess that's one thing
all of us feel bad about now, that we had to be suspicious of each other. The FBI
people began coming to our homes, going to talk to our relatives, friends, where
we worked. I guess when they got the Immigration Office working on us,
though, we knew the *Min Ching* [the Chinese American Democratic Youth
League] was coming to an end. I remember the immigration people would stop
Min Ching members on the street and demand to see their papers, just to harass
us. Once they discovered that somebody had false papers, they would begin
proceedings for deportation. I guess I've never been able to explain that well to
people who haven't experienced it, how painful this immigration harassment
can be to Chinese. Say, if a *Min Ching* member is discovered to have false papers, his whole family will be affected because probably they didn't have proper
papers either. So they'll go from you, to the uncle who brought you in, his wife,
and it goes on and on. Well, too many of us had illegal entries somewhere along
the line."

53. Xiaojian Zhao, Remaking Chinese America: Immigration, Family, and Community 1940–1965 165–184 (2001).

54. See Mae Ngai, *Legacies of Exclusion: Illegal Chinese Immigration during the Cold War Years*, 18 J. Amer. Ethn. Hist. 1 (1998). See also Mae Ngai, Illegal Aliens and Alien Citizens: United States Immigration Policy and Racial Formation, 1924–1945 (Ph.D. dissertation, Columbia University, 1998).

55. Nee and Nee, *supra* note 51, 212.

56. See Ngai, *Legacies*, supra note 54.

57. Zhao, *supra* note 53, 182–184.

58. Consider the following passage, from Henry Maine, Ancient Law 126 (1861, 1963, 1972): "No doubt, when with our modern ideas we contemplate the union of independent communities, we can suggest a hundred modes of carrying it out, the simplest of all being that the individuals comprised of the coalescing groups shall vote or act together according to local propinquity; but the idea that a number of persons should exercise political authority in common simply because they happened to live within the same topographical limits was utterly strange and monstrous to primitive antiquity. The expedient which in those times commanded favour was that the incoming population should *feign themselves* to be descended from the same stock as the people on whom they were engrafted; and it is precisely the good faith of this fiction, and the closeness with which it seemed to imitate reality, that we cannot now hope to understand."

NOTES TO CHAPTER 8

1. See Daniel Weintraub, *Crime, Immigration Help Wilson, Poll Finds*, L.A. Times, Nov. 9, 1994, at A1.

2. See Cal. Health & Safety Code 130(c)(3) (West 1996); Cal. Welf. & Inst. Code 10001.5(c)(3) (West 1996).

3. 130(c)(3); 10001.5(c)(3).

4. 130(c)(3); 10001.5(c)(3).

5. Robert B. Gunnison, *Wilson Sues Again on Immigration*, S.F. Chron., Sept. 23, 1994, at A23.

6. See *Illegal Immigrants*, Economist, Sept. 3, 1994, at 35; Robert B. Jackson, *Think Tank Supports Wilson on Immigrant Cost*, S.F. Chron., Sept. 23, 1994, at A4; Nancy Gibbs, *Keep Out, You Tired, You Poor . . .* , Time, Oct., 3, 1994, at 46; Gunnison, *supra* note 5, at A23. See generally Milton Morris and Albert Mayio, Curbing Illegal Immigration (1982); Francisco Rivera-Batiz et al., U.S. Immigration Policy Reform in the 1980s (1991) (discussing findings that although social science research on illegal immigrants generally suffers from the fact that such persons are hard to study as a

population, most studies show that they either benefit the economy as a whole by contributing cheap labor, or if they do drain the economy, they do so negligibly).

7. See Gunnison, *supra* note 5, A23; see also Barry Edmonston et al., *Perceptions and Estimates of Undocumented Migration to the United States*, in UNDOCUMENTED MIGRATION TO THE UNITED STATES 27 (Frank D. Bean et al. eds., 1990) (conveying the results of a joint Rand Corporation–Urban Institute study that shows a recent decrease in the number of illegal immigrants to the United States); Frank Bean et al., *Post-IRCA Changes in the Volume and Composition of Undocumented Migration to the United States,* in UNDOCUMENTED MIGRATION TO THE UNITED STATES, *supra,* 153 (noting that although the Rand Corporation–Urban Institute study shows an overall decrease in illegal immigration, the number of illegal border crossings by women, children, and non-Mexicans appears to be increasing).

8. See Louis Freedberg, *Wilson Defends Stance on Illegals*, S.F. CHRON, June 23, 1994, at A2; Julie Marquis, *Wilson Blames Ills on Illegal Immigrants*, L.A. TIMES, Oct. 17, 1994, at B1; see also *Indecent Proposition in California*, N.Y. TIMES, Oct. 25, 1994, at A20 (noting that although some supporters of Proposition 187 acknowledged that some undocumented aliens migrate to benefit from public services, the primary pull for undocumented aliens is the hope for employment); Elizabeth Hull, WITHOUT JUSTICE FOR ALL 112 (1985) (stating that the primary pull for undocumented aliens is the hope for employment); Linda Bozniak, *Exclusion and Membership: The Dual Identity of the Undocumented Worker under United States Law,* 1988 WIS. L. REV. 955, 988 (stating that "the overwhelming majority of undocumented immigrants come to this country to work"); Note, *The Birthright Citizenship Amendment: A Threat to Equality*, 107 HARV. L. REV. 1026, 1038 (1994) (stating that the dominant cause of illegal immigration is the hope of obtaining employment); Patrick J. McDonnell, *Prop. 187 Turns Up Heat in U.S. Immigration Debate*, L.A. TIMES, Aug. 10, 1994, at A1 (stating that jobs are "widely considered by scholars and other authorities to be the principal lure for immigrants").

9. Marquis, *supra* note 8, at B1. See also *Brown, Wilson Clash on Crime, Immigration, Taxes*, L.A. TIMES, Oct. 16, 1994, at A1; Gebe Martinez, *Illegal Immigrants' Tab for Emergency Care: $61 Million*, L.A. TIMES, Nov. 2, 1994, at B7.

10. See Karen Brandon, *Illegal Immigration: A Drain or an Asset?*, CHI. TRIB., Oct. 18, 1994, at 14.

11. Evelyn C. White, *Immigration a Tough Call for Blacks: Proposition 187 Debate Has Stirred Deep Feelings*, S.F. CHRON, Oct. 10, 1994, at A1.

12. Id.

13. John Wildermuth, *Huffington Endorses Proposition 187*, S.F. CHRON, Oct. 21, 1994, at A3.

14. See Rich Connell, *Proposition 187's Support Shows No Boundaries*, L.A. TIMES, Sept. 25, 1994, at A1.

15. Id.

16. Id.

17. *Proposition 187*, CAL. J. WKLY., Sept. 26, 1994.

18. Harold Ezell, *Enough Is More than Enough*, L.A. TIMES, Oct. 23, 1994, at M5.

19. See Brad Hayward, *Foes Sharpen Strategies on Immigration Measure*, SACRAMENTO BEE, Sept. 4, 1994, at A1.

20. *Proposition 187, supra* note 17.

21. 457 U.S. 202 (1982). See also, George Will, *Reclaiming the Right of Self-Determination*, WASH. POST, Oct. 30, 1994, at C7.

22. See Alicia Doyle and Antonio Olivo, *Proposition 187's Impact on Race Relations*, L.A. TIMES, Nov. 4, 1994, at B2.

23. Id.

24. Patrick J. McDonnell and Robert J. Lopez, *Some See New Activism in Huge March*, L.A. TIMES, Oct. 18, 1994, at B1 (quoting Alan Nelson, coauthor of Proposition 187).

25. *SOS Initiative—Costly, Mean and Wrong*, S.F. CHRON, Oct. 16, 1994, at SUNDAY PUNCH 1; Karen Brandon, *Illegal Immigration: A Drain or an Asset?*, CHI. TRIB., Oct. 18, 1994, at 1; *Why Californians Should Vote "No" on Proposition 187*, L.A. TIMES, Nov. 2, 1994, at B6; *Punishing Immigrants*, CHRISTIAN SCI. MONITOR, Nov. 3, 1994, at 18; *Indecent Proposition in California, supra* note 8, A20.

26. See Hayward, *supra* note 19, A1.

27. Id.

28. Id.

29. Stuart Silverstein, *Domestics: Hiring the Illegal Hits Home*, L.A. TIMES, Oct. 28, 1994, at A1; see also, *Developments in the Law—Immigration Policy and the Rights of Aliens*, 96 HARV. L. REV. 1286, 1436–1437 (1983) (reviewing statistics on undocumented aliens and finding that they "accept wages and working conditions that are below the acceptable minimums established by United States law but vastly superior to what is available in their home countries").

30. *Indecent Proposition in California, supra* note 8, at A20.

31. See SECRETARY OF STATE, CALIFORNIA BALLOT PAMPHLET 92 (1994).

32. *Why Californians Should Vote "No" on Proposition 187, supra* note 25, at B6; *SOS Initiative, supra* note 25.

33. See Plyler v. Doe, 457 U.S. 202 (1982); FAMILY EDUCATIONAL RIGHTS AND PRIVACY ACT, 20 U.S.C.A. 1232(g) (West 1996); Louis Freedberg, *Immigration Measure Would Cost Schools*, S.F. CHRON, Aug. 13, 1994, at A1.

34. Marc Sandalow and Louis Freedberg, *Panetta Warns State of Prop. 187 "Chaos,"* S.F. CHRON, Oct. 27, 1994, at A2.

35. Howard F. Chang, *Shame on Them, Picking on Children,* L.A. TIMES, Sept. 6, 1994, at B5; see Plyler, 457 U.S. at 241 (Powell, J., concurring) ("It can be hardly argued rationally that anyone benefits from the creation within our borders of a subclass of illiterate persons many of whom will remain in the State, adding to the problems and costs of both State and National Governments attendant upon unemployment, welfare, and crime").

36. Pamela Burdman, *Many Doctors Would Ignore Prop. 187,* S.F. CHRON, Oct. 19, 1994, A2. But see Hayward, *supra* note 19, at A1, where opponents countered that "Proposition 187's reduction in the undocumented population of our state should itself reduce the state's tuberculosis rate."

37. Gebe Martinez, *Kemp Draws Criticism for Voicing Opposition,* L.A. TIMES, Oct. 20, 1994, at B1.

38. *A Response to Anti-Immigrant Proposals,* CAL. TOMORROW, Nov. 1993, at 3.

39. See Henry P. Pachon, *A Flirtation with the GOP Turns Cold,* L.A. TIMES, Nov. 6, 1994, at M5.

40. See Pamela Burdman and Edward Epstein, *Wilson Goes after Kemp and Bennett,* S.F. CHRON, Oct. 20, 1994, at A1; *Kemp, Bennett Talk Sense,* S.F. CHRON, Oct. 21, 1994, at B5; William Buckley, *Immigrant Backlash Could Hurt GOP,* HOUSTON CHRON., Oct. 25, 1994, at B10.

41. See Ron K. Unz, *Scaling the Heights of Irrationality,* L.A. TIMES, Oct. 3, 1994, at B7.

42. See generally MORRIS AND MAYIO, *supra* note 6 (discussing the occupations of undocumented aliens); J. Edward Taylor and Thomas Espenshade, *Seasonality and the Changing Role of Undocumented Immigrants in the California Farm Labor Market,* in Rivera-Batiz et al., *supra* note 6 (discussing the role of undocumented aliens as farm laborers).

43. Efrain Hernandez, *Point of Impact; Before It Has Even Come to a Vote, Proposition 187 Has Sent Shock Waves through Central Los Angeles' Vast Immigrant Population and the Institutions That Provide for It,* L.A. TIMES, Nov. 6, 1994, at 14.

44. Ed Mendel, *Growers Fear Labor Shortage if Voters End Social Services,* SAN DIEGO UNION-TRIB., Oct. 17, 1994, at A3.

45. Id.; see Brandon, *supra* note 10, 1.

46. Susan Ferriss, *Prop. 187: A Clash of Rhetoric, Reality,* S.F. EXAMINER, Oct. 30, 1994, at A1.

47. See id.; Bozniak, *supra* note 8, 988. See generally, Taylor and Espenshade, *supra* note 42 (discussing studies demonstrating that in most sectors of the economy employers enforce illegal immigration laws only when it is in their interests to do so).

48. See Louis Freedberg, *Mexico Slowly Getting Tougher on Illegals*, S.F. CHRON, Aug. 12, 1994, at A1; NORTH AMERICAN FREE TRADE AGREEMENT, Dec. 17, 1992, U.S.-CAN.-MEX., 32 I.L.M. 296.

49. Howard LaFranchi, *Proposal against Illegals in California Irks Mexicans*, CHRISTIAN SCI. MONITOR, Nov. 3, 1994, at 3.

50. See Patrick Lee, *Prop. 187 Threatens to Disrupt Ties with Mexico*, L.A. TIMES, Nov. 10, 1994, at D1; *McDonald's in Mexico City Vandalized by Prop. 187 Foes*, L.A. TIMES, Nov. 9, 1994, at A26.

51. See Lee, *supra* note 50, D1.

52. Susan Ferriss, *Immigrant Ballot Issue Imperils Kids*, S.F. EXAMINER, Oct. 9, 1994, at C1.

53. 457 U.S. at 202, 220 (1982).

54. Leslie Berestein, *Asian Groups Unite to Educate Residents on Impact of Prop. 187*, L.A. TIMES, Sept. 25, 1994, at 3. The Asian American community has therefore, responded to Proposition 187 with concern and organized opposition to the measure. See Pamela Burdman, *A Push to Get Immigrants to Vote*, S.F. CHRON, Sept. 24, 1994, at A3; Samuel Cacas, *Prop. 187 Continues Stirring the Senses*, ASIAN WK., Oct. 21, 1994, at 3; Connie Kang, *Asian American Groups Organize to Fight Measure*, KOREA TIMES, Nov. 2, 1994, at 1; Milton Marks, *The Posing Dangers of Proposition 187*, ASIAN WK., Oct. 21, 1994, at 1; Tina Nguyen, *Chinatown; Coalition of Groups Denounce Prop. 187*, L.A. TIMES, Oct. 30, 1994, at 3.

55. Pamela Burdman and Edward Epstein, *Wilson Goes After Kemp and Bennett*, S.F. CHRON, Oct. 20, 1994, at 1; see Edward Epstein, *Brown Quotes Wilson against Wilson on Immigration Issue*, S.F. CHRON, Oct. 26, 1994, at A8 (noting that when Wilson was mayor of San Diego he opposed employer sanctions for hiring illegal immigrants on the theory that the sanctions "would very likely produce the kind of discrimination that a number of minority groups, civil rights groups, are concerned about").

56. See Doyle and Olivo, *supra* note 22, B2; Antonio Rodriguez and Carlos Chavez, *Latinos Unite in Self-Defense on Prop. 187*, L.A. TIMES, Oct. 21, 1994, at B7.

57. Joe R. Hicks & Constance L. Rice, *Pioneers of the Civil Rights Movement Would Find Common Cause with Latinos in Today's California*, L.A. TIMES, Nov. 4, 1994, at B7; see *Punishing Immigrants*, *supra* note 25, 18 (noting that Proposition 187 has an "unmistakable undertone of bigotry" and would aggravate racial tensions).

58. McDonnell, *supra* note 8, A12.

59. Louis Freedberg, *Reno Blasts Prop. 187—Questions Legality*, S.F. CHRON, Oct. 28, 1994, at A4.

60. John W. Mack, *Is Black-Latino Friction a Voting Booth Issue? No*, L.A. TIMES, Oct. 24, 1994, at B5.

61. See Doreen Carvajal, *Prop. 187 Has Even Backers a Bit Uneasy*, L.A. TIMES, Oct. 31, 1994, at A1.

62. Bozniak, *supra* note 8, 1003; see also David Ferrell and Robert Lopez, *State Waits to See What Prop. 187 Will Really Mean*, L.A. TIMES, Nov. 10, 1994 at A1 (quoting an LAPD officer stating, "It's not our job to ask people where they are from. . . . We aren't the INS. We have more important things to do").

63. Burdman, *supra* note 36, A2; Pamela Burdman, *Opposition to Prop. 187 Is Growing*, S.F. CHRON, Aug. 18, 1994, at C16.

64. See, e.g., Weintraub, *supra* note 1, A1.

65. Id.

66. See Paul Feldman, *Wilson Acts to Enforce Parts of Prop. 187*, L.A. TIMES, Nov. 10, 1994, at A1; Elizabeth Shogren, *Plans to Cut Safety Net Leave Legal Immigrants Dangling*, L.A. TIMES, Nov. 21, 1994, at A1.

67. See Weintraub, *supra* note 1, A1.

68. Connell, *supra* note 14, A1.

69. See Miranda v. Arizona, 384 U.S. 436 (1965) (delineating the right to remain silent in interactions with police officers).

70. McDonnell and Lopez, *supra* note 24, B1.

71. 20 U.S.C.A. 1232(g) (West 1996) (stating that "no funds shall be made available under any applicable program to any educational agency or institution which has a practice of permitting the release of education records [or personally identifiable information other than directory information] of students without the written consent of their parents to any individual agency or organization, other than to [education officials or the US Comptroller General]."); see Freedberg, *supra* note 33, A1.

72. Hayward, *supra* note 19, A1 (emphasis added).

73. Kenneth J. Garcia, *Wilson's ID Card Idea Draws Scorn*, S.F. CHRON, Oct. 28, 1994, at A4.

74. Note that scholars still debate whether health-care rights, education rights, or subsistence rights should be considered as fundamental as the right to speak or the right to privacy. See generally, HENRY SHUE, BASIC RIGHTS: SUBSISTENCE, AFFLUENCE AND U.S. FOREIGN POLICY (1980). The Supreme Court has been reluctant to view government benefits as "rights" to which citizens are entitled, and yet the Court often treats entitlements as rights. Compare, e.g., Goldberg v. Kelly, 397 U.S. 254 (1969) (treating welfare entitlements like property rights protected under the Due Process Clause of the Fourteenth Amendment), with DeShaney v. Winnebago County, 489 U.S. 189 (1989) (holding that a social services department specifically set up to protect children may not be held liable under the Fourteenth Amendment for harm to a child, even though it knew that the child was in danger of harm; in effect, the child had no "right" to protection under a state program charged with protecting children).

75. See 457 U.S. 202 (1982); see also Marianne Constable, *Sovereignty and Governmentality in Modern American Immigration Law,* 13 Stud. L., Pol., & Soc'y 249, 261 (1993).

76. 457 U.S. at 221.

77. 347 U.S. at 483, 493 (1954).

78. 411 U.S. 1 (1973); see also Plyler, 457 U.S. at 221 (stating that, although education is not "merely some governmental 'benefit' indistinguishable from other forms of social welfare legislation," it is not a "right" guaranteed to individuals by the Constitution).

79. *Asian Pacific Americans Opposed to Proposition 187,* Korea Times, Sept. 7, 1994, at 5.

80. Hicks and Rice, *supra* note 57, B7.

81. Doyle and Olivo, *supra* note 22, B2.

82. *SOS Initiative, supra* note 25.

83. See Paul Feldman and Rich Connell, *Wilson Acts to Enforce Parts of Prop. 187,* L.A. Times, Nov. 10, 1994, at A1 (noting that after enactment of Proposition 187, Governor Wilson responded to these concerns by ordering that all precautions be taken "to deal with any threat of communicable disease, whether through immunization or quarantine or other measures," and also ordering state agencies to protect "the rights of all legal residents" and to ensure that "the provisions of Proposition 187 [be] implemented in a manner that avoids discrimination on the basis of national origin").

84. Brian O'Leary Bennett, *An Initiative Even Conservatives Can Hate,* L.A. Times, Oct. 7, 1994, at B7.

85. See *Developments in the Law—Immigration Policy and the Rights of Aliens, supra* note 30; see also Hannah Arendt, The Origins of Totalitarianism 286 (1951) (stating that "since [the stateless person] was an anomaly for whom the general law did not provide, it was better for him to become an anomaly for which it did provide, that of the criminal. . . . The best criterion by which to decide whether someone has been forced outside the pale of the law is to ask if he would benefit by committing a crime").

86. See Michael Hoefer, *Background of U.S. Immigration Policy Reform,* in Rivera-Batiz et al., *supra* note 6, 30–31; Susan Gonzalez Baker, The Cautious Welcome (1990).

87. See Hoefer, *supra* note 86, 30–31.

88. See Baker, *supra* note 86, 16.

89. See Arendt, *supra* note 85, 286.

90. See Burdman and Epstein, *supra* note 55, A1; and Chang, *supra* note 35, B5.

91. See Arendt, *supra* note 85, 286.

92. Shue, *supra* note 74, 15.

93. White, *supra* note 11, A1.

94. Hernandez, *supra* note 43, 14.

95. Harold Ezell, *Enough Is More than Enough: We Can't Afford Illegal Immigration*, L.A. TIMES, Oct. 23, 1994, at M5.

96. *A Panoply of Emotions over Proposition 187*, S.D. UNION-TRIB., Oct. 22, 1994, at 7.

97. Id.

98. See Feldman, *supra* note 66, A1.

99. See *Newshour* (Korean Broadcasting Service news broadcast, Oct. 28, 1994).

100. John Jacobs, *For Huddled Masses Yearning to Be Free, Prop. 187?*, S.F. EXAMINER, Oct. 31, 1994, at A21.

101. See Susan Yoachum, *Huffington Hired Illegal Immigrant*, S.F. CHRON, Oct. 27, 1994, at A1; *INS Says Feinstein Maid Illegal*, S.F. Chron., Nov. 5, 1994, at C3.

102. John Wildermuth, *Mrs. Huffington Talks about Secret Nanny*, S.F. CHRON, Nov. 1, 1994, at A1.

103. James Bornemeier, *Charting Wilson's Transformation on Immigration*, L.A. TIMES, Nov. 2, 1994, at A3.

104. Ferrell and Lopez, *supra* note 62, A1.

105. Id.

106. Bozniak, *supra* note 8, 992.

107. See Burdman and Epstein, *supra* note 55, 1.

108. Henry Pachon, *A Flirtation with the GOP Turns Cold*, L.A. TIMES, Nov. 6, 1994, at M5.

109. *SOS Initiative*, *supra* note 25.

110. Mack, *supra* note 60, B5.

111. *A Response to Anti-Immigrant Proposals*, *supra* note 38, at 3.

112. 457 U.S. 202, 216 (1982) (emphasis added).

113. See Unz, *supra* note 41, B7; Wildermuth, *supra* note 130, A1.

114. See Gail D. Cox, *Calif. Law on Aliens Spurs Disobedience*, NAT'L L. J., Dec. 12, 1994, at A6.

115. See Hernandez, *supra* note 43, 14.

116. See *187: It's a Risky Proposition; Hazards of Immigration Measure Dwarf Potential Benefits*, L.A. TIMES, Oct. 16, 1994, at B18.

117. For useful discussions of the court challenges against Proposition 187, and the subsequent state actions with regard to undocumented aliens, see JoAnne Spotts, *U.S. Immigration Policy on the Southwest Border from Reagan through Clinton, 1981–2001*, 16 GEO. IMMIG. L. J. 601 (2002); Lucy Williams, *Property, Wealth and Inequality through the Lens of Globalization: Lessons from the United States and Mexico*, 34 IND. L. REV. 1243 (2001); and *Recent Legislation—Immigration Law—Education*, 115 HARV. L. REV. 1548 (2002). The new rule does not include the same tuition breaks for students attending the

University of California. The leading cases challenging Proposition 187 were reported as: League of United Latin American Citizens v. Wilson, 908 F. Supp. 755 (C.D. Cal. 1995); and League of United Latin American Citizens v. Wilson, 997 F. Supp. 1244 (C.D. Cal. 1997).

118. Quoted in *Recent Legislation, supra* note 117, 1550–1551.

119. For useful background on the Patriot Act and other developments in immigration law, see: Susan Akram and Kevin Johnson, *Race, Civil Rights, and Immigration Law after September 11, 2001: The Targeting of Arabs and Muslims,* 58 N.Y.U. ANN. SURV. AMER. L. 295 (2002); and David Cole, *The New McCarthyism: Repeating History in the War on Terrorism,* 38 HARV. C.R.-C.L. L. REV. 1 (2003).

Index

About the Author

John S. W. Park is Assistant Professor of Asian American Studies at the University of California at Santa Barbara. His research interests include American immigration law, Anglo-American political theory, critical race theory, and Asian Americans in American law and culture.